Talking Lightly

Talking Lightly

Interviews with
Leading Personalities
of New Thought

•

Interviews and Photographs
by William Koopman

CHARLES E. TUTTLE COMPANY, INC.
Boston • Rutland, Vermont • Tokyo

First published in 1994 by
Charles E. Tuttle Company, Inc.
of Rutland, Vermont, and Tokyo, Japan
with editorial offices at
153 Milk Street, Boston, Massachusetts 02109

Library of Congress Catalog Card Number 94-60420
ISBN 0-8048-3030-4

Printed in the United States of America

Dedication

This project is dedicated, with all my heart, to Aymalee, Colin, Grietje and Wiebren.

Contents

Acknowledgements

Given the nature of this particular work there have been a number of hands who have helped to mold it. In this space I would like to thank each of them. Their contributions were mighty.

First off, to all those fine sages who gave their time and put forth their elegant donations: Ken Carey, Pamela Chase, Richard Erdoes, Chris Griscom, Steven Halpern, Ken Keyes Jr., Penny Keyes, Dorothy Maclean, Jonathan Pawlik, Tara Singh, Michael Sky, David Spangler, Marcel Vogel, and Fred Alan Wolf I wish to extend a deep admiration and appreciation for all of their elevated, prominent and sublime words, here and elsewhere.

Equally as influential, kudo's go to:

Joel Friedlander, whose work with this book has been critically keen, for all his dedication and patience in editing, design, formatting and putting this baby to bed. All the fine folks at Tuttle & Co., for their efforts and vision with this project.

Dorothy Rubin for her much appreciated help with editing some of the introductory pieces; Andrea Mikana, for the initial kick in the ass to get all this started; Maureen Rawlings and Ken Bates for their content thoughts; Pamela Chase & Jonathan Pawlik for calling the right shots; Robin Mercer for his clarity; Waki and Zobra Anassazi for their most generous help, support and time; Karen Clausel for her support, friendship and lattés; all those who helped, in large and small ways, with *The Light; A Magazine Of The Heart*, which got this entire series of events off in the right direction; my partner Aymalee, who accompanied me on many of these interviews, for her deep patience, nurturing and love, all of which saw this project through and helped make it whole; and my son, Colin, for his ramrod-wit, lightening-influence and computer expertise.

Introduction

Listening has always been an adventure for me. The discovery of previously unknown or forgotten elements of living have usually been uncovered through my eyes and ears. Often, I listen to myself and wander the twisting meandering of a questioning mind. More often, I listen to others and then extrapolate yet additional twists to the serpentine trail. That is basically how this volume has evolved and subsequently been birthed.

One might notice, ever since the mid eighties and up until the present day, that the world appears to be transitionally moving with an ever-quickening velocity. The momentum of these changes has been witnessed by all. They have had a significant effect on the human community as a whole, and upon each of us individually. Personally, I have not been spared from the tide. One such flux was that for a period of four years I was involved with the publication of an exceptionally uncommon and delightful magazine we called *The Light*. The choice of that title was completely symbolic. Actually we started out as a delicate and diminutive tabloid called the *The Light of Olympia*. The name was shortened after a few months to provide both a handy moniker and a clear reference point. With the sincerest of declarations it was also, obviously, the intended direction of our efforts. As I say, it was all done with good heart and genuine honesty.

The Light was easily one of the most important things I have ever done and definitely one of the most enjoyable. The entire project was most fortuitous. It began very spontaneously and quickly became the outlet for all my creative energy. It was a labor of love and out of it came the most intense period of learning I had ever experienced. It was an education of the heart. Fortunately, my mind traipsed along. For my ego, however, it was more of a pursuit. I didn't realize it in the beginning, but later it became obvious that much of the entire effort was meant as a personal healing.

The content we sought and usually found was of the adventuresome sort. We tended towards that which would stretch our heads, and assumed that our readers would enjoy the encounter. It frequently worked quite well. We were well aware that these journeys with text would assume many forms and travel through a variety of experience. The stipulations we put into place were few. All we expected was that the substance of the logos should be conscious, real and sensitive. All we really wanted was that the significance of the material be soul inclusive.

It was a shoe-string operation. The house quickly became a design and production facility, with the basement overrun with makeshift layout tables and swing-arm lamps. The ancient manual waxer that had been generously donated to us was constantly plugged in and continually leaked its most precious waxen cargo. Exacto knives lay everywhere and I was amazed that I couldn't cut a straight line. Eventually I almost learned how. The electrical bills jumped precipitously when we bought a second-hand stat camera. Along with everything else, I became a handy halftone shooter. The world was rosy and benign because of the process itself and the content that was driving it. The two together, operating in a tandem ecstasy of creation, provided a dynamic framework of personal evolution.

Within this whirlwind of communications process it became very apparent that the inclusion of interviews with the many enlightened and articulate communicators of awareness, consciousness and spirituality was a healthy way to provide our readers with substantive content. Beyond this there was an even greater reward. Through the publication of the discourses the hope was that there would be evoked a greater depth to the person that was being interviewed. That they could become, in the intuitive minds of the readers, real people... with all the attributes of real personality. Not that they weren't before or that the interview itself was so magnificently complete. It was simply that prior to this, our reading audience only had access to the words that these wonderful people had written in a book, or perhaps only a response to a favorite concept. Now, through this manner of sharing, their favorite authors suddenly became alive and accessible. The inclusion of photographs with the text added an additional element of reality that I hoped would deliver a complete event of recognition, comprehension and—if the material suitably paralleled their personal motivations or touched them in some meaningful way—integration. As for recognition and comprehension, I believe it worked. Integration is, of course, such a unique process that there's no telling for sure how we did, but I do know we provided some tools.

Of the fifty or so interviews I produced for the magazine I've chosen the following twelve for inclusion here. These selections were not made on a basis of personality recognition, flamboyancy or to salute phenomena in any way. In fact, I believe you will find that to be rather down-played and dismissed throughout the volume by myself and all those interviewed. There has been a tendency over the past few years to place an inordinate amount of attention on that which is only superficially unfathomed. Perhaps we have a cultural bias towards it which has been propagated through sound-bites, commercials and vicarious gratification. Fortunately, real substance has its own mystique and holds considerably superior promise.

With this volume there travels an intention to provide a—albeit partial—framework for a discourse on a few of the many avenues of intuition, perception and sensitivity available to all of us. Myriad more remain to be explored. Hopefully, given our abundant resources of the heart, we will make a few inroads. In order to be as reader-friendly as possible, a quick biographical sketch of the interview subjects is presented below. This will, perhaps, help you to identify the direction of the various subject matters as well as the people themselves. Many of you will already be familiar with a number of these people. For those who are not, or if there a few names you do not recognize, here is a brief overview.

Chris Griscom

Chris Griscom is the founder and director of The Light Institute, located in Galisteo, New Mexico. She has authored several totally informative works. Two of her books in particular, *Ecstasy Is A New Frequency* and *Time Is An Illusion* rate as genre-specific classics. She was prominently featured in the book *Dancing In The Light*, which documents Shirley MacLaine's conscious reuniting with her Higher Self, which was facilitated by Ms. Griscom. Which brings us back to our Higher Selves and Ms. Griscom's discipline. She does not work alone and will tell all who ask that there are grand helpers plotting the process.

Ken & Penny Keyes

Ken Keyes, Jr. has been at the forefront of the human potential movement since 1972. Since the release of his book, the *Handbook to Higher Consciousness*, his work and teaching have slowly and surely touched an ever-widening expanse of those seeking healing in bodies, minds and spirits. With over 3 million books in print worldwide, there's little question that many, many people have found his words to be meaningful, life-enhancing and real. Ken Keyes Jr. was born in 1921. In 1946 he contracted polio and has lived as a quadriplegic, confined to a wheelchair ever since. In many ways, mostly unrecognized and unsung, the work of Ken Keyes has quietly pervaded many of the arenas of contemporary thought.

Michael Sky

Michael Sky is a workshop leader, teacher, holistic healer, firewalker and the author of *Dancing With The Fire, Breathing; Expanding Your Power and Energy*, and *Sexual Peace; Beyond the Dominator Virus*. He holds a degree in Chinese Studies. Of late he's become popular in Japan where he leads workshops and seminars. Michael has led some 4,000 people over a 1500° path. A path which does far more to their minds and belief systems than it does to their feet. While my initial surprise with the process of firewalking was centered on concern for the feet, Michael's real work with the fire begins and ends with the head.

Dorothy Maclean

One of the original founders of The Findhorn Community located in Northern Scotland. They have all been quite open and direct about the reasons for the success of their experiment. They consider it to based upon their own willingness to listen and co-create with the openness of the angelic realms. With the publication of the evocative *The Findhorn Garden* in 1975, and then the stirring *To Hear The Angels Sing* in 1980, Ms. Maclean has made an indelible mark in the annals of spiritual literature.

Steven Halpern

Steven Halpern, Ph.D., is the innovative trailblazer who has brought justification to the term "New Age Music." One of the concepts that has been integral to his work has been the physical phenomenon known as entrainment. He started his work on a very small scale and began marketing his works through small health food stores in the San Francisco area. Fifty albums, and a healthy distribution network later, he is decisively deserving of the recognition he has received. A few years back he was honored with the coveted "Crystal Award" at the International New Age Music Conference for his contributions to the field. He is a popular columnist with many publications and the co-author of *Sound Health*.

David Spangler
One of the earliest and prime definers of the new age, David Spangler has also maintained one of its more pragmatic voices. He served as a co-director at the Findhorn Community from 1970-73. During his tenure the community expanded from 15 to 150 members and Findhorn became a model for living based on non-separation and co-creation. He is a Lindisfarne Fellow and a faculty member at the Chinook Learning Center. His many books include *Revelation: Birth of a New Age, Towards a Planetary Vision, Reflection on the Christ, A Vision of Findhorn*, and *Emergence: The Rebirth of the Sacred*. He is a co-author of the now classic, *The Findhorn Garden* and the newer, *Reimagination of the World* (with author/philosopher William Irwin Thompson)

Pamela Chase & Jonathan Pawlik
The ability to extend our conceptual understandings of rapport and relationship so as to include our environment and the natural world have become an obvious and necessary next step. Toward this expansive beginning there are two who have taken the time and devoted themselves to the task. Pamela Chase and Jonathan Pawlik began their on-going connection with the Devic Kingdom, the overlighting spirits of the natural world, in 1983.

Their latest book, *Trees For Healing; Harmonizing with Nature for Personal Growth and Planetary Balance*, is a potent interpretation of expanded vision. Through the use of the words and messages within its pages, the reader may well attempt and experience a new momentum of flow towards the natural world.

Richard Erdoes

The author of the now-classic *Lame Deer: Seeker of Visions, American Indian Myths & Legends* (with Alfonso Ortiz), *Crying for A Dream*, and, with Mary Brave Bird, *Lakota Woman* (winner of the American Book Award in 1990), continues his work of pursuing the protection and understanding of the Native Americans. Mr. Erdoes, a native of Austria, made his way to America in 1940 and began a career as a freelance illustrator. His associations with the Lakota Medicine Men, John Lame Deer and Henry Crow Dog, began during illustrating voyages to the West. Richard Erdoes wrote his first book at age 50, at the insistence of Lame Deer, whose medicine indicated that he had indeed found the co-author he had waited for.

Ken Carey

An unassuming family man with seven children, Ken Carey never really intended to be anything besides a husband, father and carpenter. Now, literally through public demand, he is a widely-acknowledged author. Public acclaim for xeroxed and randomly distributed copies of *The Starseed Transmissions* eventually led to a publisher and its subsequent publication. It was followed by *Terra Christa, Vision, Notes To My Children* and the classic *Return Of The Bird Tribes*. The latest, and perhaps last, of the Starseed volumes, is *Starseed: The Third Millennium*. The evolution continues with his latest release, *Flat Rock Journal*, a real down-home spiritual adventure guide. It moves ahead in a pragmatic vein, with elevated awareness and a consciousness attuned to everyday reality.

Marcel Vogel
Dr. Marcel Vogel was a research scientist, author, philosopher and proponent of the Divine. Many will remember him for his years of research and development for IBM. There, his work led to the magnetic coating used in computer hard disks, liquid crystals used in digital displays and the red hue on your TV. Many will remember him for his work with plants and his coverage in the book, *The Secret Life Of Plants,* which dealt with just that subject. Many will remember him for his pioneering work with crystals and water. All of this is, and will be, worth remembering. To the above we may also commemorate his warm nature, moving smile, compassion and his cultivated and enlightened sense of Self.

Fred Alan Wolf
Fred Alan Wolf, Ph.D., is the author of six popular and informative books, *Parallel Universes, The Body Quantum, Star Wave, Taking the Quantum Leap* (winner of the American Book Award), *Space, Time, & Beyond* (with Bob Toben) and *The Eagle's Quest.* Dr. Wolf holds his doctorate in theoretical physics from UCLA, was a Research Fellow at the University of London, and has lectured and taught literally all over the planet. He is a lucid example of visionary physics and considers it to be an art form based upon scientific fact and consciousness. He suggests that if visionary physics are to have any value or practical application they must provide a doorway to insight.

Tara Singh
Tara Singh is best known for his lifework of teaching, instructing and sharing with students the principles of the inspirational text,

A Course In Miracles. Born in India, Tara Singh first came to America in 1947. Following close relationships with Dr. Helen Schucman, Dr. William Thetford and a period of 100 days of intensive study, reflection and "special aloneness" Mr. Singh devoted himself towards bringing the Course into application. He facilitated a one year, non-commercialized study of the Course for a group of serious students. From this core group of seekers there evolved the Foundation for Life Action which conducts itself as a non-profit, educational foundation. The author of some ten books on the Course, Mr. Singh's work continues to become more and more widely visible.

As you can see, there is a fair modicum of diversity presented here. Hopefully the material, herein presented as a collection, will keep you busy for quite awhile (or at least until volume two is ready). While the fabric of each of the interviews is distinct, I find that the substance of the whole is not all that divergent. There's a good deal of parallel movement working within all of the components of this smorgasbord. And, like all good feasts, this one also leads to dessert.

Personally, I believe that the creative forces of the universe have put us four-square in the middle of this celestially speeding dance so that we might become, and observe, the cherry pies (and the cow pies!) of our own existence. Each of your wise relations in this volume would encourage you to play along... and to keep your eyes and minds open to the spontaneously creative bakery of the soul. We are the honey, we are the spice. All this to say that somewhere in this volume you are virtually certain to encounter various perceptions of yourself.

Perhaps that's another reason why this book came into being. Sometimes it's just not enough to look at ourselves without the aid of a mirror. If the mirror can also double as a looking-glass then there's all the more to be seen. Maybe after digesting the composite of all the upcoming discourse it will become obvious that we will never see enough of the total so as to indulge a halting of the vision. When the mirror begins to fog we know we can wipe it clean and look afresh... and probably deeper.

As for any particular techniques I might have employed in conducting these interviews... there were none. In virtually all of these discourses everyone was most forthcoming. I had hoped to record vibrant orators and it turned out that way. They all had something considerate and generous to share. In those moments where true gems were pinpointed and uncovered we can truly thank the focus of the moment. I have tried throughout this volume to take myself out of it as much as possible. I think that the most I contributed was somehow locating the serendipity to ascertain the right people to question, and receiving the good fortune of their agreement.

What I particularly like about this work is the depth of the twists and the quality of the turns contained within its meanders. There's a hearty good deal of information contained in these pages. Much of it is perfectly practical and all of it is certainly quite usable for the inquiring disposition. The universe places no limits on the well-springs of our imaginations. Equally impressive—and quite possibly just as sturdy—are the potentials of our awareness, sensitivity and beliefs.

Talking Lightly

Chris Griscom

Coalescing Into the Center

"The spiritual body is like a coagulation of conscious fluid which forms out of the infinite sea of divine source. Like a silent seed, it has awaited the impulse of our distant memories to disperse it throughout the matrix of our interdependent bodies. Once rooted, it flowers. By means of its true beauty, it allows us to see our life's purpose and source. It is a poignant source of our growth and evolution at this time and the only gateway to survival."

Chris Griscom—*Ecstasy is a New Frequency*

As every New Mexican who drives will point out to you, albeit passively, New Mexico is an enchanted space. There's no question about it. The hues alone demand contemplation. It was obvious that my knowledge and appreciation of pastels was ready to be exploded. Then there's the sky, the overall scenic appeal of the terrain and the timelessness of the space. So, should it have come as a surprise that in a magical place I would find a magical woman doing magical work. No, I guess not but it always is just the same.

I was reflecting on illusion as the plane descended towards Albuquerque. Certainly I was as imbedded in my own personal apparitions as anyone. And why not? It was, after all, what I was used to. Had not all my previous pondering not brought me to where I was? Well... yes, but... the questions remained. In fact the questions were far more jarring when the reflection turned to include our social beliefs, the prevailing consciousness of our immediate environments and the priorities to which we focus our energy. All of this without even considering our relationship to time and temporal matters. Where could we go if we weren't so completely enveloped within our deceptions? Just what is the potential of the unfettered mind? The query continues as a worthwhile challenge. I went to the land of enchantment to find some answers. Timely circumstance (thank you Coyote and Raccoon) and Ms. Griscom's great and spontaneous kindness resulted in the following interview.

Chris Griscom is the founder and director of The Light Institute, located in Galisteo, New Mexico. She has authored several totally informative works. Two of her books in particular have held me in a state of expectant suspense for several years now. *Ecstasy is a New Frequency* and *Time is an Illusion* rate, in my mind, as genre-specific classics. She was prominently featured in the book Dancing In The Light, which documents Shirley

MacLaine's conscious reuniting with her Higher Self, which was facilitated by Ms. Griscom.

But first, I have to tell you about something. Ms. Griscom tells a great story about how she came to locate in that backroad, dusty and perfect one-street town. After a most meaningful hitch with the Peace Corps she was engaged in a search for the appropriate location in which to continue her undeniable work. After looking around in Galisteo she was wandering about in one of the many back-country arroyos one will find there. She felt a commotion in the sky. Looking up she saw a Pterodactyl flying by ... and then she knew she was home. I have heard and recorded like tales from others I greatly respect. A gifted sage woman from California told me about crows flying upside down at very specific moments and in very different parts of the world. In this volume you will notice Fred Alan Wolf's encounters with the Ayahuasca spirits. And there is Ken Carey's meeting with the Hoya tree. They all hold a shared thread.

Such stories hold a great fascination for me. And it has nothing to do with the internal digestion of that which might be construed as phenomenon. I have come to appreciate that such events are so uniquely endemic to the individual that they are completely, and very simply, gifts. By simply, I suggest that they are wholly natural expressions of the creative forces that co-facilitate our lives. In short, they are to be taken Lightly. To label such events as incredible, bizarre, or unorthodox (or even miraculous) is a mis-translation and perhaps a disservice to the energies that set them in motion. When it happens the best advice I've received is: be quiet, be grateful and let Be. To under-estimate such experiences as phenomenon leaves little room for integration.

Which brings us back to our Higher Selves and Ms. Griscom's bona fide avocation, discipline and art. She does not work alone. She will tell you that there are grand helpers plotting the process. Mystical love will flood the senses and You will do the work. After being with this woman for a few short hours I can tell you she facilitates a great role.

I've often wondered what such a facilitation might entail. By way of a great deal of listening I've come to appreciate it as a reunification. Perhaps the Native Americans have defined it best. The spiritual spokespersons of the absolutely original cultures of the America's frequently speak of the greater potentials of "seeing with the eye of the heart." I can understand this and in this way so too could we further clarify, interpret and illuminate our understanding of the expression, Higher Self: Welcome to your soul.

And what a grand meeting it will be. Can it be possible for one to merely imagine the wonder and utter dazzle of meeting their immortal selves... within themselves and then be content with just the imagination of such an acquirement. Such events, mildly classified as enlightening, might well change our perspective a wee bit. It takes a wholly unique type of medicine person to assist with such an encounter of balance. As I said, I found such a woman in Galisteo, New Mexico...

"Perhaps the cruelest of cosmic jokes is the illusion that death lurks around every corner, perpetually measuring out our life as if each experience or feeling must be paid in kind to an insatiable force. ...Within the deepest essence of our knowing is the unmanifest, disembodied self. Yet it is the body that holds sway in the realms of outer consciousness, that whispers its fears of certain ending we so ardently strive to delay. The energy we expend by holding the resistance to that ending is the energy drained from our life."

Chris Griscom—*Time Is An Illusion*

How about some brief background on the Institute to get started?

I've been working in clinic here for about 10 years. I've lived in Galisteo for about 20 years and I taught in a school for natural healing before that. I've been working in healing for close to 30 years. But the Light Institute is about 4 years old, in its present form.

I imagine it went through various phases in its evolution to its present form... and you probably did too.

Yes, indeed. Wisdom that has any value, that can bear upon our personal lives, always comes from the interface of our knowing with our everyday reality. In other words, experience gives us the necessary instruments for being able to manifest what it is from a place of such truth within ourselves. I just got back from a big tour in Europe and I talked about consciousness in and out of the body, radiation and parent-child relationships. People always know that I'm speaking the truth because they can feel, in the essence, the experience of that truth.

That's what the Light Institute is about. It's not about philosophies, it's not about theories of the new age or what we might become, but who we are now. We simply peel away the masks so that what is there naturally comes up without our interference, our sabotage. The evolution of the Light Institute has come only through the evolution of body and spirit through life experience.

In your books you've written about enlightenment as surrender. It strikes me that most of us have significant problems with learning to surrender.

When we are condensed into this frozen block of the ego, then everything that happens to us from the outside world feels like the possibility or probability of death. So we resist and we resist, the ego defends and defends, and everything is viewed from the perspective of survival. When we begin to disassemble ourselves a little bit, to de-crystalize ourselves, we can begin to connect with that pulse, the cosmic pulse of the universe, which means we are dying all the time, and we're breathing all the time.

Each time we have an experience like that, each time we let go, whether it's in giving up an attitude, giving up a thoughtform, saying "I'm sorry" or risking a little bit, we give ourselves a frame of reference for the recognition that we can let go and die, and that something else always comes. You know that saying, "When the door closes, the window opens"? The Light Institute is a window to the sky. That's the purpose of it.

So, we begin to give ourselves a frame of reference that the passage always brings us something good, always brings us something that nourishes us, heals us, and lets us try on a new hat. The child in us always wants to try on a new hat. The child is always saying, "Let me pretend that I'm this one or that one." It's always waiting for the adventure. The teachings of the Institute are about that adventure, that path of life, that path of light, that lets us say, "Go on, go on, jump off the precipice, there's no bottom. You're not going to hit anything. You're just going to go down and come up and so on." Surrender can become a delicious game.

How do the sessions here typically go? How structured is it?

We do have a very formalized structure of that path, because we have something very specific in mind. First of all, there is a minimum of four sessions, because when you want to crack open to your own multidimensionality we want to make sure you can shake loose from your positionality or who you think you are in the world.

As you see your multi-incarnations, as you see all the hats and clothes that you've worn, the bodies you have inhabited, you see them from a holographic consciousness. You see that you're not only the good guy but the bad guy—and within the bad guy is the good guy—and all the great hopes, dreams, talents, and relationships that are there and how they are connected. The universe is not chaotic, we must let go of the linear perspective of conclusion. In the Western world we always conclude—meaning that we always judge—that it's this way or it's that way, and this is not the way of the cosmos. The cosmos is ever blinking and rippling out of consciousness.

So, a person comes and they do four sessions. They begin by working with the child within and connecting with the Higher Self. Then we teach them how to utilize this technology of consciousness, this Higher Self, how to pull it away from the unmanifest, this speculated something out there, into something that's very palpable that you can connect with, that you can hear the answer, that you can trust to guide you.

The Higher Self energy guides you deeper into the self in a way that's safe, in a way that has purpose and always has meaning. You're always able to recognize it; "This is what is going on with me now, this is why I feel this way." To experience it from an energetic level rather than the laws of the feeble intellectual mind—but which include the intellectual mind—so the consciousness feels itself expanding with the integrity of the center, so it can risk expanding out. The Higher Self takes you through those four sessions, a holographic perspective of who you are now, what you can dare to let go of and what you can dare to reach for.

Many times people wait a few days to assimilate all of this and we go on. We also use cranial work which is a different aspect in that it's nonverbal. It has nothing to do with the mind, the body or the astral energies which come out as we explore multi-incarnations, but rather the subtleties of the energetic connection between the brain and the body and the brain and our entire consciousness. So, we wash the brain, and peel the karma.

I have developed a particular kind of cranial work which is specific to consciousness, specific to exciting the pineal gland. It helps us take all this tremendous information and data, which is sensory sometimes as well as linear. In other words, we may see a past life or we may smell it. We may sense so many things that make us understand why we have chosen a person or why someone feels familiar, because in fact we are able to perceive them with more than 70 senses, not six senses. The cranial work helps us to attune our awareness, our capacity to be awake in those higher octaves through the mechanism of the master glands.

Then we go on to another set of four sessions in which we begin something which is very exciting to me. This is the peeling away of the actual DNA so we have a chance to put our thumbs on why we have blue eyes or brown eyes, or this shape body or that shape body, why we have chosen the genetic coding of these particular parents. Actually as we go on with the work of the institute we go into the inner parents.

We are working with the fact that the DNA—or the blueprint of being in-body—is more than the blueprint of the physiological body, but is interfacing with the emotional body and the spiritual body; so we can feel the blueprint of the spiritual body, of the soul, in its holographic imprint. I feel that in another five years or so the physicists are going to be able to talk about what's coming up in our sessions. It's very exciting.

How does this aspect of your work differ or tie in with the work that you're doing with younger people?

Well, there we begin with four sessions of clearing the parents. We do that because so much of the thought-form of the physical shape of the positionality of our self in the world comes from that dance between the parent and the child. In order for a young person to access the whole soul that's struggling through the mechanism of a 12 or 16 year-old body—you know, all this knowledge all this background information, so they can break through—we focus the funnel of the parents. We explore all the hologram of our relationship on a soul level with the parents so we can merge with them. Not separate from them, but merge with them so they are no longer a force in our lives which prohibits us in our outer layers of consciousness from stepping up in the world and being who we are, no matter our chronological age.

I was pleased to do some parent-child workshops in Europe and discover how universal this dance of the self, and the self and the family is, and how it really colors an entire spectrum of our life experience. So, that's the second series of sessions, after that we clear our children, our lovers, our themes: "Why am I not successful at work. Why am I this way? How can I manifest my themes?"

Then we go on to the higher octaves I was talking about, connecting with the inner female and the inner male. Again, giving the consciousness a way, a vocabulary, of understanding from an energetic perspective that balance of the emotional/spiritual self.

We definitely choose our parents. We get all we can from that and then let it go, so we can get back to the inner world that is manifesting out, rather than projecting-out and reacting-in. That so limits the choices we can make if we do that, always projecting and reacting. It's so stultifying for a whole soul.

Do you think that we get hung up trying to entirely discount the ego? I wonder if maybe a whole soul might not have, as a necessary component, some certain aspects of ego.

The ego is crucially necessary, just as is the left-brain, for the capacity to discern, to analyze data, to constantly whisper about the center of self, so there's enough orientation so that we can function in a third-dimensional world. Now, the ego gets in the way of the higher octaves because it always sponsors a repertoire of separation.

From an enlightenment perspective, from a consciousness perspective, separation lacks enough of a holographic under-standing to function on the levels of enlightenment. So the ego is important to recognize that this self, this name that you have, is a point on your soul's hologram that was chosen specifically so that you can work out the themes that are necessary in your life through this funnel of your body, your name, your self.

But the ego can learn to expand its repertoire to include our self as a part of cosmic self. So ego is necessary, but it has to be trained, it has to be loved. It has to be nourished out of octaves of self-righteousness and judgement and into octaves of merging. This is a new game on this planet.

We have within us the whisper of those experiences, of not being in polarity bodies, male and female bodies, not being separate, of being divine, but they're a very distant whisper. Only when we can calm and prepare and support the ego will it get out of the way enough to let us go on back into the merging. It's a passage of death; death to the ego and death to the positionality of separation.

How about the relationship of the ego to the emotional body?
The ego is the instrument, the fall guy, of the emotional body. The emotional body, which is all energetic in nature... it is a conscious entity, but it has different laws than, let's say, the mindbody does. Its laws have to do with the biochemical and electromagnetic stimulus of experience, which it constantly repeats. It stirs around in its pot reclaiming and reusing experien-ces to give itself a constant stimulus of energy so it knows it's alive.

The ego does the same thing, though the emotional body uses the ego to demonstrate its aliveness. So the ego says, "I am whoever you are in this moment." And who you think you are is in the biochemistry, not in the memories, of the emotional body through eons of multi-incarnational experience.

Your books speak a great deal to our multidimensionality and present it quite beautifully. For those who are reading this, what would you say about it?

Just to say to them to think of the child within trying on all the hats. That on a soul level this is what we've done through many lifetimes; to explore being the lover, the killer, the wiseman, the fool. In each experience is a kernel of divine wisdom that helps us to grow. The only purpose in being alive is the growth of the soul. We have to begin to readdress the fact that man is basically spiritual, which means we come from nothingness. This is a great mystery, and a great miracle. We need to uphold it, and look to touch it and keep it alive within us, rather than feeling the weight of being born and struggling through our lives and dying.

Multidimensionality isn't anything esoteric, it isn't any constant to the mind. It's just a replay of potential, of human potential. There's more in us than we think there is, always much more in us than we think. Even if we think of one lifetime, all that you garnered as a child and how you're using it now. How, if you could connect with it from a point of knowing, much of it you could discard if you were conscious instead of always replaying the old hurts and the old imprints that we have from childhood. Just as it's true for one lifetime, so is it true for our multi-incarnations.

It's not esoteric to think of time and space as our own human illusion. After all, all these planets and heavenly bodies have been out there for eons of time. We are carbon, we are made of atoms,

atoms never die, never die. So, where in us is the capacity to touch the part that never dies, and in following it through the maze of existence? The richness, the stories and wonderful experiences? We're too habitual, we don't get enough out of life, we're inert and disconnected, we have nothing but our televisions and our sleepiness. We need to awaken, we need to play.

When we begin to probe, "Could it be that we've lived forever? Could it be that we've always been?", what comes up from everyone, surprisingly, are these magnificent stories of who they are which help them to recognize the possibilities, to feel alive, to risk. We don't risk enough. Whenever we risk or try something new we enhance our reality and enrich ourselves. We need that. We need to have it come from inside ourselves rather than the stultifying imprints of the outside world. It's not enough for me, not enough for me... I want more.

Well, I have no doubts but that you'll receive it too. [Laughter] Maybe you've brought some readers to a place where some comments specifically related to inertia and fear would be appreciated.

Yes, I always talk about that, because when people get overwhelmed by multidimensionality there is something that everyone relates to and that's fear. It's so impregnated within the molecular structure of our physical bodies, that it becomes our habit of existence, and it's very addictive. It literally stimulates the physiological body, the adrenalins, the adrenaline rush we get whenever we're just a little bit frightened. That's why we seek movies that are worse and worse and worse, or relationships that are worse and worse and worse, because we're hooked on that fear. Even the Earth is beginning to smell of that fear. I always say to people, "You know, you know the smell of fear." Witness how animals recognize that around us.

Fear is the only cause of disease and perhaps the only cause of death. We are afraid to acknowledge that we're infinite, our little bitty minds just can't understand it. Until we can address fear, grab it! Shake it around a little, throw it out, we'll always be the victims. Which means we'll always be inert.

Whenever I address audiences, work with people, I always have them explore the fear. The body knows where it's holding fear and our body is a profound expert of who we are. It always amazes me that people think they have to go to an outside source to find out why they're sick. We know exactly why we're sick, we want time out, you know? Stop the world!

The more we can listen inside and find the source of the fear... what I've found is that the source of the fear is not only held literally in the molecular structure of the body... In other words, if you push into the body you will come up with memories of experiences that the body has had that it doesn't want to repeat. Whether it was a little experience you had in your bathtub when you were two, or a death in another lifetime.

If you discover the source of the fear, energetically you have the opportunity to change it. Once the left brain can say, "Aha! It's because I drowned in this lifetime and my whole body is experiencing that," that fear that was imprinted in the body. The body then has an opportunity to divulge itself, to shake loose the fear of that particular experience. What happens, no matter what you think, is that people lose their fear. They desensitize. I spent nine years in the Peace Corps and we used that principle all the time, to desensitize people so that they could risk, so they could become free.

You can't do that by saying, "There's nothing to be afraid of except fear itself." That's a nice theory, yet the body will hold what it has experienced until something comes along to dissolve that experience. The work of the Institute is about getting rid of this illusion of past, and the huge bogeyman of the future. Few of us think that the future is full of light and joy, we always dread the future. So, fear is a necessary conversation.

And a long one for most of us. Speaking of the future, what do you see as happening these days, in an evolutionary sort of way?

I see that as a soul group being born on this planet we have set up a blueprint for ourselves that began eons ago. That's why that blueprint is echoed in every great book, the messages of all the seers, in all the cultures around the world. That at this time on this planet there would be famine, there would be earthquakes, there would be death and all that. Why? Not to punish the humans because they blew it, but because we're addicted to this great game of the bogeyman.

We're so inert we don't do anything until we have all the toes over the edge of the precipice. When it's the eleventh hour, then the great aspects of human nature come to the fore. We become selfless, we save each other, we honor our potential, we love the earth, we move it around, you know? That's where we are right now.

What I see coming up tomorrow is more bogeymen. We've already passed the threshold with radiation. Radiation will become the great threat of the future. Both natural radiation from the sun through the ozone layer and human created radiation dramas. These will force us into perceiving the actual truth about life and death in a way we never have. We better get busy and become globally conscious lest it all go poof. We as a species have no guarantee. We can be snuffed out along with the other species that we ourselves are snuffing out constantly.

I feel that we are now going to address the greatest challenge and one of the final initiations of human consciousness, which will force us on to a catapulting leap of awareness. It will force us out of the linear brain patternings that we've developed over 50,000 years. We must become more holographic in our consciousness. We must become like the whales and the dolphins, because we're not perceiving enough to survive.

Shirley MacLaine's experience here is well documented, and I'm sure you're bored of speaking about it.

I am, but I'll answer it anyway.

Her experience was very moving and intense. I'm wondering how close to the norm it was. Could her experience be equated to what typically happens during a session?

It's the norm. I now have eight people working at the Light Institute, and we work on thousands of people. I can't remember when the last person has ever come and not expanded into realms of new possibility. Part of that is because we do not promote, we don't beg people to come. They come because they're dying to come.

When you have that kind of intention something happens, because you're creating it. That's one of the very first lessons that we all have to learn. That we are creating our own reality. We're creating what's going to happen in the future.

I did have to give up the gold needles. It was gold needles that I was using. Because... people love glamour, especially in America, the more glamorous it is, the more that we can project that somebody else does it, you know? It's one of the negative attributes of our passive media. Forgive me for beating on the media here

It's true. I understand what you mean.

We've forgotten that we are the players. In order to let them dissolve the glamour and let them recognize that the glamour is inside us. It's not coming from me, it's not coming from acupuncture needles, you know? It's coming from inside you. All you have to do is say, "Hey, I want to know. I really want to know, how it is that I am in this life. Who I am? What I'm here for?"

All you have to do is say, "What's my purpose?" and that purpose will come from your Higher Self. It will show it to you in the most divine, laughing, enjoyable, magnificent, and relevant terms. You could never make it up. You could never think it up. So, intense experiences are the norm at The Light Institute, because people choose them. That's why they come. They haven't come to be disappointed in themselves. They've come to find what they always hoped and sensed was in them.

Basically, the truth is that we don't do any fancy anything. We just use your intention to trigger in you that coalescence into the center, that bang in the center of yourself! You don't have to think about anything when you lie down on that table. There's nobody there but you and your Higher Self. Suddenly that coalescence creates something. It's there in everyone. We love witnessing it. It's such an honor.

I think that this is very important. Could we clarify your feelings about the gold needles some more?

We didn't want people thinking that it was all about the gold needles. We didn't want people getting into the glamour of thinking, "Ah, it's the gold needles," or, "It's Griscom," because it's not. It's not Griscom. I teach all of my facilitators to be invisible. For us, it's an honor to sit at the end of the table. Because we are constantly honing our own sensory apparatus, our own perceptive qualities, we're able to ask the right question at the right time. That's all we do. We sit there, watch the energetics, ask the right question that their Higher Self wants asked, so they get it. They go, "Ah! I got it! That's it!" Then they move from "that's it," to the next "that's it," to the next "that's it."

They begin to see, to ripple the consciousness out, through their own divine plan, not mine. I'm just the doorkeeper. I laugh about that all the time. Sometimes I think, "Ooh, I wish I was having that experience." This person might be laying there having this tremendous experience. Even when they are experiencing very boring lifetimes that are out there, living, dying, shoveling the earth, they're going, "So... what's this about?" Then they ask their Higher Self. Then they suddenly get how that boring lifetime is playing itself out right now this lifetime. It's great fun.

Every so often I get busy with tours and books and stuff, and I don't get to work in my healing room. When I get back, and I sit on the edge of this table, and I literally sit on the edge of my chair enraptured, enraptured, by the perfection, the articulation, the synchronicity, the brilliance in which Higher Selves lay out for people the map of their lives.

I have never, ever, had a boring person on my table. Whether on the outside world they work in the most mundane of professions, or they are the most illustrious and glamorous beings. I learned that in the Peace Corps. Very often the only difference between the peasant and the president of some country is that often the peasants are more eloquent, more poetic, more holographic in their perception. Because they live with life and death. When we live with life and death... we're real.

At the institute we are interested in what's real. We're pragmatics. I'm a very pragmatic person. I'm the single parent of six kids! You know, when you have six kids you can't be out in fairyland out there. They've got to be fed, organized, chauffeured around, snapped to, and all that stuff. I have one grandchild about to be two and I don't have time for dreaming dreams that aren't real.

I'd like to ask you about the death experience? In your writings you've mentioned your past associations with it and their very important meanings for you. It seems to me that many people are reevaluating their feelings about it.

I had an experience of dying less than five weeks ago in Mexico. I was given an anesthesia that my body was allergic to. It stopped my breathing and actually damaged my left ventricle. I was unconscious for an hour, while an entire operating crew stood around waiting to see if I was coming back or not. They couldn't have administered any more drugs. I was completely blown out.

Again, for the sixth time in my life, I passed the passage of death. I went from my body stopping into Divine Light and experienced what's beyond. For the first time in those six times I feel that I actually grabbed hold of enough coalescence of consciousness to say "I will return," by myself. I made the choice.

When I became conscious again, of course I was babbling about divine love and divine light and sobbing in the ecstasy of that experience, and at the same time was saying to the people who were around, to sort of console them, that it was okay, that I was alright. I was saying that I choose to be here, I choose to be present. Whether that's for another day, or another five months, or another twenty years is irrelevant to me because I've played it up on both sides, and I was able to say I choose to be alive. This gives me a great presence, a great power and a great capacity to laugh.

What was your passage like? White light? Was there a dark tunnel?

No dark tunnel. At the moment the drug hit, my body responded by my breathing stopping, by suppressing my life force energy. I experienced this explosion! I still remember the concentric circles and the star pattern, the awe of that vision that went out, gold light. Then there was just the most profound experience of cosmic love and white light, which is what a lot of people talk about, going into the tunnel of light. I came away from that tunnel of light back into the body. That's what was so ecstatic for me.

Whenever I travel I come across a lot of people who are dying. I'm so thankful for that death experience because I can touch them and say, "Don't be afraid. Use it!" People say to me "Well, what's your message?" My message is, every experience you have, ask yourself, what's the gift? What's the gift? Grab hold of the gift, and use it.

I'm asking everyone about AIDS these days. Maybe we're at a good point to ask you that very question.

It means understanding how can we use the gift of anything that comes to us, whether that's a negative relationship or something that we can't avoid in the outside world. How can we dance with it and participate in it? We have the intelligence. We have the spiritual capacity to become a part of the creative force.

Radiation, for example, is only light. We are made to be light. It's quickening us, it's going to give us the opportunity to get rid of death. I always say that radiation, cancer, and AIDS are three octaves of the same theme that is coming fast and furiously upon this planet to remind each being of the Self. The theme of all of them is that there isn't enough sense of Self to survive. But if we keep our focus on survival, we'll never survive.

We have to keep the focus on the recognition, the capacity to understand that we can never be damaged, that we'll always be here. To do that the consciousness has to expand, it has to expand to the octave of understanding from an atomic point. We have this in our potential and we have to address it.

This sense of the Self begins this theme of recognizing that we are not separate and the self has to cooperate. That brings about the international play, and the global consciousness. Chernobyl showed us that. What happens in Russia, Germany, or Africa happens here. All of these things that are going on that seem to be portraying the greatest fears of humanity, the famines, earthquakes, etc., is just a symbolic message saying, "Hey, wake up you guys."

I feel that in the eleventh hour the human species will jump across. Those that are not intending to jump across are leaving. Those that are leaving are providing a great opportunity. If you will sit with someone who is dying you will learn a lot about life.

Ken & Penny Keyes

It's the Power of Love

"Over 99% of the people in the western world live on lower consciousness levels characterized by trying to find enough security, sex, pleasant sensations, ego rushes, prestige, money, power and status. This endless struggle yields lives of constant resentment, worry, suspicion, anger, jealousy, shyness, and fear. Everything people tell themselves they must do to be happy ends up yielding more frustration than joy. The more successful a person is in making money, collecting skills and possessions, developing exciting sexual relationships, acquiring knowledge and degrees, and achieving positions of status, power and prestige, the less loving peaceful, and contented he may find him or herself."

Ken Keyes, Jr.—*Handbook to Higher Consciousness*

When those uniquely individual winds of personal evolution come calling you isn't it nice to know that a helpful resource awaits? Wouldn't it be gentle to realize that a wizened old uncle or grandfather has some pertinent information? The new age movement can be very proud and thankful for its many grandparents, and there are many.

Ken Keyes, Jr. has been at the forefront of the human potential movement since 1972. Since the release of his book, the *Handbook to Higher Consciousness*, his work and teaching have touched an ever-widening expanse of those seeking healing in bodies, minds and spirits. With over three million books in print worldwide there's little question that many people have found his words to be meaningful, life-enhancing and real.

Ken Keyes Jr. was born in 1921. In 1946 he contracted polio and, as we can well imagine, this changed his life in some very basic ways. He has lived as a quadriplegic, confined to a wheelchair, ever since. Now, please pause and reflect on that fact for a moment. All that he has accomplished, created and dedicated his life toward has been done despite the most challenging of physical constraints. Clearly, he has faced many enormous obstacles and has made many challenging decisions.

Among the first of these was his preference to concentrate on his abilities rather than his limitations. Everything he has ever written or taught harkens back to that simple idea. It worked enormously well for him and has become one of the foundations of all his work. I say one of the foundations because in itself it doesn't necessarily preclude the amazing insights of compassion, love and understanding that completely permeate his work. This man has a very dynamic message. After meeting with him I can definitely say that his words are from, and for, the heart.

In many ways, mostly unrecognized and unsung, the work of Ken Keyes has quietly pervaded many of the arenas of contemporary thought. When *The Hundredth Monkey* was released in

1981 it eloquently spoke about those systems that are now in the forefront—collective consciousness, critical mass, synchronicity and quantum leaps. Today it is widely quoted and used as a possible model of evolutionary force. The Recovery Movement, with its emphasis on addictions and addictive patterning, owes a great, big tip of the hat to the man who wrote some of the very first words about addictive programming. As for some of the most definitive explanations for the concepts of unconditional love, right again, it has been Ken Keyes.

It should be pointed out that his energetics with these varying topics have not been purely philosophical. The magic in these works has not been conveyed through pontification, but rather through an art of the heart. He has communicated these frequently difficult concepts in a manner that actually provides the inquiring mind with a strong foothold toward understanding. By reading his books one can see and appreciate some of our most collective, intrinsic and unconscious foibles.

Beyond that he has consistently paved a way for personal avenues of change. The foundations of Keyes' pathways have always reflected a grounding in compassion and practicality. Certainly the destination points are completely variable but the vehicle remains the same: awareness.

Ken Keyes has written some twelve books over the years and has taught thousands—and through his publications, encouraged millions—of people to look at their existence with honesty. During our interview it seemed clear to me, however, that the overriding passion of Mr. Keyes' life has been with those two special works he created with an eye towards uplifting humanity on an international scale. The publications of *The Hundredth Monkey* and *Planethood* have in many ways defined the man and the scope of his intention.

The hundredth monkey concept is based upon the work of British science author Lyall Watson. It speaks of a group of monkeys, macaques, living on an island off the coast of Japan. In 1953 one young female began to wash the potatoes that she foraged. In the fall of 1958 all the macaques on the island were washing their potatoes and, somehow, so were the macaque communities on other islands and on the mainland. The story goes that a critical mass was achieved and the phenomenon became an evolutionary leap.

However one might interpret the original tale, Ken Keyes' popularization of it as a metaphor for nuclear containment and peace has touched millions of readers. He printed and distributed some 300,000 volumes of *The Hundredth Monkey* in the first year. Since then it has been translated all over the globe with more than a million copies in print.

It is with his latest efforts that this lifetime of consciousness takes the quantum leap. There is a sequel to *The Hundredth Monkey*. Taking the position that only a highly bonded community can truly solve its problems, Ken Keyes has turned his focus toward planethood. He does not assume credit for its formulation, as it remains a philosophy long considered but never fully calculated. It speaks of an honest "new world order" and if—although, believe me, Mr. Keyes definitely says *when*—it appears it would easily be viewed as a pinnacle, if not *the* pinnacle, of human achievement.

While the *Monkey* helped millions to realize the dangers of a nuclear world, *Planethood* sets the stage for a long-term future of international peace based upon cooperation and law. It presents eight ways through which the world community can pass from settling its disputes legally instead of lethally. Co-authored with Benjamin B. Ferencz, the book is not copyrighted so as to facilitate the potential of its grassroots momentum. As with the *Monkey* all proceeds from *Planethood* are used for reprinting and distribution.

Since this interview was recorded Ken and Penny Keyes have made the difficult decision to end their marriage. Ken Keyes continues to reside in Coos Bay, Oregon where he facilitates the teaching programs and workshops which are continually going on at the Ken Keyes College. Students (approximately 400-500 per year from all over the globe) come for weekend, week-long or seven week workshops. The facility, interestingly enough, is a beautiful structure which was originally built to serve as a hospital. The healing tradition continues within its walls... and certainly far beyond.

"Not surprisingly, being crippled by polio challenged my feelings of self-esteem and security. Inside the hospital I felt all right about seeing me in a wheelchair. But when I went out in public, I felt ashamed and embarrassed to be crippled. I thought people might perceive me as helpless, say derogatory things behind my back, or feel sorry for me or my wife.

"There is a saying in personal growth circles that what you resist persists, and what you emotionally accept disappears. I was not familiar with this principle back then. Yet I somehow found a way to apply it to my handicap. After a few months of feeling self-conscious, a strategy occurred to me. I would strike back at my crippling disability by showing myself that I was not really disabled. I told myself that it's ability, not disability that's really important. I started asking myself, 'What can I do?'"

Ken Keyes, Jr.—Discovering the Secrets of Happiness

Much of your work speaks to a topic which is widely misunderstood. So I'd like to ask you about unconditional love and what it means to you.

Ken Keyes: I tell myself that unconditional love is the greatest power on Earth. Many people might think that nuclear bombs are a greater power. I think they are a greater power. . . for killing. But for creating a beautiful life, a life with harmony, love, fun, cooperativeness, energy, insight, joy and happiness—that's a greater power. It's unconditional love that's creating that power.

This power has been greatly misunderstood. Most people are not aware of it as a power, and hence, they are not able to get a grip on their lives. Most people don't even know what unconditional love refers to. If they try to take a stab at it, they come up with something like, "You can hit me in the face and knock all my teeth out and I'll just sit there loving you." This represents a distorted picture of unconditional love.

My feeling is that the power of unconditional love begins to operate in one's life when one can separate our conditioning, our learning, our habits that we bring into the physical—our programming—from who we really are. We can love the vehicle, the soul, the occupant. . . we can love, always, that part of ourselves and every other human being on Earth that is just like us, with a heart and feelings.

No matter how misguided we may be or how skillful we may be, we are all really trying to get our lives to work. They may not work, but it's not because we haven't tried to get them to work. Those people who have withdrawn, saying, "I'm not even going to try anymore," that's their way of trying to get their lives to work. It's very clumsy and it doesn't work, but they're trying.

So, this power of unconditional love. . . to bring it out in the light we've got to understand what it means. It can be very confusing. I think the Greeks were a little smarter than we are, they had three words for it. There's *eros*, which is sexual or erotic. They had *Philos*, which refers to fraternal or our family. Then they had *agape*, which was unconditional. Somehow I can't use that word, it sounds lumpy to me, the syllables don't give me a good feeling. I'd rather work with the word love, even though it's misunderstood and mistaken for sex and all that. I'd much rather work with the word love and try to clean that up for people.

To me, love that is conditional really is not love. Like, when people fall in love it's, "Ah, I've found the love of my life." I'm sure that some very wonderful things are stirring for them, but that love is so fragile. That feeling of love and maybe temporary unity when they first fall in love together is so fragile because the minute that either one says or does something that does not fit in with their models of what they want, whatever it is, then their programming will throw the other person out of their heart. Then they have words like, "If you really loved me, you would always be on time," or "If you really loved me you would understand or make allowances for my not always being on time." [Laughter]

As we begin to focus on wanting to understand this great power that we're missing—and there are so many of us that can have this—that of creating intimacy and warmth, of relationships with people that we spend a lot of time with. Also, of not feeling friendliness and being in community with all people. Even if you never see then again or haven't met them, there's a conscious awareness of a vehicle of consciousness that's just like mine. The things that ego builds up as being so different or important—like how much education we have, status, fame or fortune or the like—those are all ego, they're not objective. They will not be the foundation of a happy life.

You can't get famous enough to be happy. So many of the most famous people in the world have killed themselves. You can't have enough money to be happy, some of the richest people have committed suicide. You can't have enough of anything external to you to live a happy life. That's another reason why the foundation of a happy life cannot lie wholly in achievement. Achievement is just a side game to the whole experience.

So, in my own mind, I don't equate love with an action, like "If you really loved me you would _____," and fill in the blank with what my programming wants from you. I find that deteriorates unconditional love, you can't do it. I find that love is a feeling in my heart of no boundaries, no separateness between your heart and my heart. You may feel very separate. That's a condition of love. I would like to feel that if I love you, you will love me. However, some people are programmed so strongly that there's no way that they're going to let themselves feel that. But that shouldn't erode the love in my heart. It's their programming, not who they are.

I think a lot of people struggle with that. What's your advice for loving someone we might not fully appreciate?

I find that when a person has blockages, the form that unconditional love will take for me is to love them in their essence. And to make it real clear that I do not care for their programming and their acts that follow. It's not who they are, it's a result of their programming. I don't have to like their programming to love them. So my love will tend to be genuine but not interactive. I may not wish to be involved with their behavior.

Say they are robbing banks. I can feel and understand that they are only robbing banks to feel secure financially. Do you want to feel secure financially? Oh you do, do you? Well, in that case you're like a bank-robber in that you both want to feel secure. Only you're more skillful at the way you work to feel secure and they're less skillful. I can still love them even if they're less skillful.

But the love will also be towards compassion and understanding, which aren't needed when the love is leaning more towards the oneness. Like with Penny and I, most of the time we're just harmonizing and playing the great adventure of life together. I don't need understanding or compassion, it's just us twin souls, kindred spirits, vehicles of consciousness living and playing with each other. So, I'm aware of two theories of unconditional love. It makes it very practical, very workable and applicable to every situation.

You were one of the first to speak out about addictions and addictive programming. I think a lot of the work we're seeing now is partially based on your models. I wonder if you might share something now for our readers?

Do you know anyone without addictions? We're addicted to money, to pride, to prestige. Theoretically, realized beings have no addictions, but I've never met one.

Addictions are things that we demand; to feel happy or to feel safe, to feel normal. Usually we don't call them addictions. It makes me feel good to eat the beautiful bread that Penny makes but I don't feel that's called an addiction. However, if I were to do something to feel good that begins to have a disadvantage to me... Let's say I eat three loaves a day and little else, I would be nutritionally deprived. We would then say I have an addiction for this wonderful bread. I have taken a vehicle for feeling good, expanded it beyond its area of adding to life and I've got a self-destructive behavior in one degree or another.

I think that this can also apply to money. A certain flow of money is needed in our society to live in a normal way. It's fine if I get a promotion in my job and I get $50 a week more, it's good to feel high and nice about that. However, if I get so addicted to more money, more high feelings, and I identify with money as

being a measure of my self-esteem, value and worth—it's unfortunate that so many people are living that way—then I think that it can be called an addiction.

Addiction has nothing to do with the activity or the substance. It has to do with the unhealthy, self-destructive, over-emphasis of it in our lives, as an unskillful way that we think will help our lives, or at least, as a temporary way to make us feel happy.

In the system of consciousness that I teach I use addiction as a key term. We apply it to anything to which you are emotionally demanding. Like the bread that Penny bakes, I would like to have it, I prefer to have it with my supper. However, if she happens to be out of it then that's okay and I'll have crackers or something. It's a preference, not an addictive demand. If I make myself upset, you know, "You should have enough bread. You know I like bread. You should bake enough. Blah-blah-blah," that's evidence of addiction.

When I upset myself, when I give out bad vibrations, when I create turmoil and go from the experience of living and experiencing the unconditional love and joy in life to grousing around about being happier if things were different. . . then we call that addictive behavior. It's a generic term that's very, very broad. It's a wonderful tool once you begin to use it as a concept for dissecting the skillfulness and unskillfulness of your behavior.

That brings up the process of personal growth.

Personal growth has to be an inside job. No one can make you grow. Even Christ couldn't make Judas grow above his 30 pieces of silver. You can only open a door. Teachers can help you, perhaps by giving suggestions—if you are open to them—or by modeling behavior. All the inner work has to come from within.

Most people do a lot of inner work that they aren't aware of. A little three year-old kid is out running real fast and trips over a log, he didn't see it. He'll get that programmed in, not to run so fast as to trip over something or to watch more carefully because it hurts when you fall on your face. So three year-olds do, I think, spiritual work in order to learn. What's happening is a kid is running along, having fun, doing his thing, then trips over something and cries. It hurt. Life is giving him a message. It's spiritual growth. We don't usually call it that but I see spiritual growth in a very broad way. It can be anything.

It doesn't have to do with religious things, or candles, or God or anything. It merely has to do with resolving the separateness, the ego boundaries. Then we go beyond that to love, compassion, cooperation. We can be just as spiritual washing dishes or mowing the grass as we can be in church singing hymns. A person can be in church singing hymns only because his wife makes him go, or he has to model it for his child. Or a person can be in church feeling a oneness with God and having a very deep spiritual experience. It has nothing to do with being in church, it has to do with the conscious space you're in.

You generally suggest that people develop a relationship with themselves before they get involved with someone else. Why?

The relationship with yourself is essential. The inner work that you have not done on yourself—that's creating pain, separateness and self-destructive behavior in your life—cannot be done quite as well in a relationship as it can be by yourself. That doesn't mean you can't do any work in a relationship. Most of your inner work will happen in a relationship if you use it for that purpose. However, you have to be at a certain point in order to benefit and use relationships in that way. Otherwise you just get more turmoil, more separateness, or whatever your ego gives you to justify it.

You see, the problem is that I project my programming on you. I don't see you as you are. I see you through the filters of my consciousness. If I ask you to think of your best friend and ask you about characteristics of your best friend you will answer me through your filters. All you can really see in your best friend, in all seriousness, is what you like and don't like in yourself. If we have big heavy programming about ourselves, we project that onto others.

When you go into relationship having a huge amount of self-destructive programming that you apply to yourself, you are going to get so indignant about the behavior of other people. You're trying to cover up or put a shell out there so people can't get close to you and reject you and make you feel bad. People get into and create enormous turmoil with their relationships because they're trying to protect themselves from being ashamed about themselves. They do it by attacking the other person. It's a great school for conscious growth if you can use it. However, most of us can't—the fire's too hot.

To the degree a person has deep inner child work, and inner parenting skills to learn, to the degree a person has dysfunctional behavior and programming, and is co-dependent in that programming, I feel that a certain degree of beginning the healing process must take place outside the relationship. Unless you just want to sacrifice it for the relationship, which unfortunately, might make you more cynical and more protective. In other words, you might protect yourself after a relationship blows apart; "I'll never let them get at my heart again. I won't be so vulnerable, so I won't suffer. No one's ever going to make me suffer again!" That's the illusion.

What we teach is that no one is going to make you suffer. You make you suffer. Then your ego hides it so as to not be ashamed of having negative programming. Having fun in a relationship is when you don't have anything to hide. Your beauty; you don't try to hide it. Your ugliness; you don't try to hide it. Your wonderful programmings, your lousy programmings, your self-destructive or unskillful programmings; you don't try to hide them.

When you get to that stage, when you can have an intimacy where ego is not trying to hide itself, to where we've done the inner work, to where we can communicate with it openly and not be ashamed, but still see that there's more to do. When we can join with another being in this mutual fun and mutual growth game and cross-fertilize each other, that's when the growth happens, the fun happens and pretty soon it's accomplished. It's there. You've planted the seed, it's grown. Now it's a big tree, but the seed needs nurturing first.

That's why I suggest that if one is severely dysfunctional, severely co-dependent or has a lot of inner child or inner parent work to do that they do it outside of the relationship. If you're already in a relationship then do it in the relationship if you can. But do it!

What if someone is already in a relationship that might not be working out that well?

If you've already chosen to create that relationship then it gives you an idea... actually the things that you're rejecting most in the relationship are the interface of your inner work. That's very hard for a person to see. But as we begin to use the tools that enable us to dissect our experience and see it for what it is, rather than through the illusion that our ego wants us to see... "They are separate." "If it weren't for them I could be happy." "I'm always right." Those are the three illusions that ego usually presents. When we can go behind them all to who we really are, that's dramatic growth.

I think that if you can use it for your growth it's your optimal way to get happy faster. But if you can't use it for your growth, I don't see anything spiritual about staying in a relationship where there's constant pain and suffering, day by day, month by month, year by year. I would say that's gotten to what is called codependence, which is a clinical sickness. So, I feel that if you're in the relationship do your best to use the spiritual principles that you've chosen for yourself to grow in the relationship. Because it's giving you a very straight dose of exactly the lessons that you need next, to learn to become a happier person. And it's very hard, at that point, to use those lessons.

How many people are coming through here each year for courses and workshops?

Penny: We have one or two courses that are happening at any given time. We have a seven week course that we offer four or five times a year and we have week-end courses, week-long courses, two week and three week courses. These are all happening all the time. So people come and go. We have quite an influx. Some trainings will have more people than other trainings. Some will have 10, some will have 25 or more. Ken and I just got back from Colorado where we did a workshop, so we're on the road a bit also.

Penny, how is it for you to work so closely together with your husband?

I love it. We work together so well, so easily, so comfortably. We both feel that our talents and skills complement each other, our interests also. We basically share the same values, have the same ideas about what's important in life and the wisest way to approach life. Out of that we have our individual emphasis that we like to have and work on having. When we work on a book Ken is the one who will come up with the basic, broad idea. He's the initiator. He'll get in there and start creating chapters. I'm the fine-tuner. I'll read it and do the proofing and the editing. I might suggest that a sentence isn't clear or that a certain chapter doesn't make sense, then we scrap it and start over. There's very little ego-conflict between the two of us and a lot of mutual appreciation that's shared on a daily basis. It's very easy. It feels very natural.

How are you feeling about the state of the world?

Ken: I cannot feel that humanity won't get it together. I would like to feel that it will get it together in time to avert a great catastrophe. Sometimes it's through pain that we gain. Our egos are so strong that oftentimes we will view the illusion that, "I must defend my power, my money, my territory, my whatever," to the exclusion of the values of love, cooperation, fairness, friendship, and so forth. I think we are still in a tumultuous situation worldwide. It's wonderful to see the nice things that are happening, such as in Eastern Europe. There's been a bloodless breakthrough there that no one expected. That shows a great step towards values of freedom and respect for the individual. I think that we are on a roll of very wonderful things happening, like a pendulum. And the pendulum can go back and forth. In general I tend to be optimistic. Otherwise I wouldn't have the energy to write anymore.

You're a big supporter of global community. In that vein, I understand you've released a sequel to your grassroots best-seller, The Hundredth Monkey.

Planethood is the sequel to *The Hundredth Monkey*. *The Hundredth Monkey* said that we are in one heck of a predicament. Let's wake up and discover it rather than be an ostrich with our heads in the sand. It was long on, "Wake up folks! Look what's happening," and rather short on solutions. *Planethood* gives a total solution, as it were, to eliminate war between nations, to create a solid way to rescue the planet and the environment. Also, to bring prosperity to the planet.

It's very simple. Once you quit spending a trillion dollars a year on killing machines or training on how to use killing machines, and you put it into something else then you've obviously created a tremendous amount of prosperity. This is a solution that Presidents of the United States have endorsed.

Einstein said that "unless we have this solution,"—he didn't use the word planethood, I coined that—"humanity has no future." Bertrand Russell said the same thing. Toynbee, the great historian, said the same thing. Anyone who really looks at the whole the best they can, comes to this same conclusion. Yet it's something that most people don't even think of.

I felt that it wasn't enough to wake people up, I felt that I had to write the solution. Now it's up to you. It's my final book on the subject. I'll revise it; I'm in the process of doing that now, but I haven't any plans to write another book like it, because this is more of the external game. I'm more interested in staying in my particular specialty of internal personal growth.

I know you're both involved with the World Service Vow. That certainly goes hand-in-hand with the concept of planethood. Could you tell us more about that?

Penny: It's a statement of a commitment that we want to make to go beyond our own self-gratifications to offer service to the world, lovingly and wisely. Sometimes it can take forms that will be surprising and unexpected. Generally, the approach that Ken and I take is one of gentleness. For me, it's really a goal that I'm striving toward in my life. I'm still very much at a time where I'm consumed with thinking of myself, making sure I'm okay, and that I'm getting what I want. Yet, this is that part of me that I want to develop more of, the part of me that is saying, "I'm going to reach the greatest amount of happiness in my life," by giving myself to the world in whatever form seems to be the most practical for me at the moment. The form doesn't seem to matter a whole lot.

You see, I've worked hard enough on myself and I recognize that this is a next step. This is where I can go from here. I'm going to keep working on myself, but I'm not going to make that more important than the service that I'm doing.

Interestingly, part of the form that it takes is about working on myself. Sometimes that's the greatest service that I can give somebody. If I'm mad at someone, then the greatest service I can offer them is to get myself clear of whatever it is I think needs to be different. Then I could go about trying to make changes, but doing it from a more centered, loving, preferential place.

From my own personal life, the form that the loving and serving is taking now is helping Ken physically and supporting him emotionally. Being at his side and playing the great adventure of life with him. Helping his energy. I have a lot of respect for what he has to offer in the world. My form is to support that. And, secondarily, to just be involved in moment-by-moment living, to be aware of what's going on around me and whether there's some way for me to offer some manner of assistance. To do it within the framework of sensing from inside what it is for me to do and what it is for me not to do, and either let other people do it or leave it undone.

Pretty much everyone has that. It may lie dormant in a lot of people. There are so many people out there who are striving to make the world a better place, to make their lives better, to get your own house in order and make your life work. That's part of it. It's all over the place. As Ken was talking about earlier, we have a lot of learning to do about what's skillful; what's going to really work for us in the world and what isn't.

It seems that in spite of our intentions and the desires we all have to make things work well, we have stubborn streaks, blind areas, blocks and habits that are ingrained. Games that aren't getting called loudly or clearly enough, until we get hit with a crisis that's close to irreparable or irreversible. It seems as though that's part of the nature of the game that we're all playing. That's the way it is.

I don't think that takes away from that side of us, that part of us, that's wanting to do good. So, I think it's alive and well. It could use a lot more nurturing, a lot more support and encouragement, modeling and recognition. I don't think it's a lonely thing at all, really. It's just a matter of tapping into that, seeing that and recognizing it. It's how we perceive. Each one of us has to choose, for ourselves, what forms we're going to follow and what paths we're going to take. In a sense, that's kind of an alone choice. But, we can choose to find glory and shared-spirit brotherhood, if we want to see it.

And if we trust it.

Penny: One of the things that Ken says about trust that I really like is that you can always trust a person to live out their programming.

Ken: I totally agree.

Penny: Good thing, because you said it! [Laughter]

Ken: You can always trust people to live out their programming, and then you don't have to be afraid. Beyond that, in a relationship trust is extremely important. It's very difficult once trust is shattered to get it back. If a person lies to you, and says, "I'll never lie." How can you trust that? Maybe they're trying to be sincere, but you don't know. It's very difficult to reinstate trust once it has been shattered. Will five years be enough? 10? Maybe 20? Penny and I have such a total level of trust.

It's like you open to new solutions that you've rejected before. When nothing is working after a desperate, anxious worry. When you feel that your life is trashed. What have you got to lose? "Maybe this will work." That's the straw you grasp for. If that straw is spiritual growth, then you will find yourself really getting into understanding and practice, practice, practice. Then, to that degree, things will begin to improve.

Penny: Trust is a process. One of the ways that we like to approach it is with the perception that life is perfect for either enjoyment or growth. So, if you're enjoying it, that's great, enjoy it. And if you're not, then what's the lesson to learn? Then it's a perfect opportunity for growth.

When you say that planethood is up to us, do you mean that you see it as an evolving process that will slowly gain momentum?

Ken: Remember, that when I wrote the *Monkey*—again I can't take credit for this, I'm just part of a big process—when I wrote the *Monkey*... did you ever see a videotape called *The Last Epidemic* with Helen Caldicott? It was produced by medical people, the Physicians For Social Responsibility. It was professionally produced, a wonderful video about the consequences of nuclear war with quotations from a whole list of prominent and well-known people. A top-flight production. I got a copy of that and sent it to the Louisville Public Broadcasting station. I lived in Kentucky then. They looked at it and sent me a nice letter saying that they appreciated seeing it, but they didn't want to screen it because the folks at Fort Knox might not like it.

That was the status of the *Monkey* ten years ago. It was doing its job along with everybody else. *Planethood* just came out a couple of years ago, we've only got 300,000 copies in print. It has not done its job, yet. It might need another decade. I don't like to make either-or statements, usually they aren't the most helpful. So I would make the modest statement that this, I think, is the best way for humanity to ensure its future. But if you give me a glass of wine and get me talking, I'll say it's the only way.

Do you know who the first President was that proposed this type of thing? You'd never think of it. If I gave you a complete list of Presidents, he'd be the last one you'd pick: Ulysses S. Grant.

The victorious general who couldn't fight unless he was drunk. While he was President he had this insight to propose planethood. So I can't take credit for the idea. However, I would like to do my part in spreading the word.

Michael Sky

"The forever self-defeating nature of the skeptical mind is such that it cannot see beyond the created limitations of its own presumptions. Thus, we could do happy cartwheels through the hottest of fires (and have), laughing all the while, and the skeptical mind will immediately explain it all away, without considering for even the briefest moment that it might be true, that there might be a very new and different way of looking at the world."

Michael Sky—Dancing With The Fire

It was my fascination with the more physical aspects of firewalking that led me to Michael Sky. After all, it seemed an odd thing, this shedding of any protective covering and walking barefoot over a bed of fiery, red-hot glowing coals. At the time it was beyond my experience and my comprehension. I was quite curious.

It was a warm Northwest day, I was just leaving the post-office with the usual odd assortment of mail that I so looked forward to. One bulky envelope contained an interesting looking volume entitled, *Dancing With the Fire*. It seemed appropriate to spend a few hours with it... right away. I knew just where to go. Nestled amongst the Madrone, the ocean waves softly walloping my mind I began to read this thoroughly fascinating book.

I was immediately engaged by three things; the subject matter itself, Michael's most eloquent style of writing and my own reaction. I was instantly swept away by my own fervent projections of the possibilities of something so astounding as walking on fire. I, not right away but slowly, began to realize that I needed to temper my reactions and I knew why. It had nothing to do with the potentials of the event itself, but rather my own shallowness. My own superficial reactions were insufficiently idle when compared to the substance that lurked just beneath the surface.

It's not enough to content oneself with the phenomenon of firewalking or, for that matter, with phenomena in general. Though one is sure to be, at first, somewhat overwhelmed with the visual experience of something like firewalking, it immediately, or at least at some point, propels the mind to find, realize and understand the deeper intricacies of what might actually be taking place. By this I mean taking it to fruition. For, in my experience, the sweetest taste of the fruit does not lie in the phenomenon itself, no matter how extraordinary, unique or dazzling it might be. Fortunately, Michael Sky was way ahead of me.

After spending a bit more time with this expansive volume it was plainly obvious that an interview would be a most beneficial exercise. As luck would have it, it came to pass quite quickly. For as I lay on the sands of the Puget Sound, Michael was waiting tables at a restaurant overlooking the same waters not more than one hundred miles to the north. A trip in the car to the ferry servicing the San Juan Islands brought me to a thoroughly illuminating afternoon with a remarkable teacher.

Michael is a holistic healer, workshop leader, teacher, and firewalker. He is as honest and effective a facilitator as anyone I've met. By this I mean an almost complete deference and reference to his integrity. (Again, another personal observation: If you're going to learn something that can literally turn you on your head it's probably a good idea that you feel that the teachers are principled.) He's basically an island kind of guy and thoroughly suited to the ocean wilderness he calls home. Two books have followed *Dancing With The Fire*. They are *Breathing; Expanding Your Power and Energy* and the potential classic, *Sexual Peace; Beyond the Dominator Virus*.

This last book opens up as much new territory as his first did. In fact, perhaps the subject of equal partnership between the sexes is, in many ways, hotter than firewalking. No matter, both are handled with a fair degree of illumination and dignity. There's no question that our author is not worried about tackling combustible controversies nor silent on burning issues.

Michael holds a degree in Chinese Studies (language and philosophy) and with this last volume his sageness has become even more apparent. I thought it would be a good idea to talk with him again so as to incorporate elements of the new book in with the first interview which mainly concerned itself with firewalking. He was still happily living on the island, though life has presented a number of opportunities since the first time we met. Of late he's become increasingly popular in Japan where he leads workshops and seminars. He was living in a different home, complete with a beautiful pond, and involved in fashioning a land trust with the aim of creating a small community.

While my initial surprise with the process of firewalking was centered on concern for the feet, Michael's real work with the fire begins and ends with the head. For him the fire becomes a metaphor for our limited beliefs. While our constricted attitudes might accept something such as walking on burning coals as being initially impossible our limitless imaginations could well open some new doors. Perhaps transformation through experience provides an easier access for integration. You can imagine your surprise as you watch yourself walking on a bed of fire. Is it possible that you might go through some changes with such an experience? Would there not be some sense of irrefutability as you dance the fire?

Transforming our fears is not always an easy matter. It can be but, as we sometimes know, it frequently isn't. However, let's dwell for a moment on the more positive alchemy of such a conversion. I'm fairly sure we can agree that the constricting energetics of fear are a hopeless and weary bore when compared to the dynamic vibrancy of affection. Occasionally it has been made very clear to me that the difference between those two widely disparate perspectives has been all in my head. A change in the current of our flow can easily alter the movement of our streams. As the adaptable human metamorphs that we are I believe that we can consciously evolve our changes.

Michael Sky is here to help you with these transitions. The author of Dancing With The Fire, firewalking facilitator, and human energy systems proponent, Michael has led some 4,000 people over a 1500° path. A path which does far more to their minds and belief systems than it does to their feet. A path that provides instantaneous feedback and irrefutable visual proof of something astonishing in the works.

"All of life is connected through energy and all of life may be affected through energy with the creative light of human consciousness. Though for thousands of years humans have created and enforced energetic patterns of domination, submission, violence, and abuse, there is evidence that we can create and enjoy patterns of cooperation and partnership if we choose."

Michael Sky—*Sexual Peace;*
Beyond the Dominator Virus

Firewalking is one of the oldest rituals known to man?

That's right. As far as I can tell from my own research it has happened in at least thirty different countries. Those cultures have it as a part of their long-term traditions. My own sense, and there is no way to confirm this, is that there are people who are very, very connected to the planet, in ways that we can only really philosophize about, wish about, because we are so far from it in our culture. But for people who have that connection, I think firewalking is a very natural extension of their experience.

How many times have you firewalked, and how hot is it?

I've led 150 walks. Sometimes we walk a number of times, so I've done lots and lots. The heat has been measured many times. It is generally between 1000 to 1800 degrees. It's very hot. A high burner on an electric stove is approximately 900 degrees.

One of the things that I found so fascinating about your work is your material on skeptical mind, belief systems, and intention.

I always talk to the skeptics in the room, partly because I've dealt with my own skeptic. I went with nothing but an open heart and belief and then, having done it, became a total skeptic about what I did. I felt that there must be some trick to this. I didn't feel like I was an exceptional person and I did it.

The skeptics' position is that there's basically nothing unique going on there. The skeptic wants to take out the idea that the human consciousness is creative. They want to say that, for purely physical reasons, you can in fact bring your foot in contact with fire and not get burned. They've given a couple of explanations. The first was that we are so nervous prior to the walk that our feet sweat and are protected from the fire by the moisture, that it provides an insulating layer. That's easily discredited by a person stopping and standing still in the coals, which has been done.

The more recent one is that wood coals don't have enough mass to burn human flesh. The heat energy of something is a function of how much mass it has. A description of that is to take a metal baking pan and put it in an oven, then heat the oven to 500°. You can put your hand in the oven and not be burned because air doesn't have enough mass to hold the heat energy, and therefore can't burn you. But if you touch the pan, it has a lot more mass, holds more heat energy, and therefore can burn you. What they extrapolate from that is that wood coals do not have enough mass. So even though their temperature is somewhere between 1200-1500°, they don't have enough mass to hold the energy to burn us. That's actually a great explanation. I lost sleep over that one, worrying about whether I was just doing a

snake-oil thing. The problem is that people do get burned at firewalks.

In what way?

We've talked to doctors about this. They say that, consistent with their experience as to what should happen if someone comes into fleshy contact with this degree of heat, they should experience instant and very severe burning. The sort of thing that you would rush to the hospital with. We've never had anyone burned like that, ever, with over 3000 walkers. As far as I know, none of the other people in this country have either. It is possible to get to the other side of the firewalk and experience a burning sensation on the bottom of the foot. Sometimes it can last for a few hours, or even develop into blisters. So when we say burn, that's what can happen. What we know, from lots of experience, is that on a given night, for a given person, sometimes that happens, sometimes it doesn't.

What that tells us is that the fire is always there, burning at whatever temperature, with whatever heating energy, people come into contact with it, they all get to the other side, and they all have a different experience. There's not one constant experience. Somehow, the difference is a function of human consciousness. If wood coals didn't have the capacity to burn human flesh, then no one would ever get burned. That's what slowly informed me about what's going on here. I had to deal with the fact that there was some burning. The burns have been the sobering and instructive influence that gives us the data. If no one ever got burned this experience would be totally without relevance. We would have shrugged it off a long time ago.

Can you find anything that is a common thread for successful firewalking?

Two factors stand out. The one that is the strongest is intention. Any person who has successfully walked on fire wanted to. They formed an idea about what they were doing ahead of time, they knew they were going to the firewalk and they knew they wanted to firewalk. That's a real leap. We live our lives with the intention not to touch fire at all. If we ever get burned, we get very clear from that moment on that we never want to get in contact with fire again.

For whatever reasons, firewalkers decide ahead of time that they want to have contact with fire. When someone accidentally comes into contact with fire with a body part, they are in direct, very intense conflict with a lifelong intention of not touching fire. That conflict causes, or allows, the burn. The life lesson there is that anytime we do anything we don't really want to do, we get burnt. Regardless of the sphere of activity. Anytime that we are stepping forward in life in contradiction to our heartfelt intention we are divided, conflicted, we are at less than full potential, and we set ourselves up for failure and disappointment.

The fire is very instantaneous and loud in its feedback. Life is a little harder to see sometimes. If we are in a job we really don't want to be in, if you are in a relationship you don't want to be in, anytime we do anything we don't want to do... we are getting burned. Energetically, my explanation is that intention sends creative energy towards the fulfillment of intention. If I really want to get to the other side of the room, my energy starts moving there. If what I want is that, and where I'm going is somewhere else, then I am divided. There's a conflict going on there and I've diminished myself. I'm much more liable to fail. But if that's my intention and that's clearly where I'm going then I'm operating at my fullest and have the very best chance of succeeding.

What you are saying is that the human consciousness, functioning with clear intention, is co-creating this, albeit, inconceivable event.

Right. We're saying that human consciousness, in interaction with its environment can change or, I like to say, slightly alter a law of nature. There's a law that governs flesh meeting fire. We don't change it drastically. We demonstrate that we're involved in the creation of reality, and even in the creation of natural laws. Through consciousness we can exert some influence.

Where some people say we create our own reality, I like to say we contribute to the creation of reality. We're a contributing influence, we're not it. What we're showing is that there is some play in the creation of reality. If we can come into contact with the fire for awhile without experiencing pain, we've demonstrated a totally revolutionary thing about human beings and their reality. We've shown that objective reality, which is supposed to be fixed and apart from human experience, is in fact connected to human experience.

One of the things that I found to be so intriguing and informative about the book was the way you presented your information about belief systems and their potential effects.

Energetically, I view belief as the software through which energy runs. Beliefs are arbitrary in a way. We can believe anything that we want, but as long as we are holding a belief it very much governs our experience. So, intention sets the energy moving in a certain way, and what we believe about what we are doing qualifies that energy and gives it strength and integrity. Belief is such a tricky one. I'm not sure if I would ever say that anything I believed in is true, but I know that believing in what I believe in with all my heart makes a big difference. I consider beliefs to be on a par with oxygen or love; I think they're a part of our being here. It behooves us to be very conscious of what we're believing in.

Can belief and intention completely explain the physical mechanics of it?

The question that comes out of whether you have a lot of intention about what you're doing, and whether you believe very strongly that your body will be safe, and whether you can walk on fire, doesn't really answer, "How does flesh not burn?" Somehow it doesn't have that response. We've also noticed that clothing doesn't burn, that hair doesn't burn. We were really at a loss to explain that. Most of the explanations that I had heard were like, if you had happy thoughts it creates chemical changes in the body. I believe that's probably a factor. That's a part of what's happening. I don't think it's the whole thing. It certainly doesn't explain why clothing or hair would be safe. Chemical changes happening in the brain and flowing through the immune system certainly can't affect clothing.

I'd known from other cultures that clothing was immune, and we've had experiences over the years that have shown that. There's one fellow back in New England that likes to lie down, and put his head right back down into the coals. People firewalking on crutches and the crutches being unaffected. People forgetting they had band aids on the bottoms of their feet, and the band aids didn't show any affect. People walking with long robes or dresses, dragging them through the coals. What I've noticed with hair and clothing is that mostly they don't burn.

What is your explanation?

My explanation has to do with human energy systems. A couple of years before I got into firewalking I ran across a book called, *Boiling Energy* by Richard Katz, a Harvard professor. He had gone to study the !Kung, an aboriginal tribe living in the Kalahari Desert.

The !Kung have a fairly sophisticated lifestyle and tradition of ritual and ceremony. Their most important ritual is the firedance. They do it when there is a felt need for some healing in the community. They burn a much larger fire than we do for several hours and dance intensely around it. After hours of this, some member of the dance will dance right into the coals and right into the flames. We rake fires into nice smooth sensible paths, they just crash on through the fire. They dance right in it, they will put their heads right down into burning flames. They will take coals and rub them into their bodies. They may swallow coals. They go much further with this than we do. There is something going on there that is way beyond Western understanding.

What is great about the !Kung is that they are not at all mystified about what they are doing. They have the most simple and rational explanation for firedancing and how it can happen. They believe there is this energy which totally fills the human form, fills every cell of the body, governs all of the body's processes, regulates all of the body's organs and surrounds the body in a protective field. A living energy that totally fills us, surrounds us, is the source of all of our power, a living energy that is the source of the human physical experience. They call this energy *num*. They say when your num is boiling over, when it's at its very fullest, you can do whatever you want with the fire. They see their energy and the fire's energy as connecting and they believe they will be improved, or enhanced, by the fire's energy.

Their metaphor is just so perfect and precise. It really is the simplest explanation I've ever heard. We are filled with energy, we know that life energy can empower people in amazing ways. My understanding of firewalking is that when our energy is at its fullest, it forms a protective field around us that includes hair and clothing. It either neutralizes or transforms the energy of fire from an agent of burning to an agent of empowerment. It somehow changes it, doesn't burn and allows the experience of contact.

Since firewalking brings up a lot of fear in people, do you see it as having a role in the process, or as teaching a lesson?
If I had to take one thing and say, "Thank God that the fire came into my life," it would be what it has taught me about fear. I have never really stopped fearing the fire. No matter how many times you do this, or how successful it is, there's always apprehension. I've learned to love that. I've learned to understand that it's there for good cause and to very much appreciate and feel grateful for it. My understanding of fear itself is that it is a generation and release, a strong charge, of life energy. Fear is a jolt of that, a generation and release, an extra movement of that through our being, that happens anytime that we feel in any way threatened or challenged. That's a good and intelligent design of the organism. Every challenge includes the energy to successfully resolve the challenge.

Classically, we have dealt with most fears through fight or flight. What we know from studies is that when we are frightened we can run much faster or fight much harder than ordinary. There's all sorts of descriptions of that. There's also the phenomenon of hysterical strength, the classic example being the woman lifting a car off of her trapped child. It's the energy pulsing through her until the threat is gone. She experiences the threat, she experiences energy in relation to the threat, and that allows her to do the extraordinary. We know that people in a state of fear can do this.

We also know that people in a state of fear often do just awful. That it can be a very debilitating condition. What happens is that the moment we feel challenge, we also feel a rush of energy. If for reasons of my own psychology or habits I choose not to act—the energy moves through me but I choose not to use it, I don't take steps, I don't somehow spend that which has been given to me—then it starts to collapse or contract inward. It starts as a flowing into action, but if I don't act with it, it contracts back into me.

Anything that goes wrong in our lives is a result of somehow not being energetically clear, of holding energy trapped within us, of being contracted, of not being a clear flow of life energy. Ideally life energy should be zooming through us at all times like an ocean, and being returned to the world as love, contribution and service. That is what is there for us.

Let's alter our course here and talk about some of your latest work regarding sexual peace. It's certainly a subjective topic, we're bound to push some buttons, but I know that we are all very interested. We've been talking about energy, so what about the energy of sex?

Sexual energy is the energy created within us for creative purposes. It's probably easiest to use it to create human beings. There's a whole set of equipment that comes that uses the energy in that particular way. It's a good thing we have this design because it keeps the species going, it's a lot of fun, children come into the world and that's good. That's one way to use this energy.

If it's the only way we are thinking of using it then we tend to put too much emphasis on sex in our life and the whole thing spins off into one direction. We might be led by that experience and it becomes addicting. When sex becomes addicting is when it becomes the only truth about spending this energy. Or we might see the sharing of sexual energy in a way that's totally tied to procreation. Then we can make it wrong and maybe it begins to look sinful and evil.

I see it as a free energy that is not connected to one specific region of the body. It flows through all regions of the body all the time. It's the spark of life. It moves through us not only keeping us healthy but it is also what we express when we create. It behooves us to learn all the ways of keeping that energy in motion all the time, to let it create.

I think it is an infinite source, but I believe it starts out finite in the body, where conservation of the orgasm becomes important. There's a practice to that. It's mostly about just keeping the

energy moving. My sense is that if this energy was always moving through me it would just be a pleasure to be alive. We should have a total experience of our bodies as a function of being here. It should be a pleasure to be embodied in the presence of other people. That shouldn't, in any way, suppress one's pleasure. If anything it should increase one's feeling of joy and happiness.

As you say, there's a practice to that and there certainly are some different schools of thought regarding sexuality. Which specific practices are you looking at?

I do some teaching in the book about specific sexual practice that a couple might follow to expand on what I'm talking about. Taoist sexuality, conservation of the orgasm, getting beyond the idea of sex as a purely genital experience and seeing it more in energetic terms. Rather than seeing it specifically in procreational terms, seeing it in transcendence. Again, it's about the whole body not just the sexual organs.

There are some differences between Tantric sex and Taoist sex. Where they overlap is in the thinking of the energy that usually moves in a sexual contact, specifically the sperm in a man and a vaginal release of a woman. Basically they are both saying there's this exchange of energies there and you can use this energy in a different way. You can use this wonderful energy to build a human being, it's a great and wonderful thing, but it may not always be to our advantage to spend it that way. We have choice about that. In my case the only way to use this energy is not just squirting out my genitals. I can control it and move it in different ways to express it and become more creative in other ways. I can use it to build children, I can use it to write books, I can use it to teach, I can use it in other ways.

The only way I'll know that is if I bring enough light to the sexual experience to keep it from being an automatic or addictive experience. You can learn, if you have a willing partner, to make love without orgasm. That does two things. One, it fosters this movement in other directions. Also, it turns out that it can be a lot more of an ecstatic practice than the orgasm. It can be a lot more fun way to make love. It's worth discovering that because it's actually great in better ways. It feels just as pleasurable but even more so, particularly for men. Women often have the experience of orgasm throughout the body already. They generally tend not to be as genitally-fixated as men. For both men and women it takes sex into another dimension. Then the energy of sex becomes available for other purposes. I think it keeps the body a lot healthier when we do this and it spends creatively.

I think that if the energy is suppressed it causes us to drop bombs on each other. Everything that I'm talking about this wonderful thing... if we turn it around and suppress it inside a human being it causes us to pick up guns and shoot each other. It causes us to slap out at innocent little babes that we love immensely, it causes us to desecrate the environment. That's the actual physical manifestation of domination, of holding the energy of life under pressure.

How did your work with sexual peace come about?
We had noticed for a few years that sexual abuse was becoming almost everybody's issue. In my work, just about five or six years ago was the first time I had ever heard about it. People just started, through the breathwork and some of our group workshops, to reveal it. I noticed it happened more and more over the next few years and it felt like I was working with that with everybody on some level.

What I see happening in the relationships where sexual abuse is being examined is that we're healing a pattern of relationship that's been going on for thousands of years. Now, that doesn't change the seriousness of it for the receiver. It doesn't make it better, it doesn't absolve anybody, but there was a pattern. So, blame is not what I'm looking at as much as a pattern of behavior that is now being questioned.

I think it's significant that we are now changing that at the same time we're flirting with world peace. I think the two are connected. So that's where the term sexual peace came from. I believe that we can't have peace between nations unless we have peace between men and women at the most fundamental and domestic levels of existence. It has to happen right there. Conversely, in having that happen, then peace becomes a natural. I see the two as being creatively connected.

When you speak of thousands of years ago you're really adding a historical perspective to all of this.

There's a human history that precedes what we normally think of as the dawn of civilization. There were cultures that existed thousands of years prior to that which, in all appearances, were not violent cultures. They were cultures in which men and women existed in peace and partnership. There were differences between men and women but that didn't become the foundation for hierarchies to be formed, either in interpersonal relationship, social structures or the family structure.

From what can be looked at archaeologically—and you never know totally what can be assumed from it—on the island of Crete, for example, there's a civilization that goes back some 6-7,000 years that had arts, literature, a certain degree of technology, traded with other people, had government and religion. They had everything we call culture and also had no weapons or battlements. Obviously they weren't warring with their neighbors. The record also shows a balance between sexes, no stratification of economics or class. It is what is called a partnership culture as opposed to a dominator culture.

Then there's a shift and everything, beginning with the old testament religions, becomes a male-based religious system. This was an event in history. It was extremely violent in regards to those who didn't agree with their concepts. That was an event, it was not the way human beings always were, or pre-ordained to be. There is this idea that we are this way because it's human nature. That men are men, women are women, war is war, that in some way this is just our nature. It's not our nature. Historically there was a time—and it wasn't caveman time, it wasn't that we were simple apes or something—that significant, sophisticated human culture existed without this, and balance existed between people.

I think that what is natural is for human beings to live in partnership and in gentle peace with one another. We have to be taught and conditioned towards distrust and abuse and there was a point in time where that started. There's somewhere from birth through the first couple of years of our lives that we're conditioned to what is considered to be normal human reality. That conditioning has a viral quality to it, which means that in order for it to stop we have to stop it in ourselves so we don't pass it on to our children.

It's a form of energy that my parents hold within them that they pass on to me in childhood. It passes on through the nature of their relationship, particularly through any abuse or mistreatment. That's where this affect and event, which started thousands of years ago, of people inclined towards mistrust and violence is passed on in a viral way for generation after generation. For so long it seems like human nature when, in fact, it's just a bad habit of learned behavior. It's what Alice Miller calls the poisonous pedagogy, the treating of children in a way that we think is for their own good when in fact what we are doing is conditioning them to domination, abuse and separation.

I would imagine that in a healthy partnership culture that energy would flow very freely and without any threat, any sense of evil or bad or in any way going off the rails into abuse. I believe it's possible for sexual energy to pass between two people, especially people that love each other very much and have a tight bond, in a way that is mutually beneficial and not a threat to society or a sin. Due to the state of the world that doesn't happen. That is where, I think, we all become damaged.

As a child, a one to four year old, our only understanding is in the teaching which is about disconnecting ourselves and often about an actual abuse of that energy. That, then, becomes reality. We, then, people the world and the world becomes made up of people who are so injured. Everywhere they go they encounter people who are so injured and no one can figure out why something like trust is so hard. It should be the easiest thing in the world. It should be as easy as opening your eyes to the sun to open your eyes to other people. We have to be taught, we have to be bent, for that to be difficult. Especially if we hurt those who we actually stand the most to love and gain from, the people in our own families. We have to be conditioned to that.

What does sexual peace actually entail? What's your vision of how it could be?

On a personal level it's about learning not to disconnect, stifle or suppress oneself in the presence of other people, and learning instead to remain connected. There's an energetic that happens. We know that we are surrounded by fields of energy. You can watch two people who love each other and basically see their fields expand. There's something that we do when we're in love that's very different than when we are in fear, distrust or hate. We have choice over that and can learn to stay extended into people and discover that, not only is it not threatening to do that, but actually improves our communication skills and makes our body healthier. It also tends to render us incapable of violence, warfare and abuse. In order to abuse people we have to learn to contract ourselves first which, again, is a lesson that starts at birth.

Sexual relations is really about appreciating differences without turning them into hierarchy. It's not about men and women becoming alike or anything like that. We certainly have our different bodies and our different tendencies but we don't have to take those into hierarchy. Any relationship, whether it's parent-child, professional-client, teacher-student, if it splits into hierarchy, I consider it abusive.

One of the ideas that's central to this whole thing with sex is that we tend to have the idea that sexuality is an animal part of self that acts out of our control. As though it was a force apart from human consciousness. I stress that it's totally the opposite from that. It's totally reachable from our consciousness. We can express it according to our desires, it doesn't have to be out of our control. That's a mistaken notion that comes from the whole mind-body split. Sex is as close to the spirit and the soul of the human being as you can get. And it's very much a function of consciousness.

When you're talking about hierarchy and abuse—some forms of which are currently socially supported—we're really touching upon denial aren't we?

The denial gets put on top of thousands of years of history and makes it hard for us to look at all this. A child who is mistreated has to make sense out of their world, and does so by crippling themselves intellectually. We deny whole portions of reality that

don't fit, and we have to. If it's bad enough we literally reinvent. There are kids who totally come up with their own fairy-tale realities. How do you make sense of your father hitting your mother? It doesn't fit. For a three year-old... no way, it's unfittable. You can't work with that as material, you just can't. To see the truth of that and hold on to who you are would be to go insane and maybe that's what happens to some kids. Children are way too intelligent to have that fit, so they deny. And it's a mercy that we can do that, that's how we cope with reality. We should be glad we can do that.

But it costs us—it causes an incredible suppression of our internal energies. We have to use a significant chunk of ourselves to keep information under suppression. And we cripple ourselves intellectually. I believe that when people talk about only using ten percent of our brains that maybe that is where a lot of the other ninety percent goes. You have to become about 90 percent less intelligent to make sense out of an abusive environment. The blinders we put on remain and we don't really perceive everything any more and we become crippled human beings.

All that is held in place by this tension of denial which is a significant part of the dominator virus. Wherever there is domination, wherever that hierarchical relationship has gone then both parties are denying. It's a mechanism that allows us to live with splits in our reality. It has to be addressed if we are going to expand ourselves. The two are connected.

There's a new thing that seems, over the past ten years, to be impacting sexuality quite a bit. Of course, I mean AIDS. How does that fit in here?

Let me tell you about a woman I know. She has been surviving AIDS and actually reversed her HIV status. She was HIV positive, her partner who gave it to her is now dead.

Okay, wait. Now this woman was definitely medically confirmed with HIV, right?

She was confirmed by two different tests, including a Red Cross test, as having AIDS. She went into the early stages, her body started to fall apart. She got it together, basically through what she calls her daily awareness program; bringing light to her childhood, her dietary habits and her relationships. She felt a healing and since then has tested, on several occasions, HIV negative. She actually changed at an energetic level or, possibly, at a genetic level.

I use that as a metaphor for healing the dominator virus. When I say dominator virus I mean it is as real as an AIDS virus. This isn't just an abstraction, it's something that you carry within you. If you have a two year-old child you're passing it on and it's changing the way they feel about being human, the way their bodies function, the way they think. What we've learned is that it can be addressed the same way as a virus.

In her story, and with other survivors, it's the bringing of light to their lives that's enabling them to survive this. I don't know of any war-metaphor approaches to AIDS that have worked yet. The people that I see who are winning with AIDS are bringing excruciating light of awareness to their lives, to who they are, to how they live, to what their purpose is, and that heals them. There are actually hundreds of people who are surviving with AIDS right now that have gone beyond 10 years of actual prognosis of symptoms. It's not that they are dormant. They came out of dormancy and are in a healthy state which is as close to curing as there is. I don't know if we'll ever cure this thing. I think it's part of what is changing us.

A lot of people are looking at viruses in a new way. The pure information that is floating around our world... if your body wanted to know the latest information of spirit manifesting in physical form it would get most of that through viruses. We have them going through us all the time and we learn from them. Sickness is a deep learning. I do think that AIDS is part of the new sexual nature—it's changing human sexuality. I don't look at it as a gun to our heads, either. I see it as a positive manifestation of that change. I don't mean to paint a happy face on what's a terrible problem for people who are going through it. But, it will force us to engage differently sexually, and not just latex protection. It will force us to actually engage as men and women, men and men, women and women... differently... from the place of Spirit.

We've been talking about a subject that throws a lot of people into extremes. Just the word tends to push a lot of buttons in a lot of ways. I just want to be sure that people don't misunderstand or dismiss your words because of the topic.

I have faith that as a natural system there would be a natural choreography to our sexual affairs if we weren't spending all our time suppressing the energy. We can trust that. I try to stay away from how it should be expressed. As you say, everybody sees this very differently. I know when I say the word sex, it's almost like people split off into different language systems completely. So, I try to talk about it at an energetic level and make the case that we have more choice. The thing that bothers me the most is that people think they don't have choice about it. That's it's beyond their reach, that they just have to act that way, they can't help themselves, and it gets supported by a lot of scholarly data that says that spirit is out of the body and sex is within the body.

I think that's very limiting. Sex is probably the part of us that is most amenable to conscious choice. It is where we have the greatest conscious influence. We can influence our sexuality consciously to a very large degree if we try to, if we make it a practice to. We can exercise choice there and out of those choices... things change.

Dorothy Maclean

"*The key to this transformation lies in recognizing that oneness of all life of which the devas continually remind us. If we can thus transform our way of looking at life, our actions within our environment will be transformed. As we begin to recognize God in every aspect of the world around us, that part of the world is redeemed, until ultimately the whole planet is redeemed.*"

Dorothy Maclean—*The Findhorn Garden*

It was long after the event that the world began to become aware of a provocative ecological experiment taking form on the far-off beaches of Northern Scotland. It had begun some thirteen years earlier when a trio of seekers had set up housekeeping in a small trailer parked near the sea. It was here that Dorothy Maclean along with Peter and Eileen Caddy (and the Caddy's three young boys) had found themselves transported. Not by chance, perhaps by fate, but certainly as a function of their inner work.

They lived quite simply in their small mobile trailer. There were interesting challenges. One can easily imagine the difficulties they faced just with regard to the space issue alone. We would do well to consider what it was that they were doing. As is so often the case, it certainly could be looked at from a number of differing perspectives. They had the courage to leave the lives they had known and were well qualified for. They had the commitment to embrace a different course not knowing how it would manifest itself. They had the faith to trust in its purpose and result.

What they accomplished can be seen as an evolutionary departure point toward the higher planes of human consciousness. They began to garden. That in itself may or may not spark your curiosity but there was a lot more. What they cultivated in that sandy and often inhospitable region was not what we might expect. The produce of their labor went far beyond what we might simply call vegetables and flowers. Through their intent and their faith the natural world came to life in a new way. However, the newness of it was completely based in the breaking free of a seemingly constricted human perception.

Dorothy Maclean had begun to recognize the importance of the voice within as an aspect of God's will. She learned to pay attention and to listen ever more carefully. She wrote down the guidance and began a process of learning to place this first in her life. She recognized it as the will of God and has explained it thusly, "To me, God is an indwelling presence, the core of what I am and what everything is. God is life itself, speaking through all life. And God's will is the path we tread which develops the best for us and for all we encounter."

Their first winter at Findhorn was particularly severe. It was unusually cold and windy. Spring was quite welcome when it finally arrived. Along With the newness of the earth's life energies there came a new message for Ms. Maclean. It was suggested that she prepare to feel the forces of nature. When these messages did arrive it was Peter Caddy who suggested to her that this guidance could be used to help with the garden.

The guidance that Ms. Maclean opened herself up to came from the nature spirits and the devas. About them she has written, "The devas hold the archetypal pattern and plan for all forms around us, and they direct the energy needed for materializing them. The physical bodies of minerals, vegetables, animals and humans are all energy brought into form through the work of the devic kingdom." The word deva is taken from the Sanskrit and means shining one.

We can see from Ms. Maclean's description that these creative spirits play no small role in the continuing energetic movement of our planet. In fact, what it continually brings up for me is the degree of divine orchestration that must be occurring within every moment. From the description above we can extrapolate an amazing amount of information about life. And, better yet, it's all so benevolent, beneficial and caring.

The Findhorn founders have been quite open and direct about the reasons for the success of their experiment. They consider it based upon their own willingness to listen and co-create, and the openness of the angelic realms towards that same co-creation. Taken together can one really doubt the potentials of that manner of teamwork?

Perhaps Findhorn presents us with an amazing display of the possibilities inherent in the human/spirit communion, the ego/angelic blending which resides potentially, if not yet factually, within us all. Dorothy Maclean would have us know that the ultimate teammate is not that far away, is quite accessible and actually awaits the union.

That's how it started for the three valorous adventurers. Perhaps we can utilize their experience as a starting point for ourselves. The implications are both amazing and wonderful. Through their commitment, hard work and dedicated cooperation with the nature spirits the results went far beyond human expectation for that desolate region.

In time the word spread and the almost mythic fame of Findhorn was born. With the additions of R. Ogilvie Crombie and then David Spangler, Findhorn oriented itself more fully towards community and in education. People came from all over the globe to witness, work and understand the garden. They came to learn and to be. The story spread and the word Findhorn became synonymous with the concepts of the practical applications of oneness.

With the publication of the evocative *The Findhorn Garden*, in 1975 and then the stirring *To Hear the Angels Sing* in 1980, Ms. Maclean has made an indelible mark in the annals of spiritual literature. One cannot help but be moved and encompassed by the warmth and totality of her words and deduce therefrom a sense of Higher Purpose and divine cooperation.

A very modest and humble woman, Ms. Maclean now lives quietly in the Northwest. She shuns the spotlight and holds no mark for adulation. She told me that she really didn't have anything to say and was going to be much too busy for the next six months for over a year and a half! Upon our arrival she was quite sure that she wasn't very interesting and probably not a good person to talk with. It's hard to differ with such a wise woman, but in actuality I found her to be completely charming and a veritable well-spring of insight. A book of her former devic communications at Findhorn has been recently published. She is currently planning a brand new volume embodying her experience and perceptions of the Angels of culture as mythical figures.

They gardened at Findhorn. They cultivated plants, higher communication and souls. How like the dormant, yet potentially awesome seed might we all be? The work done at Findhorn brings to our sensibilities a dimension beyond the traditional five senses and offers a vast potential for the recognition of awareness, life and the spiritual force.

We can think on these things, remember this work, recall this vastness of energetic cooperation and communication in our everyday existence. As we walk in the natural world we can realize that we too have a grand array of support and nourishment from those that take great delight in the light from other dimensions. They, too, are us.

"My own eternal quest took me as far as I could then go, into the hub of myself and of the universe... I learned that we can deal with all levels of our world in a truly creative, reciprocal way and, in joyous company, move to still more creative realms along with the brothers and sisters who make the totality of planetary life."

Dorothy Maclean—*To Hear the Angels Sing*

How are you feeling about all the changes that seem to be coming about these days?

I think there are changes for the whole world. Obviously the whole world has got to change, because we're on a suicide course the way we are. I think everyone is affected. I believe it's a planetary lifting of vibrations, if you want to put it in that sense. I think we've all got to get out of our old ruts and face life in another way. Of course one doesn't know what that is, because one doesn't have a blueprint. I myself have just sort of been lying low and hoping I can choose to go with any changes that come my way. Not knowing what they are, and not knowing what the result will be, but trying to be open.

You think we're on a suicide course?

Well, just from the way we are treating the planet, the Earth. We're cutting down all the trees, poisoning the air and the water and everything else. That's been going on for a long time, but it's really reaching epidemic proportions right now. And business... I mean using the resources of the Earth without putting anything back, without saying thank you, just taking. It's front page news everywhere now. It's something that you and I have known for years and years but now, at least, everyone gives it lip service.

Right. Everyone seems to be talking about it, but...

The change means giving things up and the people haven't yet reached that stage, in this country anyway. Sacrifice isn't popular. And taxes aren't popular. I mean it's just ridiculous! How can you pay off debts unless you tax more? But no one will even say that completely commonsensical thing; it's political massacre. It's daft.

I suspect that you see these changes in a positive way.

Oh, yes. I'm not worried about the fate of the world. I think all these changes, all these things, are making us change. If we're not going to do it without being forced to, then we're going to be forced to. Because change must come... we cannot go on. And, I think we see all the bad news in the papers, but we don't see the good news.

What sort of changes are you anticipating?

I don't see anything specific. We've got to change our attitude as far as living. We've got to realize that we're part of the planet and not try to live separately, and selfishly, the way we have been both nationally and individually.

So you think we'll make that?

Oh, yes. Yes I do.

Maybe that brings us to living in trust. Something I think you've had a lot of experience with.

Well, I'm still learning... to trust the process, completely. You know, one thinks that "uh-oh," and one does one's own thing, and then realizes at the end that they should have gone with the process. The Universe is on our side, God is on our side. If we go with the things that we know best, the results are going to be the best they possibly can be. It's as simple as that.

Sometimes we disregard the things we know inside.

Yes, and we all have done that. I think we are learning, certainly I am, that when one really trusts the process and really becomes 100% loving, miracles happen. That's a very powerful way to live, very effective. I've had several examples of that recently. If I'm in the flow and truly loving, something happens, the phone rings and all the problems are resolved, it just vanishes. And that... love, and being loving is such a feeble word, but in fact it's very, very powerful. We just haven't got the meaning of it right. We haven't got the words for it.

The early days of Findhorn certainly involved a lot of trust.

Yes, trust was there... but I could turn to the God within and find out... the attitude. I think it was the attitude one should take in any situation. One gradually gets to live in that attitude. Then the trust in the whole can awaken.

How do people get to that point where they can hear that, listen to that?

We all have a different way of attuning to our inner selves, to the God within, or whatever we want to call it and whatever is our way. I believe that when we are open the way opens. When we are ready, should I say. If one turns to that, asks for help from that, one will always get it.

Through the years one gets to know that it's real, the mind saying, "Oh, this is silly." Through the years on know that it's real, and one feels that it's real, and it's always t.

How one gets onto it... well, every religion has a different technique. I think we just choose our own way. The work is just changing one's attitude. I think you go beyond belief systems to knowing. To me one has to know these things. First one believes in them, but it gradually gets to a state of knowing. That's what's important so one can follow one's intuition, or right attitude or whatever you want to call it, all the time.

You've written about how much more Angelic presence is being felt on the Earth today. Is that an evolving process?

Yes. It is in my life. We are Angels ourselves. We have all the faculties. That is our Higher Self, shall we say. I've not been tuning into Nature so much recently, not since I left Findhorn in fact, but more to the higher aspects of human groupings, countries, nations, cities... any sort of grouping, even areas of a country, which have come under human influence. To me, that attitude which is at One, all over the Earth, is the dynamics that makes life happen. As we tune into that more, we're more with it.

So you're talking about relationship then?

Absolutely. To me it all boils down to that; relationship with ourselves and, in my situation, as I related to my higher self it related me to the environment. It was not a matter of trying to escape the environment or life as it was, it was to bring that attitude into one's everyday living. It's always been like that. I could never understand the people who seemed to think that it was an escape from life. I never looked at it in that way, just the opposite.

That attitude of Oneness encompasses all of life and all of living. Whatever there is, including oneself. The hardest thing for me to love has been myself. It's easy to love beautiful Nature or whatever, but one knows oneself. I think it really boils down to no judgement. No judgement whatsoever. Complete acceptance of what one is. It's easier to accept other people. I've always been able to accept them, up to a certain degree, but to accept myself, as I am completely, fully, with no judgement on anything; then the whole world is one, is ours.

What were the hurdles you had in getting there?

Realizing that good and evil were my judgement and were the way I see things. God is in all, is everywhere. I've read Krishnamurti for many years, and heard him. A few years ago I was rereading him, and he said, "All your faults and failings, just look at them without condemnation, without any judgement, without any feeling at all, just accept them completely as they are and the miracle will happen." One day I actually did that and the miracle did happen. Instead of all my faults and failings, there was the God that I had to drop my faults and failings to get to. There it was. To me there is nothing in life that is excluded.

Nothing at all...

Nothing at all. I'm still trying to, in my mind, bring that altogether. Because there are a lot of things that one doesn't like, or is judgmental about, as we see it in our limited point of view. So by our destroying—which is what we are doing—the planet we are coming to realize that we are part of the planet. That's something we didn't know before. We just took it as something we could exploit.

What do you think about the logging controversies that are going on?

You can imagine what I think about that. I don't know if you watched something on television recently, where the lumber companies... all they could see was, "that the trees would last forever, no problem." It's so ridiculous. They are such precious resources and we are cutting them down. The only real urgent message I got, the real urgent message from all of Nature was from the trees. That seemed really important. They wanted to shout to humanity, "WE NEED TREES!" The rest were all beautifully philosophical, balanced and nice and so on, but the trees were very urgent. And that was quite a few years ago.

How do you suggest that people connect with Nature?

Well, I'm one of these people that don't suggest to people. I prefer that they get on with doing it in their own way. I can share my own experiences and that's all I really can talk about. Everyone is different. Everyone is going to connect in a different way. I've been holding a few workshops, I've sort of given it up the last year, where we help people connect with Nature. We hold it in a place where each member could be alone, in silence, for one day and one night, out in nature and just be with it. That was always a very powerful experience. That's one way of doing it. But how one does it in that situation is by putting up a situation where people can find their own way better.

How do you do it?

Well, after about ten years of attuning to the God within, I was told that I had a job to relate to Nature. How I do it is the same way that I connected up with myself, with the God level of myself, which stemmed from the inner experience of knowing the God within and then choosing to be in that area. So I chose to be in that special space in myself. From that I focused on whatever it was in Nature that was coming my way at the time from the same area, that is, the spiritual side of Nature. That's the way I've been doing it.

Now I'm realizing, it's coming more, that even Nature has personality levels, is influenced by humans and that. Hopefully that's much more into my beingness now. At first the contact was very... elusive, a very precious sort of far away. Then, after years of contacting it, it settled down into me. So, I don't have to leave the rest of my life to get into it. Just keep that attunement on the upper levels and then extend it unto all the other levels, physical and everything.

I think that's one thing that's going on with the world at the moment. We've forgotten the physical. I myself have never acknowledged my own body or paid any attention to it. Fortunately I've always been healthy, so I've not had to. I've just completely taken it for granted, never given it any thanks, never given it any encouragement or care, just the way we've treated the planet. I'm realizing that now, and I'm trying to include my physical body more. I think that's, again, a world thing.

In one of your books you wrote about living in balance with the spiritual and physical worlds, and being well-grounded in both.

Yes. I'm thinking that my next book might be called *The Joy of Balance*. Apart from the physical and the spiritual there are the other levels, there's the mental and the emotional. Which are two levels that, because of my particular fate, I've rather ignored. I think at Findhorn our job was to make the vertical alignment with God, and we sort of ignored the personality level. If we had personality problems we would solve them from the vertical alignment. But now is a time to bring them all in, so they all have

an equal area to play in. I'm finding that's so in my own life anyway.

Are you finding that more challenging?

No. Well, whatever one is doing or learning is challenging, isn't it? In that sense, yes. But it's just like the next step, whatever one does. That was one thing about early Findhorn... we didn't find it too challenging because we only did one step at a time, we didn't know we were going anywhere. We had no particular vision, except to do what we had to do one step at a time. That's challenging enough. I still think that's a good way to work. Thank goodness we didn't know what we were doing because our minds would have spoilt it, completely. Or we would have run away and said impossible.

Have you been back lately?

No, I haven't. I haven't been back since, I think 1983. I was just back for a conference. I think I'll have to go back next year and renew my links. Unfortunately the last few times I've been there it's been for conferences, so one didn't really know what was going on with the community. Of course the community is now relating more to the outside world, having businesses and that sort of thing. At the moment I believe they're doing a lot of environmentally safe housing and that sort of thing.

What about the garden?

The garden wasn't really kept up with after the first five or six years. People started to come and we didn't have time to go in the garden, we had to deal with the people. The garden has really played second place since then.

Has your perception of Nature changed over time?

I don't think it has changed. When you get into that area of Nature... I mean, that's sort of the eternal side of it. And as I say, I'm not so much attuning to Nature now. To me it's almost second nature now—I don't have to think about attuning to Nature. I don't get messages now the way I used to. I feel that was a learning process. I had to get those messages to help me mentally understand because I was going into the area of feeling, not emotional, but feelings on a sort of intuitive level. All these messages were to help me put it on the mental level and understand it better. But now I think... as much as I need to know at the moment, I think I understand it. I don't think it's changed a great deal because it's an area of pure love.

When you read all these things about Nature being angry and such—that has not been my experience. Nature has not changed; humanity is causing greater results. It's not Nature being angry, it's man with his action. I tuned into an active volcano once, Mount St. Helens before it blew, it was a wonderful dance. A wonderful dance of trying to incorporate all the elements concerned, human and natural. Very intricate, intricate balancing steps trying to minimize the forces and bring out the best for all concerned. That to me is what Nature is always doing.

Yet it was such a tremendous explosion.

Yes. I was told at the time that an explosion would be necessary. I didn't tell anyone because I didn't quite believe it. It was brought on by the stresses of a changing world. I imagine that's always been so. Through the ages we've had far greater volcanos than that. In this particular case I think humanity was entering into it. The stresses of humanity were part of the whole process, part of the balancing act.

What are your thoughts on Native American teachings?

I have great respect for what they say. But, this is our life. We can incorporate as many traditions as feel right to us, of course, but our life is different. I think that we can have the same attitude as they had and bring it into our modern living. That's what is necessary for us; the attitude of reverence for the Earth and the recognition of all life. I don't think we need the ritual that they had. That was for their time, not for now.

Regarding your Devic communications, in retrospect would you have done it differently?

I wouldn't. I couldn't. We all did... I did what I felt was right at the time. Though I would do it differently now that's because I am different now. No... no, I don't see any point in going back like that.

We seem to be passing out of a phase where there was a lot of channeling activity going on. Any perceptions on that?

Yes, it seems to be dying down. It's just a learning process. A process where we can learn that there are other ways, and other ways of thinking, than our own normal worldview, that can get us out of our normal worldview and into a broader one. Then we go on, on our own. I think it's just a beginning phase. I think the whole process is to learn to depend on our own choices and our own inner guidance, not to listen to anyone else. To me, any true teacher will always throw you back on yourself.

Regarding your own life then, rather than having to tune into things repeatedly to learn, it's now more of a flow?

Yes. I stopped having times of attunement when I left Findhorn. The idea being that I would be in tune all the time and not just having special times of the day when it was holy, to be open at all times. Whereas I probably could have tuned in more at other times, I feel that it was the right move. I don't regret it at all. I think that, up to a point, it's opened the way for a more immediate attunement at all times. That's my aim still.

When you were doing the workshops with people, you tend to view that as an awakening conscious endeavor on their part to become in tune with that same energy that you feel that you've incorporated?

Yes. I can only share that, "here's the way I became attuned with the energy and here's an opportunity for you to do it your way." At the least we're all trying to do it together. When the energies are all together in one thing, it makes us strong, a force-field.

What would you say about your focus having been on Nature, initially, but now primarily focused on relationships?

Well, our problem with Nature is our relationship to it. Our problem is relationship. So, I think it's a natural follow-up.

Can we grasp that concept by learning to relate to each other first, and then relating to Nature?

I think we should do both at the same time. What we have done in the past is to relate to one another and ignore Nature. I don't think we can continue to do that anymore. I think the world is telling us that.

It's interesting that your focus has changed.

Yes, but don't forget that it's is still the Devic area. I'm still talking about... after I went to California for three years I went to Canada. I was there for eight years. The gist of that was recognizing that each country has a soul, and how to relate to that.

So you're able to apply that consciousness in your going from place to place?

Yes. It's the same Angelic consciousness, but in places instead of just nature, and what difference each one makes to us. How do we relate to that, the Angelic oversoul of a country, of a city? Because we are a part of it all the time. So it's not forgetting the Angelic world, it's putting into another area of it, cultural Angels and so on.

That's really interesting. I've heard people speak of that before but not in a Devic way.

I wrote a little booklet on it called, *The Soul Of Canada*. It's just a very small booklet, really printed for a more general outlook than talking too much about the souls, but all the same it gives one an idea of the way I was going on it.

You are doing a lot of traveling these days. What are your perceptions about the various areas you've visited?

I think it's the differences that strikes one. I find it boring to go to a western culture, Australia for example; it's too like us to be as interesting as say, Thailand, which is so different. So naturally one is drawn into the differences. From a soul level the attitude is precisely the same. What's fascinating is to see how the differences come out in a different country, and why they come out differently. I had thought that I would get a lot of attunements about this. I didn't get so much, but I got a much deeper feeling of the world as a whole, and the oneness of it.

You felt the Oneness of it, and yet a recognition and honor of all the differences that brought the Oneness to being?

Yes. And to me the differences are very important. The Angelic world has always said that; to honor and enhance the differences. They don't want homogeneity. Honor the differences. Respect them, don't judge them. They make for a richer whole.

Where did you go?

This year I had three months in Southeast Asia, Bali, which is a wonderful country. Everyone who goes there falls in love with it. Java, Thailand, India, Nepal. I had quite a bit of time in Nepal. I have a friend who has an apartment there. Then after coming back from that I went down to Brazil and Argentina, where I hadn't been since 1943. That was very interesting, to see the differences there, and see how the whole feel of the place is different and the direction they're taking. The other trips have just been to Canada, Hawaii and so on. It was fascinating. We were in Kashmir when all of this revolution was going on. We were about the last tourists there. It was all very interesting.

Part of what I realized is that we are all so culturally brain-washed. We see things because that's the way it has always been. If we are going to be like that then we can't accept the one world, because we want everyone to be like us and we think they are all so stupid and so on. That's part of the thing that I think is important for us to be aware; how our own assumptions are just that of our upbringing, and to go beyond that.

That's hard to do when we are just sitting here.

Yes. We can see it on a television screen or something. But it's very different living in the country and seeing it, seeing the people, seeing the differences. And yet, how what we might look down on and judge, is in fact a very wonderful thing.

What kinds of things did you appreciate?

Just tuning into the essence of something at the time. For example, here's a very odd one but it just sort of jumps to mind, in Nepal I saw rhinoceros. You wouldn't think that they would live there, but they do. So, I was tuning into them. I felt a sweetness, a tremendous sweetness from the soul level of a rhinoceros. It just seemed absolutely ridiculous. I almost got the idea that it wouldn't mind changing its form so that in its innate sweetness it could find a better form through which to express itself. Things like that you would never get unless you were feeling the real vibrations. They were in the wild, in a forest.

You once wrote that everything and anything that we do has meaning.

They all have meaning and it's generally so different from what one might think it is from the surface.

Your material on creative living is very interesting also.

I don't think we live creatively within ourselves. At least I haven't. I've been so in a rut about saying that, "I'm the sort of person who can't do that sort of thing." So, I would drop out of whatever that sort of thing is. So, I don't add any creativity to the situation. I think we all do that. It's only when we are in tune with the whole, in balance with the whole of ourselves that we can be truly creative. I think that is what life is teaching every one of us; to have all of our beingness in line—our Higher Self right down to the physical—so we're free to express that tremendous creativity and not have it go out in a little channel that's been culturally laid out for us, or brought in from the past.

Do you think that the Findhorn experience was an aspect of destiny?

Yes I do. When I was first aware of the Angel of Findhorn it was, shall we say, fully-formed. That, to me, says that there was a destiny there and we had to bring it out to life. That was ours to bring to life. If we hadn't then somebody else or others would have. It was something that had to be done. It became part of my personal destiny because I chose to do it. I could have reneged, I suppose.

Do you really think so?

Well, no. No, I don't. Not me. When one is given a job to do, I have the temperament that says, "Alright, I've got to do it."

Does that goes along with aspects of service?

Yes. I think we all have that aspect, we all like to be of service. It isn't popular to say that, but I think we all feel good when we do. I remember I was in a foreign city once, I had only been there for two days and someone came up and asked me, in a foreign language, about such and such street. And I knew, because I had just passed by it. I could tell what they were saying by the name of the street even though I didn't know their language and I could point and say there it is. That was wonderful to be of service like that! That made my day, several days.

Your activities at Findhorn were of gargantuan service. It must make you feel good, on a continuing basis, about what your endeavors brought to life there.

Well I don't really think of it. Every now and then I come across it and I'm always amazed, you know. I might be in a weird part of the world and hear that Findhorn is famous or something. And, golly, it's sort of unbelievable. We weren't trying to do anything like that, and we were very ordinary people. Our teacher had said that, "God uses the foolish of the world to confound the wise." So that's how we could see it. [Laughter] We had commitment and that takes you a long way. It's about all we did have. [Laughter] To us it was just doing what we had to do, you know. It wasn't amazing at all, to us, being in it. We just went on with it. It wasn't always pleasant. There were lots of things... if we had chosen, if we had a personal choice, but we were all three committed to doing God's will, as we put it in those days.

If you're doing what you know is right, you can do anything. We knew that we had to be there. I certainly knew that. That's what was so wonderful. That's what's so lacking in the world today, we have no sense of place in the whole. If people did they wouldn't commit suicide, they wouldn't be upset, because they would be part of a bigger thing. We were part of our little thing. We knew that we were doing... we didn't know what it was, but we knew that's what we had to do. So, you can put up with anything then.

Was it just as easy to release that, when you felt it was time to move on?

I just knew it was time for me to come back to my own part of the world.

But, again, you didn't know what you would be doing.

No. I just knew it was time to come back and I knew that I would write a book. And when I got back to Canada I wanted to join my friends in Wisconsin, but I knew I couldn't go yet. I didn't have a green light, I had to stay there for a certain period.

But even that sort of knowing has gone now. Things have changed. How, I don't know. I'm here, but I don't know I should be here. I'm just here. I think things are very different. It's not so... easy. There's far more choices nowadays and that's the way it should be. Instead of being told what to do, one's got to put oneself into it. To me, that's part of your training, part of the training for adulthood. I'm still trying to learn it.

It seems then that if you're not going to get the strong directives that it would take a larger trust level. How do you integrate that?

If you stop this judgement thing, judging what you do, judging what you don't do and that sort of thing, and just go with it. If you don't have judgement on all these things, whatever it is, you can go on—never forgetting that God is in it. Whatever in the moment feels right. It's a far greater openness. One should be far more open for change and everything. There's not a rock that one has to stick on, one is open to any direction... hopefully.

Change is something that we see coming along a lot quicker these days.

So quick, yes, and it seems to be getting faster. The statistics say so. There's so many things being changed too. There's so many more things than have been in the past, things breaking down and not working anymore. If you know that God is in the world and that everything is working out according to... and one is not judging then it's okay, whatever happens, isn't it?

I'm learning more and more to trust process. I'm learning that. And it doesn't mean that one sits back and does nothing, or foolishly believes that all is well with the world. I think one has to see all these things, understand them and be ready to do what one can when it comes into one's own life. I think that's very important. It's not just sitting back and doing nothing.

So there's nothing passive about the process?

No. In fact, I think it takes a greater contribution of energy than it ever has. Sometimes I listen to the news and if I'm in the right state I can really send love to the situation. I don't know what it's going to be or what the result is, but I can send energy into the situation and know that it can help. One doesn't know how, but one knows that the energy cannot but help. I don't say it always happens, but sometimes.

That's certainly bringing it back to the here and now.

There's no use unless it is brought back to here. I'm very fortunate in that any of the guidance that I've had always stressed that. "Brush your teeth with me," God would say to me in the early days. Every little thing, that attitude, that love, was included in every little thing one did. And it had to be repeated a thousand times because one just forgets, one doesn't think in those ways. I was kept reminded of those things and I still have to be.

I used to think that, "Every hour on the hour, I must remember God," that sort of thing. I was telling someone that recently. They had one of those clocks you could set, it beeped every hour. I thought how wonderful, I wished I had one of those. [Laughter] It would remind you. I would forget. So we can use our modern mechanics to help us. [Laughter]

What about our technology? Some think that it's the technology that's ruining the planet.

No. It's the humans who plan the technology. There's nothing wrong with the technology, any more than there's anything wrong with anything. There's nothing wrong with nuclear power. It's just the way we use it. It's human relationship with it. Technology is just our hands and feet really. I'm very grateful for modern technology. I can remember the days, for example, when you used ordinary soap and there was a line of grease on everything, things like that.

Don't forget that machinery has souls too. Everything has. There's a level of divine life in everything. Everything has that level of God's life—nothing could exist without it, it must have it. Nothing exists by itself, it's all part of the whole, the world.

I recall reading a machinery story in your book. Would you share that now?

Tell you abut the printing machine? Well, we got it to do our first homemade Findhorn Garden book. It had been neglected in a cellar of Lord Chamberlain's office or something. It was a bit lonely. We got it up with another member of the community who was good at mechanics, and I'm not. I was going to do my secretarial bit and run it off and he would look after the mechanics of it. We got it going, but it was always breaking down. We had a hard time with it. We just thought of it as a piece of machinery you see.

Then one day we looked at each other and said, "Do you think it could be more than that?" And we began to think of it... it seemed to have its quirks and things. When a certain person used to come in it used to go to pieces. Whenever that person came near it, ink would flow one way, paper would rip, something would happen.

We thought, "God, it's got a soul!" So I asked my connection on that level, the Landscape Angel, which said, "Well of course!. Everything has that level of beingness." I couldn't connect with it directly because I saw it as sort of dark because it was a human invention, it wasn't like the pure Nature Angels. It was a different type of energy, more focused on what I would now call the personality level, not so much on the higher level.

We started treating it as if it were alive. We got immediate cooperation. We didn't have any trouble after that and finished all our runs. It made all the difference. We tried that with the whole community. Everyone started treating their shovels and everything as being alive and the whole thing came to life. Everything became a much more living experience.

I think that's still true. Some computer experts—I heard this years ago I don't know if it's still true now—if something breaks down with the computer they don't want to know what it is, they just go and sit by it and, I would say, tune in. Then they know and fix it. They're doing that on another level. It was a computer expert who told me that.

I'm very interested in how all these things work out. You know, from the Divine level the same energies work through the Angelic level, the mental level, the emotional level, and the physical level. To me it's all the same energies being stepped down. The next book I'm writing, I'm going into things like that.

What's the title and how is it going?
The Joy Of Balance, tentatively. I've started. Of course working on it brings rise to one's own problems to think about. It's something to work on instead of just sitting around wondering what I should be doing, or feeling guilty that I'm not doing anything. I had to get over that one too. All my friends are so

frantically busy, they know just what to do. I'm fortunate, I can sit around and do nothing all day if I want. It doesn't seem fair. I've just got to learn to enjoy it and not feel guilty about it, because I was brought up on the Protestant work ethic you see.

I've got a book coming out called *To Honor The Earth*. But it's old stuff. It will be coming out with Harper & Row in March of 1991. It's a nature thing, with photographs. Kathy Thurmond, who did a lot of the pictures for *The Findhorn Garden* book, she's always wanted to have a book out with her photos and my writing. So it's finally coming out. I rewrote a bit of it this year. It's old writings. It's having unfortunate aspects because Harper & Row want the copyright. So now Findhorn will have to go to them for material Findhorn has always had. That's publishing for you.

That will be your first book in awhile. You must be excited about it.

No. To tell you the truth, I'm not. Kathy is the one who's been wanting to get it out. She's the one who's been pushing it. She's the one who's done all the work and is the force behind it. To me, as I say, it's old stuff. I'm more interested in the things I'm doing now.

The new book that you're working on is about the depth and the breadth of the Angelic realms? That's probably something that most people don't think about.

We don't think of Angels and higher levels of so many things, like machinery, or countries, and how they interact together in the whole. It's all part of the One life.

It has a lot to do with psychology. The myths are so popular now, using the Gods and Goddesses of the past. Well, I see those in a different way. I see those as Angelic forms, but on a different level than the myths are. They're coming down and have been expressed on the personality level, on the human mind and emotions. We fit them all into that and they are different with each country. But as I see it from the Angelic level they are qualities, energies, force-fields, which are expressed down through all these various dimensions and interpreted differently according to different cultures, though it's the same energy or force behind it.

So, I see the Greek myths as wonderful psychological things but they are coming from another area which is beyond the pairs of opposites. To me the Angels are not beyond the pairs of opposites. Like the Angel of Joy and the Angel of Sorrow is the same quality. But we live in those opposites and we have to deal with them in that way. We can, within ourselves, get beyond that into the higher levels, and bring those energies down, hopefully balanced in all levels. I just want to link it all up.

I think that animals, for example, can see things. I think we all had that sort of vision before we started developing the mind. To me, trying to develop those faculties is not what it's all about. We are to develop the higher faculties and the intuition, which is a knowing without seeing of feeling or hearing. I think early humanity had all those clairvoyants, clairaudients and so on and we've just grown out of it. I don't think we need it in the evolution of our vehicles. It's something we had in the past, and it may be useful now, if someone has that particular gift they've got it for some reason, but it's not something to cultivate. What we want to cultivate is that overall faculty which is intuition, which is much clearer and much better than any of the others.

What about science and intuition?

The two are starting to come together. Science is developing into an understanding of particles and waves at the same time, going into other dimensions, randomness, and odd things that are getting into the esoteric. I think everything is taking us into a greater understanding of life, science also. And I think it always did. I mean, I don't think it was a mistake that we've developed and overdeveloped our science. We had to do that and learn from it so we can use it in service of the whole instead of just for greed, as we're doing now.

Any special thoughts for women?

Well, obviously we've been put down. We women are coming into our own. I don't think we yet know what that is. I think it's part of this newness that's coming. So often you see women out there, but doing a man's job, doing a man's thing in the male way. And this recognition of the body, which is part of recognizing the feminine side of oneself. I think it's all going to be seen in a new way, hopefully.

But I wouldn't talk about the Goddess or anything. To me the new way, or shall I say our future, is male and female, balanced. It's not one or the other, we don't want that again. We've had both. We've had the matriarchies and the patriarchies, now we want the wholeness.

Completely off the subject, but still part of the whole, I'm asking everyone about AIDS these days.

I haven't anything to say really. It's a breakdown of the immune system isn't it. I don't know, what does that mean? You could look at it from a positive... no, you can't. No, I can't say I understand. I think there's a lot of things going on there that we'll understand one day, but I can't say I do now. Our immune system is a protection from the world isn't it, a protection from disease. Idealistically, if we are one with the whole we don't need that protection. But that sounds so far away from the AIDS disease, it sounds so callous, I wouldn't want people to... no, it's not my thing.

I wanted to ask you about gratitude and appreciation.

That was one of the first things that the Devas told me. I realize how appropriate that is. For instance, as I was saying, I never appreciated or was grateful for my own body, and to bring that into all areas of our beingness. It's a love, in a way. Gratitude is an expression of love, isn't it?

In the midst of the city this is a wonderful place.

It's nice, isn't it? It's quiet. And it's got frogs in the spring. They always beep-beep-beep. Real frogs. That's so nice to have right in the city.

How long have you been here?

Four years I guess. What I like about it is that I can walk right to the post office, library, and the shopping. I don't have to be dependent on a car. When I go off travelling I just have to worry about my plants. The last time, when I was off for three months, I had a Russian family in here, new immigrants from Russia, Soviet Jews. They just happened to come, they were sponsored by a friend of mine. They needed a place, it was just perfect. And they found a place just after I came back. That was very nice. Two little boys and mum and dad; young couple. Yes, I am lucky. There's a nice landlord. He loves gardening and is always putting in flowers and things. He looks after his people and they adore him.

You're a big believer in human potential.

To me the power of love is absolutely fantastic. But in one way I hate the word love, but we have no other. It has such a feeble thought. It usually means sex or something in the public mind.

But when you say love is God, shall we say the power of God, which we have because we are a spark of God. When we are really in tune with that power, it is fantastic and can change all sorts of things. If we let it happen, and go with it. Tune into it, let it change our whole being—which, I think, is happening to all of us—to line up with that divine spark within us, so it can be expressed on all levels of our being. That's very powerful.

Steven Halpern

Attuning the Instrument

"In cultures less dominated by technology than ours, performance in music and dance at celebrations are not spectator events. Included in such cultural experiences are chanting, singing, drumming, and dancing. Everyone participates actively. Such ceremonies are used by all in the community to promote physical, emotional, and especially spiritual health. More specifically, participation in such music and movement promotes release of tension in mind and body, enjoyment and ecstasy, interpersonal and transpersonal communication.

"For people in these cultures, sound and spirit are one. To make sound is to release spirit and energy."

Steven Halpern, Ph.D.—*Sound Health*
(with Louis Savary)

For the past 15 years or so Steven Halpern, Ph.D., has been the innovative trailblazer who has brought justification to the term "New Age Music." No easy task, considering the lack of support the genre receives from the larger music companies. As it was, Steven believed in the potential of something other than the popular mass-marketed music we are usually subjected to and frequently tune-out.

This potential was a quality and level of music that was inner-directed and to be used as a tool for personal growth and wholeness. Steven Halpern was among the first to recognize the dynamic and substantive force of music to catalyze spiritual, mental, and even physical change. Given this referencing framework we can begin to appreciate the added consciousness and efforts that must go into its creation.

Sound translates into the psychological effect of hearing through the physiological steps of the ear and the brain. At what point does sound affect our inner beings and just how is that accomplished? How does music affect our hearts? At some point we all have had such an experience. Is it possible that the combination of tone and rhythm can enable some manner of synergistic response within the collective consciousness or unconsciousness of the listener? It causes me to think of the music of the sixties, acting as a clarion call to a new generation and inviting willing ears to recognize each other through the beat. I recall Ken Carey speaking of particular patterns of auditory resonance kicking-in and establishing collective remembrance of being and purpose. I also remember the language of choice of the extra-terrestrials in *Close Encounters*. Is music like Dr. Halpern's another rung towards a collective evolution and/or a personal step towards a language of the heart?

Just as music can affect the mind, so too can it yield some amazing results on the body. You may have noticed that various types of music and sound might cause or contribute to stress and tension. Of course, the prolonged effects of stress and tension might be far more serious. The flip side is music and sound which encourage relaxation and meditation. In this case the prolonged effects are likely to be far different. The streets to self-healing may well be paved with a rich tapestry of tonality and inner response.

Just as I enjoy the natural tonality of our world as evidenced by the newer nature recordings, if we are looking for an orchestrated tonality of healing and inner resonance cast your gaze to the continuing endeavors of Steven Halpern. No one in the field has accomplished more for inner harmony and well-being. I happen to think this is due to his own awareness of what he is creating. As you will read in the interview Steven believes this is why he is here. As such his music becomes his service, and he has served us well.

One of the concepts that has been integral to his work has been the physical phenomenon known as entrainment. It is closely linked to resonance and helps to explain the more meditative side of Halpern's creations. The human body, when relaxed, vibrates at a rate of approximately eight cycles per second. Physicists have determined that the planet itself vibrates at this same frequency. In fact, all the life forms on this magnificent sphere in space exist in synchronization to this fundamental frequency. The resonance—or natural vibratory reality—of our universe is a shared event.

Entrainment is technically defined as a mutual phase-locking between two oscillators. It occurs whenever two or more vibrating realities are in step, or in harmony, with each other. This has everything to do with relaxation and music. It has become one of the keys to Steven Halpern's largely successful process of linking the music to a naturally responding human psyche. He has researched, developed and created a natural, relaxing sound to match an integral need within our organisms. And, by and large, we have responded.

Steven started his work courageously and on a very small scale. The chances of interesting a large record company in the then almost non-existent new age category were seemingly impossible, so he did it himself. He began marketing his works through small health food stores in the San Francisco area. Fifty albums, and a healthy distribution network later, he is decisively deserving of the recognition he has received. A few years back he was honored with the coveted "Crystal Award" at the International New Age Music Conference for his contributions to the field. In addition, he is a popular columnist with many publications and the co-author of the widely-heralded book, *Sound Health*, which is about his two favorite subjects.

I met with Steven while he was on the fly. I was to learn that this is a fairly normal occurrence for him as he frequently travels to odd and sundry locations throughout the country giving lectures and concerts whenever possible. He is often found at the various "Expos" that currently abound. On this particular day he was literally between engagements, having given a concert at a nearby Unity Church the night before and was booked for another in my hometown that evening. I had been running Steven's column, *Sound Thinking*, in the magazine for the past few months and had always been impressed with his aplomb, not to mention his flair! We had talked on the phone a few times and he struck me as a truly gracious fellow. When we finally did meet in person it was easy to see that I had not been wrong. Given the constraints on his time—the ever important sound-check still awaited—Steven hoped that maybe we could do two things at once; could we do lunch at the same time? So, there we were. . . nestled in the back corner of my favorite local chinese restaurant, dishes rattling, silverware clanking. Steven carefully asked that all traces of mono-sodium glutonate be withheld, and we began, pausing only occasionally to comment on the food. After all, we had a different sort of nutrition on our minds that day.

"Meditation is really much simpler than most non-meditators might think. Our human instrument—our body, mind, and spirit—has a built in 'deep relaxation/meditation response' that can be evoked by specially composed music or deep, rhythmic breathing."

Steven Halpern—11th Step Meditation
(with John Bradshaw)

I've been interested to hear that you're involving yourself with the Recovery movement.

The whole field of Recovery has been exponentially increasing in visibility. As a cultural observer it's interesting that some of the dynamics are similar to the growth of the new age movement a few years ago, certainly in the 1960s, as a certain quantum level of consciousness was reached. It's a little bit like the Hundredth Monkey syndrome.

Of particular importance and relevance to my work is that there is an interface between the traditional spiritual quest of focusing on, and including, the meditative disciplines of so many new age people; that part of the process of Recovery includes relaxation and meditation. What's happening is that a whole new audience segment is opening up. A great many of those people in Recovery from any one of a variety of dysfunctional behavior patterns—such as substance abuse, alcoholism, drug addiction or codependency, which is usually defined as caring more about what others think about you than what you think about yourself—have never had any contact with the new age. They are learning that by becoming a human instrument that is in tune with their bodies, minds and spirits, that they can be so much more of who and what they really are.

Particularly, I've had the pleasure and the privilege of connecting with, studying with and working with John Bradshaw, one of the most visible, articulate and charismatic leaders of this field. I've had the opportunity to accompany his guided imagery in certain emotionally charged exercises with live piano. For me it was a definite peak experience in being in the now and working in front of 1-5,000 people who are paying such close attention and who are all fused in synchronous wave-lengths, in a uniform consciousness. It was an experience of oneness that was just

wonderful; the depth-level of contact with so many souls and the comments they shared with me afterwards about how the music assisted them in their inner journeys and how the tapes assist them at home in so many different facets of their lives. It's given me a whole new perspective on how the music can assist and contribute.

What it has also done over the last year has been to really stimulate me into continuing with my *Music For Recovery* series; to include healing substance abuse, alcoholism and co-dependency. These are all part of my Soundwave 2000 audio-active subliminal tape series. The quality of the letters that I have been receiving since this tape has been out is really incredible. It's a very humbling experience for me, one that I honor deeply.

What will it mean in terms of your future efforts?

What this means for me in this year is that I'm composing new music to serve these inner harmony needs. When we understand that as we experience peace and harmony within, we can radiate that peace outward to the planet. It's a continuation of the general work of helping to create more peace on the planet.

I've also had the opportunity of working with Nigerian master drummer Frank Ekeh. My latest purely music recording is entitled *Gaia's Groove*. That has also had a very positive reception. Some of the tracks are definitely more rhythmically oriented, then we add a new age ambience on top of that and move on into some of the more introspective pieces. It's been real energizing to work on both of these musical levels and watch how that resonates out in the world. It's been a real focused time.

There are interesting parallels between various aspects of the Recovery movement and new age thought.

"Addiction is not so much a pharmacological problem as a spiritual one. Most addicts are really trying to experience greater wholeness." That's a quote from Andrew Warrel. That is why this music of wholeness, wellness and well-being is so important. Any compulsive, obsessive substance, process or relationship addiction is part of the definition of co-dependency. The various treatment plans include 12-step programs, processes involving yoga, nutritional support, meditation and music. That's how it all ties together. I think it's a holistically sound approach to addiction, and how addiction ties in with the whole raising conscious-ness movement of the new age.

You are recognized as one of the preeminent practitioners of consciousness music. I'd like to ask you your thoughts on what sound can do for people.

It does a lot of things. Traditionally, people have noticed that and have used music to send people off to war, get people dancing, or—like the blues—take their minds off of their social situation. It provides a form of escape, or entertainment, which is a form of escape. At its best, music, whether it be classical or rock or new age, can provide a vehicle through which one can tap into the inner self. When we take a look at the philosophies behind most music that's not a primary concern, though some of the classical composers did have that in mind. There is also an aspect of emotional release and catharsis, working on the emotional level.

What differentiates new age music from the other forms then?

What differentiated the new age music was that it came in not on an emotional level but on a level that might be a higher harmonic of that. So if we have the physical body, which has the most dense vibration... we could talk in scientific terms of fre-quencies of vibration, let's say 20-20,000 cycles per second. When you go a factor of 10 above that, say 200,000 cycles, you move into what might be the mental or emotional vibrations. You go a factor above that, say a factor of 10, and you might be into where some of the more etheric and spiritual dimensions begin. I'm just putting out arbitrary figures, but that is pretty well what the scientists who work with this progression are suggesting.

In the same way, we can see light at a certain frequency. We know that all light travels, whether it's red, blue, white, etc. at 186,000 miles per second but the wave-lengths differ. Red is longer than violet. When you get up beyond violet, ultraviolet, the wavelengths get shorter but it's still there. When you get beyond ultraviolet you get these other levels of frequencies.

With new age music we, back in the early 1970s, were looking for music that would specifically serve to get us in touch with our own true self, inner self or high self. And in so doing bring us in closer touch with the divine. That's not a new concept. If we go back thousands of years we can see that this was used in ancient Greece, Egypt, China and before that, Atlantis and Lemuria, where music was specifically used. Other than reading anecdotal reports in different journals and books, that would say, yes, music was used in the ancient healing temples, the question is, what music? What did it sound like? No one can tell you because we didn't have tape recorders there.

Is there an aspect of your life devoted to remembering that sound and its benefits?

I recognized early in my life that this was something that was very important to me. I needed to know what this music sounded like. I needed to know what the music would sound like in this day and age that would do the same thing. The literature can't give you any information. What a lot of individuals, such as myself and Joel Andrews, did and found ourselves doing during meditation and dream-focusing was trying to hear this music that would do these sorts of things in the late 20th century. Certainly our high-stress society would need music to de-stress.

One of the things we find about new age music is that it's stress reducing, uplifting and beautiful rather than being jagged, hard and stimulating from an aggressive standpoint. This might be stimulating from a different response, a psychic or spiritual resonance as well as one that literally works to tune the energy systems in the body. I believe that part of why true new age music works as it does is because it works with the built-in energy systems and etheric energy centers such as the chakras and the more subtle energy systems in the body.

Itzhak Benthov pointed out in the early 1970s that when you allow the body to literally bio-entrain and to work as a tuned oscillating system—when all the energy systems work in phase with each other—what that feels like is what people call a spiritual experience. Now we have a scientific paradigm, a model, of understanding how some of that works as an energetic expression. It demystifies the process and gives us a more repeatable technique for getting there.

Some of the newer recordings being advertised that have extra things built into the music will guarantee that your brain will be pulsed and entrained to work at a certain frequency. There are simple techniques that can do that. I've been doing that, with other techniques, since I began. That's why *Spectrum Suite* had such an effect and why, if you listen to it every day, it will still have that effect. It doesn't wear out. That's the overview of what the new age musicians, in the early days, were doing and why they were doing it.

There's also an inner need. We were told by the people we would consult with, that this is the reason we incarnated. This is part of our mission this time around. I knew that for myself. I knew this at about age 13 and probably before. I never dreamed it would be my full-time work. I always assumed I would be doing something else and doing this on the side. Things began happening in the late 1960s that made it clear that this was my full-time work. The hardest part of it was to handle the business end of it, because no one gives you grants to do this sort of thing. Getting the music was the easy part, but learning how to do business and share the music with other people was the hard part. That's part of the reason why I go around the country and offer presentations and concerts and do the writing that I do.

Your book, *Sound Health*, was recognized by many as being a departure point. Are you working on a new book?

Yes, indeed. The next one will be more practical in terms of giving exercises and techniques to specifically enhance how you can use music with color therapy, color healing, relaxation. The whole field of sound and health is one that a lot of people intuitively know about and know that it's true. It's one that we get virtually no instruction in, or real information about. Certainly the record company isn't going to tell you that certain music is going to hypnotize you, that certain music will make you buy the product that's being advertised right after a certain song. Or that certain rhythms will have such a physiological hook that they will be addicting and you will have to go out and buy that song. They are not going to tell you that. I will, because that's part of my job. But I don't say it too loudly, so I can stay alive. When we talk about the addictive quality of certain rhythms—which can be fun—it's not to say that all addictions are bad, there are positive addictions as well. We're suggesting that when you understand the effect of rhythm on the heart and the breath, you'll find as well that any external stimulus will automatically override the natural beat of the heart and put you into a manipulated situation. Some of these feel great. If you know about these things then you can choose more specifically, just like knowing what vitamins to use if you have a deficiency.

Right. Now you're talking about using music as a tool. Many people are trying to utilize it in that fashion.

There are certain things that you can do to enhance your effectiveness, your efficiency, your general well-being by using certain types of music at certain times. What we find with most classical music is that rarely does a piece of classical music work for one person as it does for another. With certain kinds of other music, such as *Spectrum Suite*, which we researched very fully, we find that it does do the same thing to a high percentage of people, like 95%, which is unheard of in the annals of music therapy. So we can talk about a specific response, we can talk about balancing the hemispheres of your brain.

If you need to relax you would use something like that rather than *A Whiter Shade Of Pale*. Not to say that one is better than the other, but there are times when you need to relax and be. The medical professions are coming to understand that relaxation is really a pre-condition to maintaining health. The more stress you are under that you don't handle, the more you're going to exacerbate all the diseases of hypertension, stress, ulcers, migraines, and so on. It also decreases the function of the immune system and makes you more susceptible to the diseases of the immune system, cancer, AIDS, and so on.

When I'm writing I've found that I can put on certain music and I won't get anything done. It's great music, but not necessarily something I can work with. I put on some subliminal activation, or self-help tapes and suddenly ideas come into my head, my energy stays high, the motivation is there, I get my work done.

We're certainly seeing a lot of subliminal material in the marketplace these days.

The use of the subliminals takes the effect of the music up another octave, another dimension. Until I made my own series of subliminals I tried some of the other ones on the market. Some of them worked okay for the first time or two I listened, but were in many cases ineffective after that. Or they had the sound of the ocean but it was a fake ocean, it was a synthesizer. My body would say, "this is not real," and I would have a counterproductive reaction.

If one is massaging their significant other, or making love, there are times when it is maybe appropriate to have loud, pulsing music. On the other hand there is a whole other order of experience that happens when you have music that caresses you. It opens up the sense organs of the skin, it opens up the receptivity of the whole body. We also found that certain music can get both partners breathing in harmony at the same rate, in synch with each other. That sets up a very powerful dynamic between the individuals; the energy fields can pulse and attune much more effectively when the breath is coordinated. It's something that should be experienced.

I go into all these things in the next book, along with specific ways to listen. We look at ways to enhance your own sense of well-being. Another thing to do is to learn how to do some more things with the voice. Typically if you were in school, at singing class, you would learn to read little black dots on white paper written by dead white European musicians. The same thing occurred if you were studying music or learning piano or something. There's a lot more to music than that.

Definitely. It's clear to me that, based on people's response to music, there's a whole lot going on.

In many cases people who sang those little black dots sang it so badly that they were told to just mouth it. In my audiences I often find that the majority of the people will admit to that experience. So for years, the rest of their lives, they go through that experience of being inhibited or feeling that they can't sing, cutting off this whole avenue of experience and enjoyment. So, we reopen these channels. It also turns out that when you use your voice in certain ways, like toning or singing in the shower—I'd like to point out that our bathrooms are our cultural equivalent of the ancient cave where the yogis and the mystics would chant and sing—the more you do it the better you sound. The more feedback that supports it, the more endorphins you will release and, ultimately, the better you'll feel. It's a great self-perpetuating cycle.

What I found in my own research was that many times what people think is happening is not what's happening at all. One of the ways you can find that out is by using some sophisticated bio-feedback telemetry and monitoring equipment, which we did. That's one of the reasons why I'm here today, because what we found was so radically different than what the classics were doing. Again, not to say that there is anything wrong with them, but if you want to concentrate... Because of a very recognizable phenomenon, what I call the anticipation response, if I were to sing Do-Re-Mi-Fa-So-La-Te, most people hear the last Do in their heads even if I never sang it. What happens is that you get hung up waiting for the rest of the phrase, so you're never in the present. This pattern is built into most of the music we hear. If you're listening to music in the background your brain is subconsciously analyzing the structure. Which means that part of your attention is being ripped off by the music rather than assisting it by getting the whole brain to focus on the situation at hand.

If you have young kids under five... we find that many parents just let their kids listen to rock and roll, these kids are doing break-dancing and Michael Jackson moves, which is all cute and fine but their little tiny nervous systems are not adapted or equipped to deal with the level of volume some people use. Also, those rhythms on the formative neurological systems in their bodies are having, from what we can see, a very powerful effect. One that is not completely natural. There have been no

long-term studies done on the effect of disco or rap music on people, it's pretty much illegal to do that. The studies that have been done with certain animals suggest that it's not that great a thing.

How do you see the music as having evolved since the sixties?

There is a difference between the rhythms of most of the music of today and the music that was happening in the sixties. As a musician I point this out: if you listen to the bass and the drums, in the early days there was this bouncing, rolling rhythm; rock and roll. Then rock and roll became just rock, heavy metal; up and down, machine-like—that's a counter-rhythm to the natural beat of the heart. Which is one reason why its weakening and stressful. Now you get these rhythms played by machines, digital drummers, where there is no human contact. Many people react to that, sense that it's not real, and get stressed by that. We haven't seen the long term effects of this yet.

Some of the things called new age music coming out now have these mechanical drummers on top of a piano player or something. To me that's a real abomination and a rip-off of the true essence of new age music, which is not just something which is easy-listening. We've had that. We've had a whole generic form of audio wall-paper. What's so extraordinary about some of these recordings that are out now is that it's as if we are seeing the reincarnation of disco in the guise of progressive new age music. Some of the drum parts are exactly the same. It's one thing if it's played by a person, another if it's played by a machine; the body can tell the difference. Dr. John Diamond has written extensively on that in his books. There's really no question about it if you take the time to check your body out.

If you stick your head in the sand and ignore all this, saying it couldn't happen or you're immune to it... just like people living near to traffic or an airport and saying they get used to it. They all say that. Well, the studies have come out of UCLA saying that children that go to school near airports never get used to it, they just get dumber. They cannot concentrate as well as their peers in the next school over that has a similar socioeconomic basis but is not under the direct flight path. We see the incidence of mental health problems, drinking problems, birth-rate fatalities, all are enhanced in loud-noise areas. It's not something you get used to.

It's interesting that this work can be so expansive, and yet it's such a new field.

I'm finding that my work goes on in a lot of different arenas. A lot of it relates to getting information out there and letting people know. I see myself as an intermediary on some of these levels, between the people who are doing some of the serious scientific research and who never get published beyond some arcane journals. I got a letter from Dr. Harvey Bird in New Jersey who's doing research that shows, using the neurological structures of mice, that noise such as heavy metal music or gas-powered leafblowers will actually cause structural damage in brains. It will cause the neurons to grow asymmetrically. It can change the chemistry of the brain, that means that it's changing personality. Now, that's with mice, but you know it must be affecting people too. Mice are mammals, we share some things with mammals. If it's affecting them it's affecting us.

I look at this whole field of sound health and consciousness the same way we looked at cigarette smoke and health 20 years ago. Some of us who could not physically handle the smoke, objected to it and got very little support. Now there are no-smoking sections everywhere; consciousness has been raised. We're seeing it with pesticides and food. Many people have known this for a long time. My body tells me in no uncertain terms when I eat fruit that has certain pesticides on it; I go into a certain form of shock. I have no choice, I either buy organic fruit or I don't eat fruit. Now we're having a number of revelations about the risks.

We'll be seeing that happening with sound. It's a less glamorous field on some levels. It's not as dynamic as dealing directly with AIDS, but in the long run it has an incredible impact on how we live, feel and work. It's the sort of information that people need to know about.

Steven, lately I've been asking everyone about AIDS.

I have read and heard Dr. Strecker, Tom Beardon, and others speaking about the origins of AIDS. I understand how it can be viewed as a spiritual opportunity for self-healing and growth. From what I've seen, it is such a clear case of biological warfare. The facts are written up in several books now about how it was originated at some Institute, developed at a chemical warfare laboratory and spread by the World Health Organization, by accident or not. It's clear to me that it's not just an accident.

On the other hand, the positive outcome of it—if it's possible, if it's allowed to happen—will be that the only defense we will have for it will be electromagnetic medicine. It could really catapult the whole field of medicine into the 21st century, because we are never going to find vaccines for it. The virus mutates too fast. They haven't found the vaccine for the first form, and now it's mutated into all these other forms. But when you find the frequency and find the keynotes you can jam it, as you can jam radar, according to the scientists I am in contact with.

I think that's where the blessing of it might ultimately be. In the meantime, it's all a tragedy for everyone, especially those who have it. It has certainly changed the way a lot of us deal with life. It points out the need to have some more sophisticated, higher dimensional energy electromedicine at our availability and disposal. I see that as a very clear possibility.

Interestingly, it will probably be the insurance companies that will push this into the mainstream, not the physicians. The whole AIDS epidemic is costing the insurance industry so much money that they will want something that works, and what will work is this space-age, new-age medicine. Sound may well be a part of that.

Many people associate your work with the spiritual component of music, so I want to ask you specifically about that.

There are many paths up the mountain, "There are many mansions in my Father's house," there are many soundtracks to the Ascension. We have all those aphorisms, different strokes for different folks. Yet, we find a similar pattern happening when you find music that works for you.

Based on the feedback that I've gotten over the past 20 years plus conversations with many other musicians, particularly with gentle, more ambient new age music there's an opportunity to hear that still, small voice; to tap in. The music can help the body calm down, can help the mind calm down and be still and know that "I am God." That's a phrase that's been around for several thousand years. It's still true. Music that brings us to that stillness can be from a variety of different contexts. There are certain examples of classical music that will do that, certain parts of rock music will do it.

What an individual has to do is to find the music that works for himself or herself and then use it. Maybe give yourself 20 minutes of a sound-bath, focus on the music with headphones, be with the music. Don't just have it as background, don't just dance to it, be with it, let your insides dance. Close your eyes, don't try to watch a video, watch the video inside your mind; go totally into the music, become the music. Don't think about it, don't analyze it; just float with it, ride with it. The music will often just trigger those things. Maybe we have some pre-programmed responses in the brain, that the level of echo and reverberation that are built into the music—that I and many other musicians record—is the music that takes us back into the ancient caves, takes us back into the pyramids, where we would hear music. Maybe there's a collective unconsciousness that, when we hear music that has such an element of space in it, creates that awe inspiring response.

There are so many variables that it's hard to pinpoint them. We know that so many people have these experiences and yet, will still watch TV, watch a video, rather than... In the sixties I remember calling friends, or being called over to friends homes, when someone got a new record that was just a knockout. We'd turn off the lights, light a candle, and listen. Now people don't do that, they have all these other distractions. If you shut down all the visual distractions you can get much more into the music. I highly recommend it. To really open up to the pure power of sound you need to focus on the sound, not have 85% of your attention focused on the visual. Gregorian chants can open up that space for many people. For others, depending on belief systems or if they were burned at the stake or something, when they hear Gregorian chant they begin to freak out. So, again, we can't say that any one music will necessarily work for everyone.

It would seem that there are any number of meaningful possibilities.

The possibilities are endless, and they are very, very profound. The key is to give yourself the space to be in that space. Even if it's five minutes, after you come home from work or before you go to sleep, to build that into your daily lifestyle. Give yourself the opportunity to immerse in the music, to be one with the sound. It's an incredible gift that you can give to yourself as part of treating yourself well and, literally, tuning your human instrument. It may well be that when we allow our human instruments to be tuned, we tune into All That Is and we tune into God. That's what the keynote of our human instrument is.

There's a certain resonance that tunes into the overall key of God, the key of G and D at the same time, the key of God. We have the Zen parables of searching for a key one has lost, not where one lost it, but where the light is. We have a lot of people saying we hid the key to self-knowledge inside ourselves, that we can access it through meditation. The key is hidden inside and it's the key of the universe. We just need to go within to do it.

You're a great spokesman for motivating people to explore those avenues.

Music is some of the most fun you can have in life without laughing. It can release a lot of endorphins. You can just close your eyes, you don't have to do anything else. So often in the 20th century we get involved in doing so many things at the same time and we lose something. My suggestion would be to consider building some of that space into your own life. Make some music yourself, whether it's with your voice, Tibetan bowls or those beautiful crystal bowls. You can make them yourself, have them right there in your house anytime you want to use them. Take a two to five minute sound break and you're right there.

These don't have to be all day affairs. This is 20th century America, we like to have instant gratification. Sound can take you there instantly. So, take the tools and you're on your way.

"Give yourself the opportunity to immerse in the music, to be one with the sound. It's an incredible gift that you can give to yourself as part of treating yourself well and, literally, tuning your human instrument. It may well be that when we allow our human instruments to be tuned, we tune into All That Is and we tune into God. That's what the keynote of our human instrument is."

David Spangler

The Potential Sacrament

"We now anticipate more rapid change and evolution in the various cultures of the world than ever before. It is entirely possible—and most analysts and futurists I have read or talked to agree on this—that the most profound transformations are still unfolding or have yet to appear. In their view, and in mine, the whole twentieth century and the first part of the twenty-first century represent a vast metamorphosis of human consciousness and behavior whose only historical equivalent would be the invention of agriculture and the rise of civilization itself thousands of years ago. We are in the midst of a process of reimagining and reinventing ourselves and our world."

David Spangler—Reimagination of the World

I t sometimes occurs that the worth and validity of various social movements—particularly those involving elements of grandiose change and alteration—are determined, in part, by the quality, sincerity and vision of their spokespersons. The developing current of the momentum of new thought has been fortunate to have been associated with David Spangler for more than two decades.

One of the earliest definers of the new age, David Spangler has also been one of its more pragmatic voices. This practicality of expression has served so many so well not only because of its reasoned, theoretical advances but also due to its poetic vision. His vision is so organic that the veracity of the content cannot be denied.

This style is aptly suited to the subject at hand: the metaphors through which we might seek, find and embrace a more holistic reality. Certainly the seeking and finding present challenges, but isn't it often the embracing that proves the more difficult? The integration of concept and perspective which may be wholly new and at odds with the norms of convention can literally turn our heads inside out. While at times this can be great fun it also yields, at times, considerable frustration.

I have frequently observed that it is the quality of one's teachers and/or resources which, at those moments of grave consternation, provide either a guiding light or a material folly. While the follies probably have their place, they generally do not bespeak a higher place. I bring all this up so that we can better appreciate the, to my mind, truer services of the honestly honorable new age sages.

It was during the 1980s that various aspects of the new age movement really began to coalesce into a formative ideal and, perhaps unfortunately, a marketable force. As we have seen, there were plenty of folks, many well-intentioned, that were ready and able to cash in. One of the voices that arose to criticize and question the validity of some of those representations was David Spangler's. His point was that some of the more doubtful depictions of psychic phenomenon were simply diversions from the more important and far-reaching aspects of our new age.

Likewise, he has been opposed to the "gloom and doom" schools of thought that have run rampant over the years. His writings have consistently downplayed the seemingly intrinsic need for some to project cataclysms onto mankind. The apocalypse through which many have indulged their sense of drama is, as viewed by David Spangler, a non-event.

It could be that his most memorable works are those that have revolved around the subjects of cycles and time. Just when is the new age supposed to start? What particular event is predestined to mark this beginning? The Spangler answers would be; it already has, and none. Rather than partitioning ourselves with linear fences, illusory events or divisive projections perhaps we might further our aspirations by viewing the new age as a process. Such processes take all the shortcuts and long detours that we, social circumstance and creative spirit give credence to. Within the writings of David Spangler the word *now* takes on an ever more exciting and hopeful definition.

Could it be that we might effect those changes in compassion, empowerment and peace that we so long for in a truly civilized world by realizing—and integrating that realization—that we don't have to wait? That it is happening now, has happened before, has already happened? Of course. For just as the new age is a human event, so too is it an event of the planet. David speaks of this as an event of dimensional shifting designed to present greater access and expression to the interblended networks, webs and geometries of Gaia and humanity. It is a new definition of relationship with the formative forces of the higher dimensions and ourselves.

David Spangler was born with the ability to access the inner dimensions of spirit. He has spent the last 47 years cultivating that ability and creatively associating with it so as to manifest an alignment with the "sacred elements that are within all of us and our world." Some 25 years ago Spangler contacted the inner-plane being he calls "John." It was through this relationship that he learned to see and appreciate the depth and potential of both the inner and outer worlds.

One of the more profound experiments with the new world paradigm was exercised in the Findhorn Community in Northern Scotland. The Findhorn gardens sparked the creative imaginations of many and spurred countless other such experiments around the globe. Findhorn served as a beacon.

David Spangler helping to guide, shape and orient that light, and served as a co-director there from 1970 to 1973. During his tenure the community expanded from 15 to 150 members and became synonymous with new ideas such as cooperating with Nature Spirits and Devic communication. Findhorn became a model for living based on non-separation and co-creation.

Born in Columbus, Ohio in 1945, David spent a good portion of his early years in Northern Africa. During that time he began having stirring mystical encounters. While a university student, those experiences led to a vision of an approaching new age. David left school and began his true vocation as an author, lecturer and philosopher on the themes of spirituality, cultural change and personal transformation.

David Spangler currently resides in the Pacific Northwest with his wife and three children. He continues to involve himself in a variety of experience. He is a Lindisfarne Fellow and has worked as a consultant for Lucasfilm Games. He is a faculty member at the Chinook Learning Center of Whidbey Island, Washington and does curriculum design for Seattle University. In addition he teaches on-line computer courses on manifestation and spirituality for students all over North America.

His many books include *Revelation: Birth of a New Age, Towards a Planetary Vision, Reflection on the Christ, A Vision of Findhorn*, and *Emergence: The Rebirth of the Sacred*. He is a co-author of the now classic, *The Findhorn Garden* and the newer *Reimagination of the World*. This last volume was created in conjunction with author/philosopher William Irwin Thompson from a series of workshops they did together in 1988.

It is primarily within the context of this last volume that the following interview was conducted. It does include some segments from a piece that we had done a couple of years earlier. They were gently spliced together here to present a more meandering stream. So let's row our boats, it was a good trip.

"Man has the divine power of transcendence, of moving beyond pre-set patterns, of bridging the dimensions of form and spirit, potential and actuality, image and fulfillment. Humanity is the Race of the Garden, the Race of Eden, expelled from paradise in order to discover how to be paradise's creator and not just its child. Man is learning how to be a gardener on all levels, a co-creator with God, a re-creator of the Earth."

David Spangler—*The Findhorn Garden*

Can we start this with some background comments on your Findhorn experience? What was it like when you first got there?

I arrived at Findhorn some eight years after it had actually begun. It was just entering a new phase in its growth. What in some ways had been a large extended family began developing into a large community. I was in on the ground floor in that development. It was a very exciting time, a creative time.

It was very small and very dynamic. It was still in the time when Peter & Eileen Caddy basically ran the place. I came at the tail-end of the time when the garden was the primary emphasis. I arrived as part of a wave of a number of folks that came in, most of whom were artists, performers, musicians, craftspeople, and some educators. In that first year the place tripled in population, but not very much in physical size. It really began to become a community then. Before then it was like a very large group, but now we had these diverse enterprises. Eileen had received guidance that we were to start craft studios and emphasize the arts and music, and begin building the foundation of what she called the City of Light.

It was a very creative time. In effect, I arrived at a time when Findhorn was hatching itself, cracking out of an egg that had defined one level of its development for eight years. Now it was moving into this other level. It was very accelerated. I was there for three years and it went from those 15 people to 150 people without adding much in the way of land. They were just renting the land anyway, they didn't own the land. They rented trailers and brought them in. Most of the people that came then couldn't afford trailers. There was a big influx of young people whom the community had to support.

When I arrived in 1970 you could feel the energy. You knew that it was right on the brink, it was right at the beginning of that change. I had actually started to go there the year before. I had gotten within 15 miles of the place and had inner direction not to go, so I just drove past and went on to Edinburgh. That was in 1969.

Really? You had already heard of it, it had sparked your imagination, and you didn't stop?.

I had heard of it for a couple of years. I first heard of Findhorn in 1967. I was quite interested in it. I had met people who had come back from there who were singing its praises. But when I was in Scotland in 1969 I had this strong sense not to go, so I didn't. Then the following year I went back, and had the feeling it was time to go up there. In talking about it with Peter, he said that they would not have been ready for me the previous year. The energy just wasn't there, it was focused on the ending of the first cycle. I was in a similar situation myself that year. I was ending a cycle of work and I really wouldn't have been ready for Findhorn myself. So by the time we came together in 1970 we were both very ready for each other and our respective energies matched.

At that point I could give what they needed and they could give me what I needed. That wouldn't have been true the previous year. Had I gone I'm sure I would have had a nice encounter, but it would not have gone anywhere.

It was a magical time. Roc [R. Ogilvie Crombie] was there on and off then, he lived in Edinburgh. It was a time when Findhorn was redefining itself and that's always an exciting time. It was pushing its boundaries and exploring new avenues of expression; very, very creative. It seems to me to be in a similar state right now.

Findhorn is viewed as an intentional community with core beliefs regarding the Spirit realms, certainly the work with the garden is well documented. Relating to Spirit in new ways is paramount to many people today. How was it back then?

The whole process of touching in with other realms of existence was important to Findhorn, because in many ways Findhorn was a theocracy. A lot of policy was developed based on guidance that was received, either by Eileen, Dorothy Maclean, or myself. But that only went so far, actually. Then you had the whole area of human relationship, community building, and everyday work which could be influenced by that guidance, but had its own dynamic to it. It was like there were two things going on, which influenced each other, but also had autonomy.

A lot of my work was with the community building and human relations side. My role in the community—much more than the lecturing I did or what I did administratively—was helping people go through rather intense personal experiences. The attunement to other levels was, many times, irrelevant to that process. In fact, a year or so after I left Findhorn went into a phase where it just jettisoned anything dealing with the esoteric, or with metaphysics, or with contact with the other levels. In fact, getting guidance became a bit of a no-no.

Now I think the community has reached more of a balance. Peter himself, and Findhorn in general, felt that there was a particular message they wanted to put out that was inspirational, that discussed the relationship with nature. Dorothy, for example, was always putting down her experiences with the Devas because she is totally opposed to the glamor. So, in midst of all this work she was doing with the Devas, about which she is very serious up to this day, she didn't want it held up as a model. So people would come to Findhorn, and they would want to work in the garden. They would want to learn how to talk to the Nature Spirits, how to talk to the Devas. Dorothy would say that you have to find your own way to do that, it might not come in the way as it has for me. And Roc was very much that way in his contact with the Nature Spirits.

In the books that were written, particularly in Paul Hawkin's book, *The Magic of Findhorn*, there was some mythologizing that took place. He didn't say anything that was untrue, but it was given a certain shine. What happens there is that you're emphasizing the positive elements of the story, and it's not that there were that many negative elements either, but just that you had 150 normal people trying to live together. To me, part of the strength of Findhorn is that they were successful. That, in spite of some very real personality differences and personality clashes, people had a genuine commitment towards making that community work, and towards resolving conflict and embracing each other in powerful ways. Individuals would go out of their way to rise above immediate emotional reaction in order to find some way of achieving cooperation. But that didn't mean they weren't having those reactions.

What were some of the differences between Findhorn and other intentional communities?

We had some people who came from Auroville [an intentional spirituality-based community in southern India founded by Sri Aurobindo] who stayed for a while, and they contrasted life at Findhorn with life at Auroville. The way they dealt with conflict there was to relate everything to a higher level, and the way we dealt with conflict at Findhorn was by relating things through the personality. If we can't communicate talk together and deal with our everyday human feelings and emotions, then we might lack the foundation on which something of a more transpersonal nature can rest. If you had been at Findhorn in the early 70's— and this may be even more true today, I'm not sure—most of the time it would have seemed like a kind of very ordinary trailer camp, in which some unusual conversations took place. People would talk about Masters and Devas, communication with God, and things like that. But on the whole, what really surprised people who came were two things; one was the genuine sense of lovingness that was there, a palpable sense of caring energy. The other was how ordinary it was. It had none of the particular trappings that might be associated with a spiritual community.

When did you leave, and why?

I left in 1973. Dorothy left about six months later. Peter didn't leave until about 1975 or 76. Eileen has never left. It is still Eileen's home. She travels, but her home is still at Findhorn. I felt my time there had come to an end. I felt called back to the U.S. That was essentially it. It was a strong sense that I had done all I could do, needed to do, or was able to do, and knew how to do [Laughter] at that time. I needed to move on into other kinds of life experiences. There were places the community needed to go and things it needed to experience that I did not, and vice-versa. There was just a sense that it was time to establish a new relationship.

How did the shift in receiving guidance at Findhorn come about?

Eileen had guidance, while I was still there in 1972, that she should stop getting guidance for the community. It was a fairly major shift. One of the reasons that happened was that people were beginning to over-rely on the guidance. The other was that there were people who began to mimic Eileen, using her as a model, rather than finding their own unique way of accessing their deeper selves. So Eileen felt that she should just stop. It was hard for her because it meant breaking a pattern of very long standing. It was especially hard for Peter. He was obedient to it, but his habit pattern was perhaps stronger than Eileen's. He was accustomed to getting the guidance for the community every morning. To have to give that up was not easy.

What's your affiliation with the community now?

I have no official affiliation. I was on the Board of Directors for a couple of years after I left in the mid-70's. That became impractical because I couldn't get back for the meetings. They went through a time where they definitely didn't want anything to do with any kind of psychic or esoteric work, and the community didn't want a lot to do with spiritual work either. They were into a real survival mode and working out their patterns as a community. They had really gone through a psychic burnout in the late 70's. So, there was a period there when I had little contact with Findhorn. We were definitely on friendly terms but we didn't have much to offer each other.

Last year I got the feeling that it was time to go back, so I did. Julie and I went back with the kids for a month last year.

We're doing the same again in the spring of next year. I'll probably be going back, at least for the next two or three years, to work there and build the links again. I'm mainly going to work with the community. They're in a time of transition again and developing new patterns. I'm going to help them with that in whatever way I can.

You've written, and have had a lot to say, about the differences and distinctions between psychic abilities and spirituality.

I think the main difference I would make between psychic abilities and spirituality is that psychic abilities, to a certain degree, are form-oriented and basically extensions of perception. So in qualitative terms there is no difference between my seeing an aura or my seeing your body; I still have to process all of that in my being. And I'm still having a sense of me seeing it. The observer and the observed.

Spirituality, to me, works at seeing in a very different way; seeing from the inside out, so to speak, in which the observer becomes the observed, without necessarily denying any appropriate distinction that's there. I don't feel that spirituality necessarily needs to deny the phenomenon of differentiation. I don't have to say that you and I are one. In the sense that we are, we sort of merge into sameness. But, I can certainly say that our well-being and our natures are very dependent on each other; we're in a symbiotic relationship. And I could go further, I could certainly say that we are One spiritually. That may give me a very different way of interpreting data that comes to me psychically. It may give me a whole different set of data, as far as that goes.

I guess for me, spirituality and psychic abilities are a bit like apples and oranges. They're both tasty, but they're different. I may never develop psychic abilities but I can certainly develop my spirituality, in the sense of attunement, wisdom, alignment and compassion. I think part of the problem is that we view God as a kind of phenomenon, you know? We talk about God a lot as though God were a phenomenon, as if we can somehow connect with it like we can connect with a river, or an ocean, or a television, or a computer. We don't think of God as something from which phenomena themselves emerge. If I think of God as a phenomenon, then it's easy to begin thinking of psychic abilities or channeling as a way to come closer to that phenomenon. If you give me phenomena that seem more and more expansive, then eventually I'm going to come to the biggest phenomenon of them all, which is God. However, to me, they are just two different journeys. They're almost at right angles to each other. In one the sacred underlies the other and supports it, but is in no way defined by it.

I feel people are looking for a number of things in our time; security, certainty, power, information, comfort. Psychic abilities, properly understood and used, can provide some of that. But it is always limited in what it provides, because ultimately we are still dealing with form. Even though they may be psychic forms or etheric forms or what have you, you're still dealing with phenomena that can be located in space and time in some fashion. I might go in consciousness to a place that seems timeless and spaceless to me, but in the act of bringing back whatever I can bring back from that place it comes into space and time. It has to, otherwise there's no way of relating to it and no one else has a way of relating to it; it remains purely subjective. It still remains a phenomenon, and I can only place so much of my spiritual weight, so to speak, on a phenomenon to support me before it collapses. The interesting thing is that we live in a world that is so rich in phenomena, that we really don't need to introduce psychic phenomena. We haven't really exhausted the powers of the natural world to exalt and inspire us.

How did you and Dr. Thompson come to do the book, *Reimagination of The World*, together?

Bill and I have known each other for many years, since 1972. We've worked together as friends and colleagues since then. This particular project began out of a television project that Bill and I had been invited to do for a Canadian producer. It was originally going to be a short miniseries on cultural transformation, the new age, planetary culture, that kind of thing. We worked out an outline, then the project got slowed up. We decided to try out some of the material in a seminar, and use the seminar to generate some more material through the dynamics of presentation. We had the tapes transcribed and we were going to boil it down into a script for the television program, but the TV deal fell through.

Then we had this manuscript. It was some 300 pages. Bill said we should just go ahead and edit it, and turn it into a book. In the process of doing that we decided to do another seminar the following year and just add the material to it. It would be an opportunity to fill in some gaps. That's how it developed. After the two seminars were done we took all that material, edited it down and created the book. Actually, Bill and I had wanted to do a book together for some time. We just had never gotten around to it. So, this was a nice excuse.

What does it mean, to reimagine the world?

I live in a relationship with my world. I define it, it defines me. There are qualities about me, possibilities, expressions, things that I will do, things I will think I'm capable of doing, the way I will order my life, that depend on the way I image the world. If I image the world as a scary and dangerous place, I'm going to order my life differently than if I image it as a friendly and supportive place. In either case I may be open to risk-taking, but I will take risks in different ways. In the former, if I take risks at all I will tend to do so in a much more constricted and protected stance. But in the latter case, where I image my world as a benign and supportive environment, I'm more willing to trust myself to it in more expansive and fluid ways.

This, to me, is more than just a psychological construct about what my prejudices, opinions and perspectives are. It's also a kind of field that I create around myself which the world inhabits. The world meets me through my image of it. It incarnates within me through my image of it. Then I incarnate through that image too. It's almost like one of these halls of mirrors with mirrors on opposing walls, where you see reflection on reflection on reflection. It's a recursive pattern where I incarnate the world, which incarnates me, then that incarnates the world and so on.

The imagination is a form of perception. It's not just a fantasy-creating fantasy in my mind. It's a way of seeing that allows me to see what isn't there but what could be there or, what is there in non-visible ways. At a very basic level, everything I know about my world is basically imaginative. It is constructed in my mind through a process of image-formation based on sensory data. But I have control over my imagination. I can invite other images to arise within me, I can weave other images into the matrix of my world-view and transform it.

What I'm doing there is that I'm not just trying to see the world differently. I'm creating a different mode of interaction and creation, co-incarnation, between myself and my world. Because things in my world that were not there before—because I couldn't see them, wasn't open to them—can now live in me. If I reimagine my world as an empowering place, then the empowering aspects of my world can live in me and act in me, where before they could only act on me from the outside in ways that were usually unconscious.

How we imagine our world is very important. Not only in the way it shapes our reactions psychologically, but also in the way it creates a garment that the world soul can co-inhabit. The world inhabits us as much as we inhabit the world. The world imagines the trees, nature, mountains. . . and we inhabit that. But it has to inhabit the landscape we create. It may feel a bit pinched at times. We don't tend to create very elaborate or well-balanced inner ecologies. We want all mountains and no deserts, all meadows and no swamps.

So, that's where the re-imagination is so important. When we re-imagine ourselves, what we're capable of, who we are, we're also imagining our world and creating the conditions through which it is inhabiting us. If we want a new world to come into being, it's not that the world doesn't already exist—its just not inhabiting us yet, we're not inhabiting it yet.

So, just as it's possible for us to re-imagine the world, it's possible for the world to re-imagine us?

Yes, very much so. In one sense the most biological metaphor that speaks to this is puberty. The hormonal changes that take place are very real, but they are intermeshed in a synchronous way. It's difficult to say which is cause and which is effect. They are mutually codependent with a whole shift in ideation, feeling, thought and behavior. Our bodies re-invent us when we go through puberty, but we reinvent our bodies too. We reinvent our images of who we are physically and mentally so possibilities become available that weren't available before; the whole reproductive possibility is there, where before it wasn't. It was

always inherently there, but it just hadn't been turned on, so to speak. [Laughter]

I feel that something like that is happening now. To the extent that we want to see the new age as an event, something is being turned on that is opening us to new possibilities. But not just humanity, the whole world system. It does call us to reinvent our images of the world and, the world is reinventing us too.

You end the book with some thoughts on Eastern Europe. Since you wrote that a lot has happened. You mention in the epilogue that events there aren't happening by chance and talk about the speed and timing of it all.

One of the points I wanted to make is that change can happen very quickly and in ways that defy conventional analyses. I think that was particularly true for Eastern Europe. What's been going on in the Soviet Union has actually been looming on the horizon for some time, but again it's happening very fast. That simply suggests to me that the potential was there just waiting for the opportunity to come out. Essentially I feel that the communist state has always been a kind of overlay on the Russian psyche and doesn't really represent the country. It was like it was floating on the surface, it had no deep anchors and just ended up collapsing of its own contradictions. Given that there's not a lot of deep historical energy supporting that state—which for all practical purposes was an empire—it's not surprising that when it starts to unravel, it unravels very fast.

The challenge now is, what replaces it? That's probably something that won't exactly be a western-style democracy. I think there's the opportunity for some new patterns to emerge although I'm not sure what they will be. For myself, I just look for a time of continued—I don't know if I would call it instability, but muddledness—for a while, two to three years or so. I think the pattern may be very similar to what our country went through after our revolution. We created the Confederation and then that didn't work out. Then we eventually came up with the Federal system we have now, but that wasn't our first government. It wouldn't surprise me to see that happening there too, that there will be interim forms. However, it may be a decade or so before the full-flowering of that national being really begins to take place. In whatever form it will be.

In the book you also make the point that transformation is a beginning and not a destination in itself.

Yes, I think it's important to realize that. New age thought, especially, is event oriented—the moment of change. It's oriented to change but not to assimilation and maturation. Even if something changes you still have to integrate its effects and be assimilated, it still has to mature into full form. That can happen fairly rapidly as far as historical time goes. I would rather expect that it would, given the nature of things today with technology and planetary communications being what they are. Things tend to precipitate a lot more quickly than they used to. I don't know if that's necessarily a good thing. [Laughter]

What does the new age mean to David Spangler?

I feel that what we're talking about, really, when we talk about the new age is something that is very organic. By which I mean it's living. There's lots of images that cluster around us. Some harken back to our history and some go forward into our dreams and aspirations. The new age is like that for me. It has a constellation of images that can define it. At its most basic level, for me the new age is a metaphor, or maybe a myth might be a better way to put it. It's the myth of what I call the sacred world.

The sacred world is a condition of conscious harmony and mutual empowerment between all that makes up the Earth: humanity, nature, spirit. The image of that sacred world is one of those deep images that's written into our psychic structure. Part of our human identity is the drive to bring that world into being or to participate into its coming into being. I don't think we can actually make it happen, but we are a component of it. We have to find how we fit into it before we can do our part.

Each culture as it develops has its own way of addressing that, and then it gets stuck in that way. Then you have something like a new age image that surfaces from time to time and says: "Wait a minute, you're not there yet, the future is still virgin territory, there's still creativity to be expressed, there's more discovery to be made." The past, in the sense of our personal and cultural habits, does not have to define our future—there can be transformation. I see the new age as an image that reminds us of that. It can put us back in touch with that power of co-creativity, that sense of building our future. That's one definition that's very important to me.

And the others. . .?

Another way of looking at the new age is that it's a phenomena that's made up of at least four parts. One is an invitation to discovery, to push beyond our boundaries of what's familiar to us and open up to new possibilities. They could be old possibilities to other people, but they may be new to us. Then there's an element of empowerment; on one level we're here to feed and nourish each other. Your power and my power are co-dependent on each other in a good way. That's a risky word to use these days but. . .

Interdependency?

It's more to me than interdependency. They would not exist without each other. There are ways that I find I can empower my world, the people and things in my world, then I'm in turn empowered by that. Those two elements, empowerment and discovery, are what most people who think of the new age will think of. Most workshops deal with some kind of self-empowerment, self-discovery, self-exploration beyond what's familiar, new paradigms and so on.

The third element is an attention to the planetary conditions, both social ecology and natural ecology, and how do we work on that level to create balance and wholeness. The fourth element is a realignment, a re-perception of the sacredness that is within the world, within ourselves. It's a re-integration with the spiritual domain at a deeper level than just everyday religiosity.

For me, if something is really new age it has at least three of those components. It has the personal side of discovery, empowerment and self-discovery, but it also needs to have a planetary perspective, a perspective of a larger whole. Some form of working to assist at that level in ways that take you outside of your own self.

One thing that's real hopeful to me is that in the past year I've seen some good, responsible analyses of the new age. There was an absolutely wonderful piece defining and analyzing the new age in the *Religious Studies Review* a while ago. I've finished a chapter for an anthology that's coming out, called *New Age Spirituality, An Assessment*. It's published by a religious press associated with the Presbyterian church. It's a very solid analysis of the new age, both in its weakness and the more flamboyant things, but also in the really important contributions that it's making. Seeing these things makes me hopeful that we may be moving beyond that very narrow segment that the media inflated, and said this is what the new age is all about. That's just a slice. It's like defining Christianity on the basis of a televangelist.

What do you see as the meaning of the new age to the planet?

I think there's two things operating there. In some respects I don't think it has any meaning to the planet. It has a lot of meaning to humanity and to what we do with our consciousness, our belief systems, our insights into ourselves and the world, how we define ourselves and relate to the world. From that sense, to the degree that it affects human behavior, it has a profound meaning. You know, I think humanity could cease to exist and the planet would keep on. I don't think in any way that humanity is absolutely indispensable to the planet. However, I do think we are a very cherished part of it. It would not be the same planet without humanity.

I don't want to imply that at deep levels there isn't concern or interest, but the perspective is very different. It's not exactly identical to a human one. In that sense the new age can act as a

doorway leading us into perspectives that broaden our human one, and help us to be less anthropomorphic.

At another level though, there is an aspect to the new age that seems to be structurally inherent to the planet. That is, the changes going on in the body of the world itself. That would also have an affect on humanity because it is all interrelated, what affects the world is going to affect us. I see that as a trigger.

Whichever language we use—the vibration is speeding up, new energies are being assimilated, whatever—to metaphorically try to say something is happening to the psyche of the world, that may be a force behind the acceleration behind the human consciousness that's been going on for the past 150 years. Then, that would be like saying that humanity has to adapt to some changed conditions, or there are some new possibilities that are within our reach if we can expand to encompass them.

There is also the side to the new age that is not time-oriented. It's not just related to an event, something that can be pointed to on a calendar of some kind. It also relates to a state of mind, to a perception that part of what constitutes consciousness exists in an unconditioned state that is not caught up in a temporal / historical / habitual condition-lineage, but can act from outside that to introduce change and transformation that may not be possible from within that lineage itself. I may not be wholly able, caught within my own life-system, to bring myself to change. Something might have to come from what appears to be the outside in order to trigger a new perception. I do feel that is happening for humanity, because something is shifting within the planet itself.

You often refer to the planet as a living being and as having a soul. I want to ask about that beingness and the nature of that soul.

I think we have an opportunity to see the soul from a new perspective. We have been seeing it, and thinking about it, in a very specific and particulate way: my soul-your soul, as if the soul is a thing. A material thing, but a thing nonetheless, that lives on after I die, maybe looks a bit like me—who knows what it looks like?

Now we are being given a language and a metaphor that can enable us to look at the soul in a more dynamic way, as a process and not just as a thing. As a process, or something like a field, I can't say it's bound to my space. If I accept the idea of non-locality in physics, or the idea of non-locality in mysticism, then I would have to say that my soul doesn't really have particulate boundaries. At least it's not confined to them. It may choose to focus through some boundaries or specific patterns, but it's not confined to that. Maybe my soul itself is an extension of the world-soul, the planet's soul, and it is an extension of a cosmic soul and it is an extension of God's soul.

I think we are moving away from becoming very literal in our interpretation of soul and body as two separate entities. Perhaps we are beginning to appreciate ways in which they are interrelated, and may in fact be the same thing viewed from different perspectives. The point I would want to make is that, just as it is very difficult to define God, it is equally difficult to define the soul, and for the same reasons; that it doesn't fit wholly within a single linguistic structure or set of images. It's more dynamic and larger than that. It doesn't preclude me from talking about my soul, but it invites me to recognize that there is more to my soul than what I would normally call mine.

When I think about that in terms of the world, I feel the planet has a soul. That's a way of saying that what the planet is extends beyond its material form. There's more to it than just what we experience in this dimension. A way that I experience the new age is that the non-material part is going through some kind of opening and realignment with larger aspects of itself that might be called cosmic. I feel it's doing that interdependently with humanity, because in doing that it is invoking a similar response from us to both keep up with the world, so to speak, and to assist it. I think we are simultaneously both that which helps invoke that larger resonance, and that which must learn how to receive and embody it ourselves.

We might say that the Earth is hatching some sort of new soul for itself that incorporates the human dimension more fully than ever before. The arising of the human dimension, with all of its imagination, power of thought and feeling, is part of what is hatching this new planetary soul. It's making accessible possibilities that weren't accessible before.

If a particular kind of planet-wide transformative experience has come into being, has been turned on, what turned it on?

In part it is a drive toward the experience of planetary wholeness. The experience is the important thing, not just as a concept, but the experience and the ability to inhabit bodies of incarnation—physical, mental and emotional—for which the systemic nature of the wholistic nature of the world is a given.

However, I also see that state of wholeness as an enabler. It is that which allows something else to also happen, which might be the equivalent of a kind of planetary reproduction. I don't know. If that deeper thing wants to happen which... when I try to tune into it or meditate on it, I always come out with this image of a very profound kind of creativity, a co-creative energy. So, I think of it as a more co-creative state allowing possibilities to emerge that cannot now emerge, because the co-creative vehicle and the energy of that vehicle are not yet available.

I keep wanting to bring this back to an everyday level to solve the worlds problems.

Well, let's take a look at the Soviet Union. What Gorbachev did was to invite people to re-imagine themselves and their relationship to the state. When the coup took place, it did not take place in the same country of imagination that the coup leaders lived in. I mean, as so many accounts have said, had the coup taken place 20 years ago, or even 10 years ago, or even 5, it probably would have been successful. The people had been invited to imagine themselves as a different kind of country and people, so the coup didn't fit.

One reason it didn't fit was that the people could now imagine themselves as being able to resist. They could say no. Then you have Yeltsin standing on top of a tank saying, "We will resist this thing." And it was the spark of imagination that said "Yes." People were already imagining that and, somewhere in their being, they had imagined themselves on top of a tank, metaphorically speaking. So their own inner Yeltsin climbed on their own inner tank and said "No."

That just broke everything open. Now they're having to reinvent their own country, to imagine a new country. In a sense you have an interplay of imaginative states where one leads to another. Gorbachev and Yeltsin could not have done what they did if there were not already some imagination going on to re-imagine Russia. They gave it room to operate and to develop. Then the coup happened in the context of all this new imagining, which spurred on new imagining. And now they are in this wonderful, scary place of having to re-imagine their country.

We haven't had something like that happen here, not yet. I think it may. I don't mean a coup. We might have a coup, but I would really doubt it. But I do feel there might be other things that might be more partial to our national history and character, that speak to our re-imaginings.

There may already have been those things. Personally, I think that Jimmy Carter was a potential opportunity to re-imagine some things about our country. But his imagination fell on not-so-fertile ground because we weren't individually grasping the possibilities of re-imagining ourselves. That, I feel, was one of the great services that Reagan offered. He just brought our imaginings up front. That's one of the roles of a movie actor, to embody our collective imagination. He brought some of these things to the surface; about America and standing tall, being wealthy and powerful, and all this that we are still playing out. Reagan said, "look, this is the country that you really want to imagine." And never mind that it's partly illusory and that there's all this stuff going on in the country that's contradictory to it. [Laughter]

At some point those contradictions come to a point where we can see that there's dissonance here and we need to imagine what's going on differently. And different images come to the forefront. I think that's what really happened in Russia and Eastern Europe. I mean the democracy movement just didn't spring out of nowhere. It wasn't that suddenly, poof!, and democracy appeared and communism collapsed. There was a buildup that led up to it. There was some imagining that was going on and that got triggered.

I think that kind of imagining is going on in this country. We obviously haven't yet hit the trigger point that enables us to re-imagine this country. I feel that it won't be a liberal vs. conservative imagination, or a Democratic vs. Republican imagination. Those polarities are out the window as far as the deeper nature of what's trying to happen.

Neither you nor I are big fans of prognostication, but where is it headed in this country?

Well, in America we have this profoundly synthesizing element that we both accept and reject. We accept it in images of the melting pot, the global society, the differing races and ethnic

backgrounds. Unlike Russia, which in effect had the same thing but never brought them together. It basically conquered these other peoples. Here we've been assimilated because people, on the whole, come here voluntarily, except for most of the blacks who were brought here against their will. At the same time there's resistance to that which lies behind all kinds of subtle segregations, intolerances and conflicts.

I feel the deeper message of America is to imagine, in a micro-cosmic way, a truly planetary society. We may not be able to do it until that planetary society develops elsewhere as well, to help call it out. We are being challenged by the world to come forward as a planetary society. All nations are. I feel that it's a particular dharma of America—by virtue of what it set itself out to be—to be this demonstration of peoples of all kinds working together in liberty and freedom to create something that could not be created by any one of them alone. That's the ideal that we've never fully realized. I feel that to negotiate ourselves successfully in the kind of interconnected world that's developing we need to develop that planetary sensibility. That's what I mean when I say the deeper level of America.

All of this is talking about whole systems and planetary stuff. But it comes down to our ability to deal with difference. How does that work for you, personally?

It's my family, my friends, my co-workers; they are all different from how I am. Even my kids, you know? I can see how they have similarities to me, and I can see where they look a bit like me and all that, but they're really different personalities. It's brought home to me and I need to accept that John-Michael is a not a clone of daddy, that Aidan is not a clone of daddy, they are different.

Sometimes their otherness challenges me. They see things differently than I do. For instance, I have always been verbally skilled and was reading by the time I was 3 or 4. But when it comes to mechanical things I'm illiterate, I really am. If I have to put something together, even a bunch of Leggos, my mind doesn't create images like that. It never has. It used to be troubling to my father, who was an engineer, that as an engineer I am illiterate. But John-Michael, my oldest boy, still has difficulty reading. It's as if his mind doesn't quite grasp the whole concept of words yet. But he constructs the most amazing artifacts out of anything he can lay his hands on. He's already taking things like telephones apart. Anything that I give him that's electronic he'll disassemble and try to put back together. He's literate in ways that I'm not. He can see things that I don't see. So, there are times when that bothers me because I'm confronted by the other. And Julie and I are different. We're alike in a lot of ways but we are still different. That, for me, is actually where the rubber meets the road. It has all these cosmic overtones, but it's really down to the level of, "How do I deal with that which is the Other?"

It doesn't make a lot of sense to me to say that we are all One. On some deep level I know that's true, but our creativity does not rest in our Oneness, it rests in our difference. [Laughter] Our ability to bring that which has never been known before into being emerges out of the fact that we are different, not out of the fact that we are One. I'm resistant to ideologies that want to reduce us to oneness. I think that oneness and connectedness have to be acknowledged. Paradoxically we also need to acknowledge and honor the differentiation and diversity that exists. For me, the place where that most comes into play is family and people I work with. How do I blend my consciousness with theirs so I am not the prisoner of my own opinions and perspectives, or theirs, but we can really be co-creative? The ability to do that is part of what the new age means to me.

So we need to honor our diversity as much as we honor our Oneness?

In my particular cosmology, my approach to things, I don't feel that our differences are illusory, that we're a oneness that has somehow been forgotten and gotten trapped in an illusion of separateness. I feel that we are a Oneness, that there's a level where we share the same being, the same ground of being. However, we're also different. We're each unique. So I look to a spirituality that honors that uniqueness but also honors the ability to share out of our uniqueness, in ways that co-create something that's new. For me, the place of creativity, the place of unfoldment and revelation, is the place where differences meet. But they meet in a way in which they are not in combat with each other. They're not trying to overcome each other in the name of a false oneness which often simply masquerades as an inflation of one's own sense of being.

I want to be very careful when I talk about Oneness—since I'm going to be talking about an ultimate state—that I'm not projecting onto that a sense that Oneness means that everything is like me, that I am the measure of that Oneness. If I truly, in a mystical and spiritual way, seek to enter that state of Oneness I recognize that it's going to be a radical encounter for me. It will change me. I will not go unchanged and, in fact, what I have come to know as myself may undergo a form of death, a form of radical transformation, in order to experience what that Oneness is. However, I look at the universe and see that the cosmos itself manifests diversity and I don't believe that's a mistake. I don't interpret that as being illusion. I interpret that as being a teaching in its own right. So, while I can say on the one hand that we are all One, and I want to come to that point of recognition as a context for our differences so that our differences are mutually enhancing rather than adversarial.

On the other hand, I want to have a perception that honors those differences, the uniqueness that lies behind them, and works with the phenomenon of the Other. I don't feel that the Other is anything more than a metaphor. It's nothing more than a condition of perception. For me to say that God is the Other, at one level is false, if God and I are not different from each other then there is that ground of being. In another way it's very true because God represents a very profound kind of Otherness to my finite creaturely mode of being.

I feel that the spiritual path engenders paradox. There is room for the perception that says there's a Creator and there are creatures who have been created, and they are not identical. There is part of me that is definitely a creature and then there is part of me that definitely partakes of the Creator. For me, it's not a matter of choosing between those two perceptions, even though at a logical level they may seem exclusive of each other. Both of them represent facets of the mystery of who we are and what the cosmos is.

How are you feeling about community these days and how does it relate to your worldview?

I'm very supportive of the idea of intentional community. There's always going to be a role for intentional communities. I suppose where my interests lie, these days, is in unintentional communities [Laughter] or communities that are formed without necessarily living together. Maybe I should call it an unconscious community. Humanity is an unconscious community. We exist in community but we don't wholly realize it yet. We don't experience it as such, though in some ways we're beginning to more and more. So, what I'm interested in is how are we to recognize the process of community in non-community settings? That could be in my work and my everyday encounters. There are certain states of mind that go into creating community. Once you've created an intentional community that state of mind can build into something that transcends them. For example, at Findhorn you definitely create a field of mutuality where you are empowered by a collective component in a very conscious way.

Yet, to build a community requires certain practices like honor, respect, willingness, listening to each other. Behind that there is an assumption of community-ness. It's the assumption that we are in fact part of a community and it's up to us as to whether we want to externalize that or not, or whether the conditions are appropriate to externalize that. But it can always be externalized in some way. At the very least, it can be externalized through a graciousness towards each other. That attitude lies right at the heart of community. When I look at our world, I see a world that is being forced by circumstance to acknowledge ever-increasing layers of inter-dependency; to acknowledge in effect that we are in a *de facto* community together. What then, does it take for me to go beyond my perceptions and prejudices to see other people who are very different from me—belong to different cultures or religions, have different attitudes—as being part of a different community? It starts with a perception.

The advantage of an intentional community is that you know, when you come there, that's what you're getting into. It's made very explicit. However, we all live in these unintentional communities, these unconscious communities, that are trying to become more conscious of the community spirit that is within them. I feel that this is every bit as important, and as challenging, an issue as the ecological one. It's one of the places where the evolutionary ratchet is being turned up. What that evolutionary need draws forth is all those elements in our society, and in ourselves, that don't want to see that, or want to see it in a very limited way. We're dealing with this cusp between a negative tribalism and a truly planetary sense of community. We're at one of those stages where we're drawing creative energy by the heightening of the polarities.

What will the next stage be?

I personally believe that the function of all this is to drive us beyond our normal definition of community into a state of awareness that can experience and perceive the planetary community, whatever it may mean. I certainly don't think it means something like a world government. I do believe it means something more like the ability of a society to exist that supports and empowers a high level of diversity within itself. And, where that diversity is not stratified in a hierarchical fashion, but is seen horizontally. We could certainly create a lot of diversity by having classes, the poor and the rich and so on, and hardening the boundaries between them. I certainly see that kind of energy, that kind of trend, at work in our society. But that doesn't represent a real systemic community, a community that operates as a mutually reinforcing system. I feel that the next step is definitely symbiotic in its nature. A lot of intentional communities are not symbiotic by nature. They're organizationally hierarchical. Of course, the next step could also be that the whole thing falls apart. [Laughter] Then we start over again from whatever pieces are left. I view apocalypse as a regression; I'm rooting for our ability to manage complexity.

So far we haven't been particularly good at it. How do we manage that?

The very first step is acknowledging and feeling comfortable with our own complexity. A lot of spiritual and psychological systems that we use are geared to reduce complexity and make things appear simple, reducing the paradox. We have to come to a point of accepting and living with ambiguity. Things are not black and white, right or wrong, or stretched out between two polarities. To me, the universe is multi-polar. I need to acknowledge the complexity that is me. Am I one self, many selves, or both?

I also don't think that I can manage a complex system as much as I have to become part of it. It's like having to surrender to the rhythm that's there. You just have, as Heinlein would say, "to grok" the pattern, and you give yourself to it. That's part of what is meant when we talk about Oneness. It's a rhythm or pulse that's moving through the whole dance of life. To really understand life and to work with it in a co-creative way, I need to have some sense of that rhythm. How to blend with it and not stand back from it and try to analyze it, pick it apart and try to put life together like I put Leggos together. One of the first steps in dealing with complex systems is to recognize that I'm a complex system.

How do you deal with the complexity of your relationships?

It's easy to sloth my wife and my kids into familiar forms and patterns; this is what Julie is like, this is what Aidan is like, this is what John-Michael is like. But in actuality they are always slopping over those boundaries. [Laughter] When I try to impose a certain pre-set boundary and say, "well, this is what you're going to be," I'm really trying to reduce the complexity of their beings to match the ways I've reduced my complexity. Sometimes my kids ask me to be things for them that don't fall into simple categories of father or adult. I think that's a common experience for all of us in relationships. That's why relationships can be so challenging, because they're not simple. But we think of them as if they should be simple. So, coming to see and work with the world as a complex system begins when we see ourselves and our lives as having that complexity. Complexity is only overpowering when I'm trying to analyze it or deal with it piece by piece. I have to deal with it as a whole and that takes practice. It takes a different kind of perception.

You have three children under 10. You're 47 now. You've come to parenthood late in life. How is that for you?

I'm a late-bloomer. [Laughter] I really love it. Looking back I feel the timing was really good. I have much more to give as an older dad than I might have had when I was in my 20's. I probably don't have the same level of physical energy, [Laughter] but it hasn't been a problem. I find my family to be a real school for me, it's my training area where the rubber meets the road. [Laughter] Kids definitely have a way of bringing things out of the unconscious. [Laughter] It puts me in touch with elements of my own childhood that I've forgotten, and puts me in touch with ways of seeing and thinking about things. That's a lot of fun.

On a personal level, how do you keep your relationships together?

I never take these people for granted. I never assume I know who they are. Habitual ways of relating to each other are what causes a lot of problems. Another thing is that I'm very attentive, consciously, of empowering my relationships. One thing I've learned is that I've taken on, culturally and so on, different images of what a dad is; how and when a dad should respond, get angry, and about what. I realize how mechanical that is. In the reality of the situation, when something comes up I don't have to respond in these pre-programmed and pre-packaged ways. That's been good for me to experience. So many of the ways of responding are not necessarily empowering responses. They often project one's way of being onto someone else. It comes back to accepting the differences. I can't expect these people to be like me. It's actually more enhancing to what I am, for them not to be like me. [Laughter] I want to empower those differences.

I'm very careful with my children to be aware of the kind of perceptions that they are developing and how their minds work.

I remember that before John Michael was born I had a dream. He came to me. In the dream he was six or seven years old. He came up to me and said, "I'm going to be your son. I want you to know that I'm not coming to have anything to do with this new age stuff. I want to be a doctor." [Laughter] At the moment he wants to be an inventor. I don't know whether he'll be a doctor or not. It was a wonderful dream, saying, "Look Dad, you've got your way and I've got mine. They might be the same and they might not. So let's be cool about it. I'm giving you advance warning." [Laughter] So, I'm careful that way. I've learned not to project my own sense of things onto someone else, but to just see who they are and deal with that.

How are you feeling about the world that we will be leaving for our children?

I would say that there's a lot of hope in the world. I don't feel we should make assumptions about the future. A lot of folks, for a long time, have been predicting really rough times. And I think that's possible, certainly all the potentials are there. But the ingredients are also there to bring things into being that we can't now, or don't, expect. I just don't feel we can make assumptions and say Armageddon is on its way, or it's all going to be sweetness and light. It's going to be what it is. If we can take it on a daily basis and maintain our own center, it may turn out a good deal smoother than we anticipate.

We really do have the power to make our transitions smooth. They don't have to be bumpy and painful. It's just that we don't have many models for changes that are empowering and uplifting without being painful at the same time. All that says is that we have a lot experience in waiting until the last moment to change and then getting hit between the eyes. It doesn't really have to be that way. One way to keep it from being that way is not to procrastinate. It's the old "wait to the last minute to do the term paper" syndrome. And then you have to pull an all-nighter. I don't think that, culturally, we have to pull an all-nighter to get through it, though that option is certainly there.

There's a lot of sheer goodness and power out there in the world that just doesn't get acknowledged very much. I don't at all feel that it's hiding one's head in the sand to acknowledge that, I think that it's hiding one's head in the sand not to acknowledge it. Idealism is probably one of the most repressed emotions at the moment. It's not considered sophisticated to be an idealist. But this is not necessarily the worst period in the world, and humanity has come through other bad times.

I think we need to be realistic optimists. If we acknowledge the power of Spirit then we recognize that there's a tremendous and inexhaustible level of compassion and love and assistance and empowerment there to draw on. We have an incredible ally, the greatest ally of all—God—to work on behalf of humanity, and all the world, moving through this incredibly rich and important evolutionary time.

Pamela Chase & Jonathan Pawlik

"We wish to add our own experiences to those of all the others who have said that it is time for Humankind to learn to work with Nature for personal and planetary healing. Once you get over the hurdle of thinking that it is unusual to communicate with trees, perhaps you will feel the suffering that we have felt expressed from the trees about being misunderstood. Our own connection with Nature has developed out of what we have needed to learn and what we love to do best. As you declare your intent and your willingness to work with Nature, your own way of connecting will open for you also."

Pamela Chase & Jonathan Pawlik—*Trees for Healing*

The 90's hold great promise as a decade of learning and transition. Concurrent with this perspective is a view of the decade as an epoch, or cycle, of communication. The resultant conferencing and discussion will invariably take place on a number of levels; communication amongst ourselves, with ourselves, with our Higher Selves, with Spirit. If we have an appreciation of this, then the dexterity to extend our conceptual understandings of rapport and relationship to include our environment and the natural world becomes an obvious, and perhaps even necessary, next step.

Toward this expansive beginning there are two who have taken the time and devoted themselves to the introspection prerequisite to comfortable and meaningful connection, contact and interchange with the more subtle aspects of our world. Although I'm quite sure that Pamela and Jonathan would not refer to it in this way, I have noticed another aspect to their work. Concurrent with the above seemingly necessary restraints there is yet an additional element of sacrifice.

If one were to categorize and rank, by degree of challenge, the varied outlets of human and etheric interchange, then certainly spiritually coalescent communication would tally right up there as a most sensitive and demanding discipline. It has so much to do with where one attenuates one's focus. A mind engrossed within (or perhaps even dissipated by) the seeming demand of day-to-day hurdles of our times and social systems might not apply itself to the natural subtleties that so many, somehow, know or feel abound.

This manner of communication, when done properly, is not an idle or indulgent task. It requires a very clear and honest intention and, dare I say, a literal mountain of integrity. It is far easier to do it poorly (and the last few years have provided many distinguished and undistinguished examples of this) than to do it well. All of this by way of saying that snake-oil and truth blend well only in a needy imagination. Fortunately, the far grander potentials of truth hold the far greater grandeur, substance and reward.

Pamela Chase and Jonathan Pawlik first met in Pennsylvania in 1981. They soon found a mutual interest in outdoor activities and just being in the woods. In 1983 there began a period of connection with the Devic Kingdom, the overlighting spirits of the natural world. In 1988 their volume, *The Newcastle Guide to Healing with Crystals* was published. This was followed, in 1989, by *The Newcastle Guide to Healing with Gemstones*. Of this period Pamela wrote, "Working with the stones was a journey of the Soul, and like the journey of the tarot Fool, we learned the lessons of many lifetimes. Our personal journey was filled with joy and a sense that all was unfolding according to plan."

With the publication of their latest volume, *Trees For Healing; Harmonizing with Nature for Personal Growth and Planetary Balance* (Newcastle Publishing, 1991), the plan has unfolded in a very expressive way. Through the use of the words and messages nestled within its pages, the reader may well attempt and experience a new momentum of flow towards the natural world. In this book Pamela, Jonathan and the Devas invite you to co-create within a new paradigm of energetics.

Over the course of, at least, the last one hundred years, we as a species have shown a bizarre disregard for the planet and its occupants. If we are fortunate, future generations will only have to consider it a puzzling anecdote concerning their forebears. If the future does not work out so favorably, then perhaps we will have the unenviable distinction of being damned by the lips of our very own grand- and great-grand children. What else will they have to say about those who squeezed the last natural resource out of a poisoned-beyond-understanding world? And we will have no legitimate excuse... none. There aren't any.

However, just as the natural world has provided all the sustenance we have required to become, on occasion, so awkward, so too does our precious planet offer us insight into our healing. Both personally and collectively the balm of living in harmony with nature, as all good stewards should, at the very least holds the promise of a sustainable future. At the very most... perhaps it will provide for a much easier access to that grandeur mentioned earlier.

I have always found it quite fitting that these two wonderful folks have lived in the Northwest. Their work has provided a fitting counterpoint to the environmental battles that have been waged here over habitat and timber. Hopefully, balance will occur and make a lasting impression.

Actually, we all live in the same town and have the pleasure of each other's company as time allows. I mention this while thinking of a dinner we once had together. Jonathan is normally such a serious and intent fellow, but he has this mirth which can be quite funny. On this occasion he was relating some rather humorous stories from his college days. At one point he divulged this tremendous secret of having been a business major. I remember being completely dumbfounded for a few moments and then just laughing and laughing. The idea of it was just too astonishing and seemingly absurd. Given his personality and present work, it just seemed so charmingly ludicrous. However, in hindsight, I now see this as a representation of evolution that is perfectly appropriate to our times. It is certainly a process that has served him well, as the followers of their current vocation would no doubt agree.

Readers of *The Light* were well acquainted with this eloquent pair. For about three years their column, *Moving Upstream,* was a genuine favorite with our readers. When we learned that their third book was at the printer and their time slightly freed up it seemed inevitable, and certainly quite timely, that we presented their audience a more in-depth and detailed look at two of Nature's favorite examples of the Human Kingdom.

"When you work with stones, you interpret their Consciousness according to your own spiritual understanding. You tend toward consistency in your belief systems and consequently, you do one of two things: either you interpret your perceptions in a manner consistent with other things that you know and understand, or you dismiss the perception from your conscious mind."

Pamela Chase & Jonathan Pawlik—*The Newcastle Guide to Healing with Gemstones*

How has it been for you to work together as a couple and, more importantly, how do you manage it?

Jonathan: I was mentioning to Pamela earlier that it's been 10 years we've been together. If you had said to me 10 years ago that this would be happening... uh-uh. I would have never, ever thought that this would be happening, that three books would have come through us. It's pretty incredible.

Pamela: And that we would be interviewed because we had written three books that have to do with celebrating nature. It's been fun. In the times that we feel that we haven't grown very much, or are wondering why we might be working on an issue... looking back 10 years... we can see that we've come a distance. I think we're lucky because we have complementary skills. I also think that we are blessed because there's enough of a similarity in outlook that it's easy enough to agree on the main ways that we want to get there and each of us has an individual part to play, a role to fill.

Jonathan: In addition to having a similar focus spiritually, we also bond together well in terms of our lifestyle on the physical plane, which helps with what we are doing. In terms of working together as a couple, we tend to know and have a sense of where each of our strengths lie. We balance each other.

Pamela: I tend to pick up perceptions that are emotional in nature. Jonathan tends to pick up a broader spiritual perspective. We would share them and see what the common themes were. If we didn't get a common theme we would assume that one or the other was out of tune, and go back and work with it some more. Sometimes it's a matter of working from different perspectives. One of the values of working together is that although we may pick up differing qualities... when we could see a theme we could also see what the different facets of the perspectives were. It was helpful, actually, to have the two of us do it together.

Given the work that you two do, the types of books you write in terms of content, I'm wondering how does your work affect your lifestyle?

Pamela: We've found that in order to reach the level of spiritual attunement that we've had to reach to work with the trees, we've needed to spend a lot of time alone. Part of that has to do with personal issues that sometime get stirred up when we're with people. When we are around people we operate more on an emotional/mental kind of framework. When we're attuning to the stones and the trees it's a higher frequency. That's been both wonderful and difficult. It's been incredibly peaceful. One of the wonderful things about writing the tree book was the time we spent alone with the trees... incredibly peaceful and joyful. Probably one of the most incredible experiences we'll ever have.

The difficulty is that sometimes we're lonely and have to deal with the issue of loneliness. It comes from facing things

inside ourselves that are difficult. It's been difficult to be or talk with people who don't understand what we're doing, or think it's strange. We haven't grown past the point where it isn't hurtful in some way, although it's getting better. That's the flip-side of the joyful part of doing this kind of work.

Jonathan: It feels like the journey we have chosen to follow in this life has meant that we were, and are, really pioneering—a little bit different than the early settlers and what have you, but yet very much out in the wide expanse of things. I know that, at times, I've had thoughts of, "Why am I doing this?" If I look at the main arena of the world and what I'm doing, it's like black and white. At times there's no gray area I can enter or feel comfortable in.

Pamela: The more we work with spiritual energy the more we have to do things. We have to be careful with what we eat, we have to watch our rest and our nutrition, because the more sensitive our bodies get the less they tolerate stuff that isn't healthy. Sometimes being careful is a pain, but I think we are more healthy now as a result.

One of the first lines in your book, *Trees For Healing*, has to do with belief systems. Now that everyone is more aware of them and how they affect our whole being, why is it important to look towards altering them as regards to the natural world?

Pamela: I've come to feel that everything in Nature, every physical form, is here to teach us. Biblically it's said that man is to have dominion over the earth and the creatures. The way that many of us see natural things is that they are there for our use. It's a belief system that things are here to be used and what it means for trees to be here to serve us is that trees are to be used. From science we learn to see things as objects with no spiritual life, just physical life. When you put those things together that's a very different way of perceiving things than native cultures perceive things. They have been, all along, much more aware of the spiritual consciousness that I perceive to be in everything.

What the trees continue to teach is how to be spiritual in a physical form. We have found many answers; how to deal with death, how to be ourselves. To me it says that all forms of Nature are incredibly wise and spiritually involved and evolved. The whole concept of plants and animals being here to serve takes on a whole new dimension. It's like they're the teachers and I'm the student. That is a very different concept from what most people have. It's one that I didn't have not so long ago. Now I wonder how I could have thought anything else, but I know how long it took for me to get there. It's a very important thing for us to learn now because it's part of preserving the environment. If we understand that the environment is here to teach us, to heal us, to work with us, then we're not going to misuse it and destroy it the way we as a culture do now.

Jonathan: One of the things that the kingdoms of Nature teaches us is about timelessness. We so often hear people say, "I just don't have the time," to do this or that. When you open yourself up to bond with any of Nature's creatures, plants or minerals, the connection in what you receive can occur instantaneously. It's not like it's going to take you hours or days. That's one aspect of it. Another is the fact that they teach about patience. Sometimes we want to have things right now, and if we don't get them we get all bent out of shape. What we have found through Nature is that when you orient your thoughts and feelings to a purposeful flow, then things will come to you and things will be for you, effortlessly. Sometimes healing takes a period of space before it is complete. Sometimes it's a lifelong process. It may require your entire span on the Earth-plane. Does that make it wrong? No, not a bit. Every moment that you're healing is a moment to learn. Every moment that you're healing gives you more opportunity to work on behalf of not only yourself, but on behalf of others.

If we relate your work to science it might be said that it takes something like the Gaia hypothesis to an evolved culmination. How do you feel about traditional science?

Pamela: I think the scientific view is limited because it only deals with material reality. When you work with spiritual consciousness it becomes a very subjective process, because your beliefs and perceptions are always an integral part of what it is you're working with. That means that science itself is going to have to go through a whole shift in terms of methodology and basic concepts if science were to open to a spiritual dimension.

Jonathan: I think that how we view this in terms of what we have put forth, is that those who have an immediate resonance with what's there will be impacted, perhaps instantaneously. For those of the scientific realm we see this as planting a seed of light whose germination will take place in its appropriate time, whatever that might be. Ultimately, our feeling is that more light will create space for a reassessment of one's stance as it relates to the spiritual part of being. We release it without expectation as to what will manifest, or how it will manifest. Our feeling is that even if there is a minuscule or small adjusting that takes place, it's part of the healing process for the whole planet.

The beginning of the book looks at some historical perspectives of trees as sacred beings. What can you share about that?

Pamela: To me, in part, it's the coming together of the East and the West. The Eastern tradition of mysticism and the understanding that there is God and spiritual consciousness in everyone, coming together with the West which has developed a lot of technology, but has somewhat spurned spiritual development. I think this is a very significant time in human development because we're bringing together both aspects; learning to honor both our material existence and our spiritual existence.

Jonathan: It's like a marriage. Instead of its being between two people it takes place within Self. You come into this world as a soul and the first thing you learn is about materiality and what it means to be in a material world. Your focus is very strongly in that particular realm. Ultimately though, you have to have a blend. You have to develop the consciousness of your spiritual nature as well. The consciousness of your material nature continues to affirm to you throughout your life that we are all One. All aspects of Nature are One. We are part of that, so we are One with Nature.

Pamela: Trees, as well as many other natural objects, were regarded as sacred. In some of the ancient cultures, certainly with the Greeks and maybe with the Druids too, it was the priests who fully understood that concept and acted on rituals that then gave things to the people. The people may not necessarily have made the connection. The rituals may have been developed to be a possible path to lead people to the consciousness, but the power and the understanding of it remained with the priests. This time is significant because each of us has to learn to do that on our own. Each of us is our own priest and our own guide. At least that's our belief and what we see in this movement of spirituality. It's probably a blessing that many of us are increasingly able to take that step, make a choice, make that connection. Because... to find God, to look within for the answers... it does seem to be a difficult step for many to make.

How do you see that movement and momentum evolving in our world at this point?

Jonathan: There's a gradual process of spiritual maturity taking place on the planet right now. There is a growing interest among religious institutions that they have to give more. And give more in a broader spectrum; to be facilitators for the spiritual growth of their flocks. In other words, I see progress being made. I feel that it will ultimately change the very structure of the major religions. It may or may not happen in my lifetime, but that's the direction; much more openness, less consolidation of knowledge and the sharing of that knowledge, a true giving and receiving in Spirit.

Pamela: I've often wondered how the energy of change works. The people I know who are involved in spirituality find this time intense, with the intensity increasing toward change and growth. Those whom I know who are not involved in personal growth... I'm not sure they feel that there is an acceleration in the intensity of living. Perhaps how one perceives this time depends on the choices that one is making.

Jonathan: Even if there is, or you notice that certain religions are opening up more, it becomes individual choice even then. The patterns run deep. The patterns are programmed within self. You truly can't know how that's ultimately going to unfold. If anyone were to pinpoint a time and say what's going to happen—it's impossible anymore. The intensification for change is accelerating. How someone responds to that intensity is really anybody's guess.

Pamela: I guess those are our beliefs on predictions. We question predictions on the basis that it's each individual's choice, and there are many choices one makes moment by moment.

Jonathan: I think it's also a product of the environment, where the person is. You can read all the good books on the spiritual expansion, but if you remain in an environment that is not conducive to that growth, then it will be much harder to determine what the path is going to be like.

Pamela: When I look at my own emotional growth, there are times when I know, or that my Higher Self tells me, that it would be good to do x, y, and z. But the emotional part says that I can't possibly do that, or it fights on some level. Those kinds of changes or growth take a long time to work through. The changes depend on commitment. The choices to make a growth step are there. It just takes some people longer to make the choices—maybe more lifetimes—than it does other people, for a variety of reasons. It is a matter of choice. It's impossible to predict choice.

Jonathan: There's also this idea of making mistakes and also self-judgement. The moment that you put judgement on yourself you abort or curtail, you slow down your progress with what you are doing. Sometimes you will actually come to a standstill. Who knows judgement better than self?

Pamela: I think self-judgement is probably the biggest thing we all work to overcome.

As humans we can only see self-judgement in linear time. As such we're halting and continuing on through our immediate history, instead of viewing it with perfect clarity, from the ultimate macro-perspective.

Pamela: It's definitely a lot of back and forth, a lot of meandering. It's more picturesque than a straight line.

Jonathan: The thing here is that if you can see that no matter what direction you take off your main course, you are learning something, then self-judgement will not limit you. Because you are allowing your experiences to teach you. It doesn't matter if it's linear, it doesn't matter where it takes you, ultimately you are learning. By learning, you're growing. By growing, you're being. By being, you are becoming more yourself.

One of the biggest lessons we are learning on the planet at this time—I'm talking about humankind taken as a whole—is compassion. We're learning about forgiveness, we are learning about acceptance of self. The more we can forgive, the more we can be gentle and kind... kindness has to start inside. You can't be kind to another being until you are kind to yourself. You can't give anything from your heart to anyone until you can give to yourself first. That's why we are all here on this planet. We're here to learn how to give and receive within self, so we can give and receive outside of self.

Pamela: The trees and the stones, Nature, already know that. They live in a state of being able to constantly give and receive love. By learning to bond and attune with them I can learn what that feels like, what that is.

Jonathan: There are many levels to unconditional love. The more that you give yourself to Nature, the more Nature gives. There are infinite ways that unconditional love can be expressed by a human. When you enter into communion or attunement with Nature, it will teach you about those levels; what they are, how you can integrate them back inside yourself, and then extend them out to others. When we're here on this planet, the planet itself becomes our school. When you're out in Nature you enter her classrooms... to learn.

Reading your books certainly gives one a perspective on how much there is to discover. What about the soul of a tree? What have you perceived about that?

Pamela: We then definitely get into the realm of belief systems and how one translates what they perceive into a reality. We make the assumption that, for example, because we in our egos compete, we therefore describe events in the natural world as being competitive. When two animals are fighting, to us it might look competitive. For them the experience isn't like that. They don't have the same ego attachment, the same emotional attachment to the experience. For them it's not painful or a struggle as we might project it would be for us.

When the ancients said that animals have souls, I would say that yes, animals have spiritual consciousness. We're talking about the same phenomenon, but we have many different beliefs and perceptions about how we interpret what that phenomenon is. It seems to me that everything in physical form has a soul, by which I mean spiritual consciousness. Everything takes on a physical form for a particular purpose; something that the form is learning, something that form is giving. When what is learned and given is done, that physical form disappears or changes and the spiritual essence is left. There's a constant changing and shift of life-force energy that goes on all the time.

I know that sometimes, for me, trees can also take on human attributes. There's a favorite tree of ours that is very young, it reminds me of a puppy. I think of it the way I think of certain friendly animals that I know. Sometimes trees can feel masculine or feminine in the kinds of energies they put out, or the things I perceive from them. I think those are perceptions or ideas that I use to help me explain or understand what's being taught. I don't think that's necessarily the reality of what the spiritual consciousness of the tree is for itself.

I guess I'm trying to get you to say something about those beings not in an egoic state being closer to the cosmic mystery than we are.

Pamela: I think that they are closer to unconditional love. Their being able to give and receive is an example of that. The way they see time, work in time and see themselves operating in time is, essentially, timeless. They don't have the same sense of time as we do. Those are all ways that they are connected with the mysteries that we are not; that we have become separated from but have in our memory.

Jonathan: They operate in a parallel reality to our own. They teach us about simplicity and practicality. When we come as a soul onto the Earth, what we seek to learn is about balance. Not only how to give and receive but when to let go and when not to let go. The cycles that trees go through is part of the yearly season. In the Fall you find a lot of trees drop their leaves. There's not a sense that they have to have them forever, but that it's a part of their cycle and evolution. We can learn the same thing in our reality. When is something no longer needed? When is its time?

Pamela: The parallel reality is that we are still learning how to use our will. In Nature the will is already merged; the Divine Will is not separated. Nature teaches by example about what it is to merge your will with Divine Will.

What do you feel Nature teaches us about that? And about surrender and trust?

Jonathan: I've had experiences where I have bonded with trees that had been hurt by having lost major limbs, and so on. In the course of bonding with them I would ask if it wasn't very painful and awful. They would say, "No." They would say, "When you resist the process it becomes painful, when you surrender to it, it

is no longer painful. There's no longer an attachment, there's no loss."

There's another aspect to this too. In many places in our world we are taught that whenever something dies, that it's forever gone. What Nature says is that nothing dies... everything continues to recycle.

Pamela: I'm remembering when we were visiting some oaks. I had the distinct impression that I wouldn't be seeing them again. I was feeling sad about it. The message I got from the oaks had to do with just being in the present and knowing that the abundance of Nature is always with you. There's always something that you can attune with. There's always love there. It becomes a matter of opening your eyes to what is here in the present. I find now that when we're out in the woods it's a blessing to look and see what's new there. It reminds me that even though forms change, that people may come and go in my life, there's always love there if I look for it.

We've talked to a number of trees that know when they're going to die... they convey that sense. I always have a duel reaction. There's a part in me that finds that very painful. The sense I get from the tree is not that. It's a sense of living in the present. "I live my life, however it is. When the time comes for me to die, I let go without resistance and there is no pain."

Having said that, this is going to sound contradictory, but... when humans do things that are unloving to trees or animals or plants, there is an energy of pain that is transmitted and remains in the memory consciousness of the tree. We have found that there are some trees that don't have as much energy to give humans, or don't wish to be as close. It just feels like they don't want to talk to us right now. Our guidance indicated that was because they have a memory of pain which needs to be healed or worked through.

Jonathan: An example of that was when Mount St. Helens erupted back in 1980. We visited there a while back to get a sense of how the trees felt about that experience. From the human perspective, it was ghastly to look down from the air and see that there were just a few green things left. We attuned to those that were there, that had survived. For them it was a way of saying that there is a tomorrow, it doesn't all just end. It's like surrendering to the Light. After a period of time there's greater movement in that direction. Thus there is a rebirth. No matter what the natural event may be, whether it's a volcano or anything, there's something very special that we can learn and apply in our own lives.

We've been talking about trees, plants and animals. Is it similar to be in tune with the seasons?

Jonathan: On a different scale. Certain animals, like the bear, go through their life cycle and they spend a period of time, months, totally going within Self. Then they re-emerge back into the real world. They don't fight doing it. They don't fight giving themselves permission to have that space. We humans are learning to do likewise, perhaps in a little different way, yet it's similar. If I need to rest, or get away, or change my pattern of how I am living, I need to give myself permission to do it, not feel guilty about doing it and, literally, get on with it.

Pamela: Just observing the life cycle of a particular animal teaches you something about life's rhythms. The seasonal cycles also teach that. The energy of Spring is the most interesting to me. It's possible to address yourself to what's going on when you're in it; "What can I learn from the Spring energy?" It's a very good thing to do at equinoxes and solstices, but you can do it at any time. To me, the Spring energy feels very intense. There's this incredible movement to emerge. It feels something like the labor and delivery process. It takes a tremendous amount of energy and momentum to open up a bud; intense almost to the degree of being painful. Then there's this incredible upsurge that I find just awesome. For me the energy of Spring is very helpful for personal growth.

Jonathan: Sometimes you may need to take the little steps before you can take the big ones. It's like saying, "I value every part of my journey," and really appreciating all that it takes to emerge. If it's a shift in how you feel or sense in your given space, it may require the little things you do that build a pattern. Then you can feel comfortable in going forward into something more dynamic.

**We all seem to be working on our interpersonal relation-
ships these days. Maybe if we could heal those we could
heal everything. How do you feel that Nature exemplifies
that?**

Jonathan: We learn from nature that we can, and that it's
important to, claim our own space while, at the same time, living
in harmony with those around us. When you walk in the woods,
you see all the various forms of life that are beneath a tree and
actually grow on the very trunk and bark of the tree, the ferns
and what have you. There's a sharing of the space, there's a
mutual giving that provides a positive space for all there. In other
words, the ferns provide a certain type of nutrient balance that
helps to provide a life-support for the tree, but the tree also
provides cover, shelter and life-support for the ferns.

Pamela: When I go into the woods with the intent of working on
an interpersonal issue and I say to the tree, "I'm not happy about
x, y and z," usually—well, not usually, always—what it does is
give me love in the area where I'm having trouble loving myself.
Once I understand that, it's easier for me to see both what and
how I need to continue nurturing myself, and also how the other
person needs to be nurtured. Often what happens in interpersonal
communications is that you feel that you're not getting enough,
that the other person isn't giving you enough love, they're not
understanding you somehow. Your space gets limited and you feel
threatened that you're going to lose what space you have. The
tree teaches how to give yourself space and give somebody else
space at the same time. It almost always comes back to helping
me release judgements that I have more often about myself.
That's sort of a bottom line.

I also remember a time when I was expecting to be in some
way nurtured by the tree. Instead the tree seemed to tell me,
"Well, if you want to feel better you need to make a choice to

stop thinking in a certain way." It surprised me. I guess what I'm saying is that whatever I need, the tree can teach me. And in such a way, because it comes from unconditional love, that it helps me understand what I need to give to another.

Would you like to share anything further about utilizing Nature's resources to heal ourselves and the environment?

Pamela: In the language of Alcoholics Anonymous and the Adult Children of Alcoholics, one of the Twelve Steps has to do with relying on your Higher Power. Nature is an incredible resource for learning how to do that. An important part of personal and spiritual growth is learning how to be by oneself, because it's your own inner experience that teaches you about what God is and what God is not. It seems like the connection with Nature is a personal kind of relationship. For people who are dealing with co-dependent types of issues or depending on other people for one's approval or support, learning to connect with Nature teaches you how to give yourself support.

Certainly we've become more aware of the environment than we were before. There's no way we could avoid it. In some ways that's problematic because we've become sensitive to the ways that we're not as sensitive as we could be. When you work with Nature it becomes even more imperative to save our environment and to help other people save it too.

Jonathan: The environment represents an avenue that helps the healing of not only the planet, but the healing among people. When you learn to be more conscious of the environment so that whatever actions you're taking are in harmony with her rather than abusing her—and you see the positive affects that it has on those who are in the same or surrounding space where you are—that provides a catalyst for greater interchange and greater healing among people in an ongoing way with the environment and the planet. People learn through example. If you clean a stream that's been polluted very badly so that lifeforms can inhabit it, and others come to it and they can appreciate it—they love it for the beauty and the purity that's there. That helps to consolidate more consciousness from the Human Kingdom in moving further and further in that direction. It's like building a collective will to heal.

Richard Erdoes

A Witness for Tradition

*"The light was extinguished and we were left with our
thoughts—human islands in a sea of darkness. The
drums throbbed as many voices rose in a quavering
chant. The steady rhythm of the drums transmitted
itself to the walls from where I absorbed it into my
body through the shoulder blades. I not only heard the
drums; I felt them physically. Lights appeared out of
nowhere like so many fireflies. They came floating up
out of the darkness for a fraction of a second and were
gone almost before eye and brain had been able to
register them. The spirits were coming in."*

Richard Erdoes—*Lame Deer, Seeker of Visions*

A s you all know, there's something quite remarkable about life. It frequently maintains this unique tendency to cre-ate myriad opportunities for significant and differentiating experience. Such a life is Richard Erdoes'. Such an experience was my opportunity to interview the man who, for the past 30 years, has so honestly portrayed the Native American experience.

Not content to sit back and relax after 80 years of energetic effort, he continues working, generally on several projects at once. With twenty-three books to his credit, the author of the now-classic *Lame Deer: Seeker of Visions, American Indian Myths & Legends, Crying for A Dream,* amongst others, continues his work of pursuing the protection and understanding of the Native Americans. It is not an endeavor that is easily cultivated. For Richard Erdoes it has meant thirty years of living life as a shared event with those of the Native American Nation who have come to know and honor him as a friend.

His accomplishments take on an even more dedicated quality when one understands that English is a second language for Mr. Erdoes, a native of Austria. Owing to family circumstance the young child Richard Erdoes travelled and lived in vastly differing areas of the European continent. He was studying art in Vienna when, in order to elude the rising Nazi tide that was sweeping Germany and its surroundings, he was forced to escape.

Actually, he was forced to flee on two occasions. As an underground student activist in 1930's Berlin, he and his friends published anti-nazi literature. Needless to say it was not par-ticularly popular with the roguish brownshirts that had infested the area. Their operation was eventually betrayed. His partner was publicly executed and other friends were shipped off to concentration camps. For Richard Erdoes fate allowed an inter-cession, and kindly circumstance allowed an escape to Vienna. Eventually the Germans arrived there also, so he made his way to America in 1940. He than began a career as a freelance illustrator for such publications as *Life*, *Time* and the *Saturday Evening Post*. As an artist he developed a distinguished reputation.

His associations with the Lakota Medicine Men John Lame Deer and Henry Crow Dog began in the 50's during illustrating voyages to the West. These friendships provided him a unique view into Native American perspective and a new direction in life; a path that would compel him to document the profound, interpret the mysterious and give voice to the indigenous sacredness of America.

He wrote his first book at the age of 50. This occurred through the continued insistence and provocations of Lame Deer, whose medicine indicated that he had indeed found the co-author he had so long awaited. As he stated, "I always wanted somebody to help me write a book about Indian religion and medicine, and when I first met you I knew that you were the man I had been waiting for. Your coming was no accident."

During a sacred yuwipi ceremony (a very ancient medicine stone ceremony of the Lakota peoples) the spirits told the Lakota Medicine Men to give Richard Erdoes a name, the name of a human being. They now called him Inyan Wasicun, the White Man with the Rocks. Apparently the spirits recognized him, knew him. They played with his camera gear. His name signifies that he is a spokesman, a communicator for the people. The Lame Deer book followed shortly thereafter.

Beyond that there was his time during the siege of Wounded Knee, accompanying the Hopi to the United Nations and numerous other adventures. After a lengthy time of involvement he was so trusted by the Sioux that he was invited to photograph the revival of the Ghost Dance. He is the only white man to have ever had that privilege.

Through his perseverance in accurately and sensitively documenting the Native American culture, experience and presence, Richard Erdoes has preserved a legacy for all those who wish to understand. Through his connection with and love for living legends he has become one himself, for many believe him to be America's greatest living ethnographer. If this introduction is brimming with platitudes it is only because I, like many others, have been deeply moved, by the man and by his works. His words, the words he has compiled, and his photographs have indeed been a selfless service; a service for all people.

It was during our interview that the clues which signed the way to understanding this preeminent author became apparent to me. I was most curious as to the how's and why's that have fashioned a life so in accord with the timeless traditions he has so aptly documented. For myself, two things clearly stood out. The first, that Mr. Erdoes is a man of many cultures. It could well be that when one's mind is attuned to the world as a whole and not necessarily affixed onto one particular cultural bias, a variety of appreciation and experience may more readily be assimilated. You will see that in our time together Mr. Erdoes extended a similar metaphor for Medicine Man Archie Lame Deer.

In addition, and perhaps more importantly, Richard Erdoes is an artist and a perceptive human being. One has only to read his books, and gauge the subject matter, to ascertain that fact. Lakota spiritual leader Leonard Crow Dog has made this very clear, albeit vicariously, in the interview. While Richard related the story, I thought I detected a twinkle in his eyes. He was obviously honored and delighted by the words. Of course, in his most modest way he related the incident as an honoring of its source.

Unquestionably there have been great issues of awareness, sensitivity and trust involved in the production of his works. The Sioux and the Hopi do not believe that their cultural heritages are without substantial meaning. For the Native Americans, life is an interconnecting circle which encompasses all living things. And by no means is that circle separate in any way from Spirit.

Lame Deer must have known that his circle would remain whole through his collaboration with Richard Erdoes. He must have understood that the timeless traditions of his message, and of his life, would glide gently and true through the Erdoes filter. And, of course, the choice was perfect.

We met in Santa Fe on a warm spring day. Inyan Wasicun and his wife, Jean, having left the bustle of New York City to bask and create in the New Mexico landscape. Their work continues quite diligently and with quiet industry. He was very pleased that *Lakota Woman* was finally being published. Mary Crow Dog and he had been waiting a long time for its appearance. To me, his demeanor indicated that he was a patient man. He related a humorous incident, that won't be repeated here, and we began.

"To Native Americans, dreams have an importance unimaginable to the non-Indian. Gods and supernaturals manifest themselves in dreams. Revelations from the spirits reach the supplicant through dreams and visions. Through dreams are conferred magical powers, the gift of prophecy, and the ability to cure illnesses and heal wounds.

"Among many tribes it was the common belief that visions had to be earned through fasting and suffering. Hence, for the Sioux, hanblecheya, a vision quest, is a 'crying' or 'lamenting' for a dream. There is often the feeling that, compared to the reality of a dream, the White Man's reality is a mere fragment of the imagination, maybe a nightmare."

Richard Erdoes—*Crying For A Dream*

Talking Lightly

I've really enjoyed all your works a great deal. What can you tell us about your latest book, *Lakota Woman*?

It's a book I did together with an old friend, who's still a young woman of 36, Mary Crow Dog. She gave birth to her child during the siege at Wounded Knee. She had wild teenage years. She lived with her Grandmother, Turtle Woman, who was a Medicine Woman. Turtles were her totem, she carved turtle images. Turtles are used as a fetish. You have a turtle-shaped, beaded image, in which you put the navel cord of a child, and you also have a second identical image. The one with the navel cord is attached to the cradle. The other one is hung up somewhere in a tree so as to confuse evil spirits. It's a protective charm for children.

Mary was forcibly taken away. Her original name, before she married Leonard Crow Dog, was Brave Bird. She was taken to a Catholic missionary school where the kids were beaten if they spoke in their native languages or performed ceremony. They weren't well fed either and were, more or less, used as servants for the nuns. She hated every moment there. The children were beaten on their naked buttocks with swats, flat boards. The boys were beaten by the priests, the girls by the nuns. So, she ran away. By age 11 she could hold a whole quart of liquor. She ran in groups, wolf-packs, with other kids of similar circumstance. She lived by stealing. These kids roamed from Vancouver to L.A.

They were originally coming from South Dakota?

Originally. There were lots of Indian kids who were put into foster homes or missionary schools. They tended to run away if they could. Then they would form groups which would roam through the slums of various cities; Rapid City, Denver, Chicago. They always found somebody to take them in. In a way they were roaming Indian juvenile delinquents, they did a lot of fighting.

Finally the American Indian Movement (AIM) came in and gave these kids an aim in life. They became militant, joined AIM, stopped drinking and formed friendships. In 1973, Mary got pregnant from an inconsequential affair and went to Wounded Knee in order to have her baby during the siege. There she met Crow Dog and became the very busy wife of one of the top Medicine Men in the country. She and the baby were arrested after the siege. She attends all manner of ceremony, she's also a Peyote lady and a Sun Dance lady. She has the Sun Dance piercings; the women do it up on the collarbone or at the wrists, the men do it on the breast muscles.

I did the book with her while her husband was in jail. He was in jail for political offenses. He was the Medicine Man at Wounded Knee and was the Medicine Man of AIM. They put him in Lewisburg, in Pennsylvania. It was hard for her to get to him from South Dakota so she and the baby stayed with us in New York in order to be able to communicate with him. We were in charge of his defense committee and, because he was a Medicine Man, eventually got support from the National Council of Churches. They originally gave him 23 years, but with the money we got from the Council we got the best lawyers and got him out after 18 months.

The book has apparently been ready for awhile. Why did it take so long to reach the shelves?

I had done the Lame Deer book for Simon & Schuster. The editor I worked with there left when it was taken over by Gulf & Western. The man who became the head editor called and asked me to do a parallel piece on an Indian woman. I told him I would like to do it with Mary. He signed us both to a contract and we delivered the book two years later. He felt the book was unacceptable. He said, "My good fellow, the sixties are over, this radical shit is out." I said it was a spiritual book, not a radical one. He wanted me to make her into a female Don Juan [ala Castaneda], flying through the air and so forth. I said, "Michael, you are Castaneda's editor. You have told me, with big grins, innumerable times, that Don Juan exists only in the fantasies of Castaneda. My friends exist in the flesh. They will come after you and scalp you if you try to fake it. I won't do it." So he threw me out and would not take the book. He didn't pay me for the two years of work and seized my royalties from the Lame Deer book.

I've just had the book laying around. Suddenly a man from Grove-Weidenfeld who had heard of the project, came by and asked to see it. He took a look at it and immediately took it. Now it's coming out and it's making a big splash. I can't account for it. Maybe radical Indian women are suddenly in again, I don't know.

You were at Wounded Knee when it was all going on. It was such an incredible and important event. What was it like?

I was there. I can't say I played any great role. I went out with my camera to shoot the marshalls and the so-called goons, the private army of a little half-breed mini-Hitler named Dickie Wilson. They grabbed and arrested me. They might have killed me if I had not suddenly screamed, "I am a West German journalist!" Which, of course, was not true, but then Wilson came running out. "Oh! Come in, come in," he thought I was a Nazi. He had a private army of about 80 people, supported by the FBI. They killed people left and right because he didn't like AIM, which was a competition for him.

He was a fearful character, and an embezzler. He was a tribal president. He was voted in because he said, "Look, you poor fullbloods don't know anything. I'm a businessman, I know how to get money for you," and so on. So he was elected. Then they found out that he was a crook and a murderer. But they couldn't get him out because he'd made his brother the chief of police, another brother the tribal judge, another brother was head of the election board, and his cousins were something else. He immediately took all the tribal offices and distributed them amongst his cronies and relatives. That was the situation at the time. It was wild.

I was actually in Wounded Knee for two days before they arrested me. I wanted to go back in again but then they sent out a delegation to meet with President Nixon. They came out and said that they would be staying at my place in New York, so I could arrange interviews and things for them, and then we would all go to Washington to see Nixon. As it turned out Nixon wouldn't see them. The delegation was led by Russell Means, Crow Dog, an Indian lawyer by the name of Ramon Rubido, and an old, old treaty chief named Tom Badcob.

Why did they let you, a white man, be there? How did the relationship begin?

I was in practically all of the confrontations. Not because I'm a radical by nature; I'd rather sit in the grass and smell the flowers. It's only if a bumblebee stings me in the rear that I get very angry, because it reminds me of the Hitler time in Europe.

Up until age 50 I was a magazine illustrator. I generally describe myself as an old decrepit artist and a young budding writer. I started writing *Lame Deer* at age 50. *Life Magazine* had sent me out to do a painting portfolio on the Sioux reservations at Rosebud and Pine Ridge. Two old Medicine Men, Lame Deer and old Henry Crow Dog, both dead now, took to me. They suddenly appeared back in New York, separately, each with a little cardboard box containing their belongings, saying, "I like you and think I'll be staying with you awhile," and stayed and stayed.

Lame Deer always said, "You are going to do my book." I would say, "I'm not a writer, I'm an artist." "My medicine tells me you are going to do my book." "Not only am I not a writer, but English is my second language." "My medicine tells me. . ." This went on and on for two or three years until I couldn't stand it anymore. I told him, "Look, I know all your stories backwards and forwards, I'll write a trial chapter and an outline. I'll take it to the men for whom I illustrate. You are not a writer, I'm not a writer, they'll throw us out on our ear and that will be the end of it. Then you'll leave me alone." Well, in 48 hours we had a contract. Since then I've been a writer more than an illustrator.

That book is such a classic. What could you share with us about Lame Deer?

Lame Deer was a Medicine Man. He had a wicked sense of humor. He could be absolutely wonderful and breathtaking. He could do all sorts of weird things which he claimed came from his contrary Heyokah nature, the up and down Sacred Clown. He actually was a tribal Heyokah for awhile.

I remember when the book came out, they sent me and old Lame Deer out cross-country to do interviews and our song and dance on TV and so forth. On one occasion we were in Cleveland. There was a woman with flamingly-dyed red hair, she said, "Come on Lame Deer, don't put me on. You say you can understand the language of birds and animals? This is the 20th century, don't do this con game on me."

He looked at her and said, "Lady, in your good book a woman talks to a snake. I at least, speak to eagles!" That brought the house down.

In Chicago we were sitting with a very nice man, Father Powell, who speaks Cheyenne fluently and is very pro-Indian. He said to Lame Deer, "You should know that my church is built like a teepee, my vestments are beaded, the pipe hangs next to the cross, I go to the Sun Dance, I go to Eagle Butte for my ceremonies, and I go to the sweat."

Lame Deer looked at him for a long time and said, "Father Powell, does your Bishop know that?"

"Oh sure, my Bishop approves of this. We are not the old horrible missionaries, we are now very supportive of Indian culture. The Great Spirit and God are the same, Jesus and sweet Medicine is the same, the Cavalry and the Sun Dance is the same, the cross and the pipe is the same. It's all the same."

Lame Deer looked at him for awhile and said, "Father Powell, in your religion do animals have a soul?"

"Chief, you got me!" This he couldn't say without the Bishop going after him; their credo says that only human beings have a soul. Later, he winked at us and said, "Of course I know that animals have a soul. I just can't say it on television."

We had a good time. Lame Deer could always surprise you with things. In Los Angeles there was an interviewer, she was with a woman's program and wanted to know what he could tell her about the Indian diet. Lame Deer said, "Indians diet spoiled by white man." "Well, how did white men spoil the Indian's diets?" "They bring in those cans of baked beans. Air in teepee no good anymore." You never knew what he would do.

His son, Archie Fire Lame Deer, is quite well known these days.

His son is very different from him. Old Lame Deer's horizon was the reservation and nothing else. His son left at age 18, when he couldn't speak a word of English. They were filming a movie, *The Great Sioux Uprising*, on what once was Sioux ground in the Black Hills of South Dakota. They hired Archie. They needed someone to jump down from a very high tree. You know, the cavalry man shoots and the Indian falls down. They thought he was good at this and told him to come to Hollywood and become an Indian stuntman. So Archie, the son of old Lame Deer became a stuntman and lived in Hollywood for years. He has some hilarious stories about it. But his horizon was no longer on the reservation.

When Old Lame Deer died he gave his son his power, and told him to go on with the Medicine. Archie is a fullblood Sioux, a traditional Medicine Man, but with a slight difference; his horizon is the world. He has given sweats for the Dalai Lama and has had furious arguments with the Pope. The Pope won't go into the Sweat Lodge, so Archie won't kiss his ring. He sits with Japanese Zen masters, with Laplander Medicine Men in Scandinavia. He spends a lot of time teaching outside this country. He does basically the same thing that his father did. He relates it to a universal spirituality, but always as a traditional Sioux and doing it in the traditional Sioux way.

Universal spirituality? That intrigues me.

That's one of the oddities that we have today. Tibetan Llamas appeared suddenly on the Hopi reservation out here. There's something going on between spiritual people of all kinds, different cultures, different races, who come together and they know what each other is doing and have similar concerns about the environment and so on. You would be surprised by those who appear at the Sun Dance. Archie and Crow Dog run the Sun Dances at various Sioux reservations. People come from Chile, Mexico, Japan and other areas. People who have never done a Sun Dance are coming to dance with the Sioux.

Dennis Banks [one of the founding AIM spokesmen], besides being a traditional Ojibway is also a Zen Buddhist. When Dennis was being tried in 1985, I went to testify for him at Custer, South Dakota. There were two Japanese monks sitting at 6 a.m. in front of the courthouse in Custer drumming and chanting for him. There are things going on, via the "moccasin telegraph" that white people generally don't know about. If something happens in Patagonia, people up in the Arctic Circle and the Northwest Territories will know in two days. The communication that is going on is quite amazing.

What does it all mean?

It means that there is a certain spiritual revival going on that is all-encompassing. It's not compartmentalized in a lot of different little boxes; Japanese box, American box, Chinese box. It's all coming together now.

I seem to recall that you were with the Hopi delegation that went to the United Nations.

Thomas Benyacya [a renowned Hopi Elder] is a friend of ours. In the 1970s the Hopis went to the United Nations. They went to warn them that we better get our act together, or this world will be wiped out like other worlds have been wiped out previously, or that another world will be superimposed and only a few people will go through the hole of emergence into the next world. They stayed up in our apartment. Our place was called "Sioux East."

The Hopis were very excited. Their prophecy says that if you see people fly through the air, if you see a black sun rising, and if you find the House of Micca, then things are becoming very dangerous. Well, they saw people flying through the air in airplanes, this they were used to. Then, the other two things happened. They were driving through Gary, Indiana and there was so much smoke from the factories that the sun was blackened out. When the sun rose it looked black through all the soot. When they got to the U.N. they found the House of Micca because it's totally glass-covered. Then they warned the U.N. about the prophecy. Then they went to my place and had a big discussion about photography.

If they were talking about photography then it must have involved you.

The Sioux would come to me and say, "Look, we have a certain ceremony, like the revival of the Ghost Dance, and we invite you to come and photograph it. But you must make two sets of identical photographs. There are only a few old men around anymore who know how the Dance should be done. When they die we want to have a record, a complete visual and taped record of the ceremonies we perform." The Sioux were very proud of it and bragged about them to the Hopi.

The Hopi were totally flabbergasted. They couldn't believe that it would be allowed. I told them that I only photographed if I was specifically asked. I wouldn't intrude. They had a big discussion about that. I felt awkward. I had photographed a number of Sioux ceremonies because I had been specifically invited to make a record for them. Their religion was under a lot of pressure by the whites, and they wanted to have a complete record.

The Hopis decided against it. They were sure that they wouldn't forget anything. We were friends, it was all very nice. However, it did show a cultural difference between the macho Plains Indians and the feminist-oriented Pueblos.

You had the honor to do that which no other white man has ever done. I won't ask about the Ghost Dance ceremony itself, but I've got to ask you about your experience there.

Well, it was no trouble at all. I was invited to do it because they wanted to have the record. We had a little problem because the F.B.I. was very interested in what was going on. In 1890 they thought that the Ghost Dance was the signal for general uprisings. I think the FBI thought it was still 1890. We found two FBI agents at the sacred ground, which is in the middle of nowhere. There's nothing there except maybe a coyote and an eagle, but no human beings or houses, nothing. But suddenly there were these two guys in mod clothes. It was 1974. They said they were life-insurance salesman. [Laughter] The idea of these guys out there in the middle of the prairie, or that Indians would pay for life insurance... so we made a citizen's arrest and took them down to the tribal judge.

They identified themselves as FBI agents and I had to photograph them. The problem was that before this the FBI had a plane flying over watching the Ghost Dance. So I had a real long lens on the camera in order to get a picture of the plane, and I had no chance to change the lens. So I had to go back and back and back, 100s of feet, before I was far enough back to shoot the picture. They were scowling at me.

It was a very interesting ceremony. I took my daughter out, she was then 15. Leonard Crow Dog said that only those people who were going to make the vow to dance for four days, without eating or drinking, should step into the circle and hold hands. Before I could say anything there was my little daughter in the circle. Afterwards I said to Leonard, "She's only 15 and four days is a long time. What if she faints?" He said that was his business

and I should worry only about the photographs. They were very sweet. They made her a Ghost Dance shirt, gave her an eagle feather and a medicine bundle. She was very impressed by this.

I have the photographs. They look like the old photographs of the Ghost Dance of 1890. People wrapping themselves in their Ghost Dance shirts. People fell down in a trance. Some had visions. It was like going back a 100 years. It was very impressive.

Crow Dog says that the old Ghost Dancers had misinterpreted Wavoka [the Native American prophet who saw the Ghost Dance in vision]. They believed that if they did the dance the Earth would roll up and underneath they would find those killed by the Whites, who would then come back to life. That their lands, now filled by stinking pig-farms, towns, and telegraph wires would disappear and the world of before, the world of the Indian, would be underneath. Crow Dog said that was a wrong idea; "First, we must know ourselves before we can change the world. We are dancing this to go back to our old beliefs and to reexperience thoughts of long ago. Only when we know who we are, can we try to change the world." It was very impressive.

One of the most dramatic and powerful Native American ceremonies that I can think of is the Sun Dance.

I've seen it many times. When we first came out, old Lame Deer was running a very small Sun Dance where he lived, in this very small hamlet. He had an old tar paper shack with an outhouse, and so on. At that time there were few dancers, and they pierced their skin only a little bit and only on one side. The Sun Dance had been forbidden under the Indian Offenses Act for over 80 years. Even the Sweat Lodge was forbidden. Now if you go out you'll see 100s of dancers at Crow Dog's place. The Dance itself has become more and more severe every year. Now they hang themselves up just like in the old paintings.

We knew a young guy, 16 years old, Bobby LeaderCharge. He danced for the purpose of getting his brother out of jail, he had been jailed for taking part at Wounded Knee. Bobby dragged around six buffalo skulls attached with thongs imbedded in his back, and they wouldn't come loose. So, people grabbed him under the arms and whirled him around the dance circle. They still wouldn't come out. Then they had little kids sit on the skulls, and the weight finally tore them out. This went on for over an hour, Bobby was so exhausted.

Another time Crow Dog had four horses, two attached in the front, two in the back. They were driven off in four different directions. Another time he hung himself from the Sun Dance tree and fell through almost at once, but another man, Jerry Roy, an Ojibwa, was hanging for hours. They finally came and grabbed him by the leg and yanked him down.

The Sun Dance is totally misunderstood by white people. Many people think it is as it was documented in the film, *A Man Called Horse*, for macho purposes, to show how strong you are. It has nothing to do with that. You make a vow when a Sun Dance takes place that you will dance the next time. A man dances to have his son safely return from Vietnam or that his brother will get out of jail, and so on. It has nothing to do with adoption by the tribe, or puberty, or becoming a man or anything like that. It is simply like Lame Deer always said, "You Christians let Christ do it all for you. We are not Christians, we take the responsibility and the pain ourselves." That's the philosophy behind the Sun Dance.

Your experiences with the culture are clearly very vast. I'd like to ask you, what changes have you noticed in the Native American Nation over the years?

When I first went out there everyone thought that the Indian religions would die out. I was astonished to find them flourishing in so many places. They were revived in certain places to the point that the missionaries were running scared. I have also seen reservations where everything is lost and has disappeared.

When our children were small we went to Zuni. They had some absolutely fantastic dances, Kachina Dances. They were so breathtakingly beautiful that I don't have the words to describe them. They had the Clowns, with very sexual jokes. They were watching to see how we would take it. We laughed. Afterwards they said that we were okay. Our Accoma friend who took us—we were the only whites—comes from the Turkey clan. The languages between Accoma and the Zuni are totally different, but they recognize clan relationships. So she was invited by a friend, A Zuni lady of the Turkey clan. They had an adobe house right at the plaza where the dances were performed.

While we were looking out the window at the dances, the kids of the family were watching television. They were watching John Wayne slaughtering Indians. So, you have that problem. Our friends were afraid that their children would learn English first and that there would be a competition with their own language, that there would be influences that they didn't want their children to have.

When Jean first took me to Accoma Pueblo there were three rows of Pre-Columbian houses still there in pristine condition. Now they are all gone. Now they have these little Mexican style things. So you have this aesthetic devastation. At Taos, the whole thing is disfigured by the tourist market that mars the appearance of the village.

On the other hand, the tradition is very strong. A friend of mine, Alfonso Ortiz, was asked to take a few big-shot politicians, including some governors and their wives, a whole bus load, to Taos and explain to them what the Pueblo culture was like. When they arrived—generally you can drive in, they have a little house there, and they charge fees for entrance and photography—when they arrived a woman came out and said, "Alfonso, you can come in, but they can't."

Alfonso explained to her that they all had cameras and that there was about $1000 worth of fees in the bus and how could she say "no" to that. She explained that a tourist woman had previously disregarded the no-admittance signs on one of their sacred kivas, went into the kiva while ceremony was in process, and tried to take some pictures with flash. Her camera was opened, the film confiscated and she was escorted form the village. As a punishment for her deed, no tourists were being allowed in for a whole month. It did not matter that it was going to cost the village a lot of money. It was a matter of principle.

So, there is an element, amongst the Pueblos at least, which keeps the traditions. But amongst, let's say, the Ojibway and others, the language is mostly gone, the ceremonies are mostly gone. Many of the mid-west cultures now go and Sun Dance with the Sioux so as to be Indians again.

We had a friend who was a wonderful painter. He was also a Sacred Clown, a Heyokah. He was the last Sacred Clown at San Ildefonso Pueblo. When he was very old, his son came to him. His son was a computer programmer in San Francisco. His son told him not to worry if he couldn't do it anymore, that he could paint himself with the little stripes and do the dancing around. The old man said that it wasn't that easy. He asked his son if he would stay for two years by the kiva and learn. The son thought that was crazy, he didn't have the time to spend. So when the old one died, the Pueblo had no Sacred Clown, they had to borrow one from Santo Domingo. That's how things get lost.

Have you noticed any impact from AIDS?

I will mention that something horrible happened. It shows how something that seems far away from the reservation can intrude upon it. It was two or three years ago. Archie Lame Deer told me about it. He said a man appeared at the Sun Dance claiming he was an Indian, that he had made the vow a year ago. Of course, they believed him and took him at his word. The belief is that when you are at the dance and under the Sun Dance pole you won't tell a lie, otherwise you will die. So, they let him dance.

It turned out that he was not Indian at all, but a Puerto Rican who had just been released from prison. He had AIDS. They had used the same knife, as they always do, on three or four other people. Lame Deer will pierce four or five people, his son will pierce four or five, Crow Dog will pierce some. They all use their own knives. Well, four people contracted AIDS.

So now they are wearing surgical gloves when they do it, and using disposable scalpels from the tribal hospital. To think this happened at their most sacred ceremony; it's gruesome to think about.

What can you tell us about Leonard Crow Dog?

Well, he is a controversial person. Now, the Lame Deers, both father and son, always said, "It's fine to be a Peyote Man. Be that. It's fine to be a Yuwipi Man, be that. But peyote is a foreign introduction. It's fine if you are a Peyote Man—Native American Church, be it, but don't mix the two things." But Crow Dog does. He's quite happy running the traditional Sun Dance and at the same time running a Peyote meeting. He's also very strong-willed.

He's also illiterate. His father drove off the truant officers with a shotgun because he saw his son had dreams and talked of sacred things. He felt his son to be "wakun," sacred, and believed that white learning would spoil him from becoming a Medicine Man.

Crow Dog is a very remarkable man in many ways. His father brought him to New York when he was very young and spoke very little English. He made a great impression on me for this particular reason. . .

At the time, I had a typical Madison Avenue type of guy at the house; we had a large apartment between Broadway and the Hudson River. There were 70 units with a great mix of people. This Madison Avenue creature was with an advertising agency, and he came down two floors to borrow a T-square. The moment he saw my Sioux friends he was a gone-goose. It changed his life immediately, in a very strange way. Before that he had been into Tibetan things, but now he had found his Indian guru. The Crow Dogs were not quite aware of what was going on. They both came to me and said, "This man questioned us about all kinds of things and found out that we are Peyote Men. He asked us to have a ceremony for him two floors up."

I said, "Oh my God, don't do it. He doesn't believe in what you are doing, he just wants to get his Madison Avenue advertising people in there to say, 'Look, I'm having a peyote ceremony here.' I know it's legal for you if you do it on the reservation with Indians. You let me sit in on some at the reservation where I was one white man sitting with forty Indians, each with a function; cedar man, door man, and so on. But here, you will have 40 Madison Avenue people. You don't know what this means. They are flaky from your point of view, and you will be the one Indian. How will you handle this?"

Old Crow Dog said, "You're right. I won't do it." Then, a little later, he came down and said, "I told him I can't do it. But I have to do it, because he said I promised him this and he will tell everyone that Indians don't keep their promise, so I must do it. You must come and back me up." So I went up and he did the ceremony. The people behaved very, very strangely. The host, the Madison Avenue guy, literally tried to drown himself in the toilet bowl. Another guy crawled under the couch because he was being attacked by giant bugs. Others danced on one leg and uttered horrible screams. I was nonplussed. I had been at meetings among the Sioux and it had never affected me in any of these weird ways. The Indians tend to sit very quietly and be very contemplative, nobody dances or screams.

After it was all over and we were back at my place, I was sitting down with young Crow Dog, we were overlooking Broadway. He had never been off the reservation before, had never been exposed to any white philosophy. I said, "Gee, I can't understand that. Why did those people behave in such a weird way?"

He said, "Well, look down there, look at all those unfortunate people who squeeze themselves into the subway to punch a time clock. It's the most horrible thing in the world. They think that it's reality. But it is not. The reality is underneath. That is the trouble with these people, they don't know this. They accept the Whiteman's reality as the real thing. But when they take the Medicine they find out that they are not what they thought they were, that society is not what they thought, that happiness is not what they thought. That drives them crazy."

I said, "I'm a Whiteman. Why doesn't it drive me crazy?"

Then this noble child of nature said something very profound, "It's very simple. You are an artist. Each time you paint a picture you change this Whiteman's reality into something else. When you were in your first meeting and you discovered that you are not what you think you are, that the world is not what you thought, it didn't bother you because you knew it already, because you are an artist. They don't know it. If there had been an artist among them, they would have been sitting quietly too." That really impressed me. I thought it a profound observation. He was 18 at the time.

He takes his religion very seriously. I've seen him, during the Yuwipi ceremony, burst into tears. He's macho, as all the Sioux are macho. This causes certain problems with Mary, who is a feminist, but they get along somehow. I suspect they have the occasional philosophical tussle about the role of woman in society.

The Sioux are very pro-woman though, aren't they? Don't they have strong views about women and their moontimes?

The Sioux have very strong views about menstruation. Very different from European or Hebrew religious things, which consider women unclean then. Quite the contrary, the Sioux believe the woman is not only very clean during this time, but also very powerful. If a woman is menstruating—is in her moontime—during a ceremony, the ceremony will not work. Because her power will negate the power of the Medicine Man. So you have to deal with this.

On one occasion we had a ceremony—for Dick Cavett, oddly enough—at our place. He comes from Nebraska and lived for a while, as a kid, just five miles below the Pine Ridge reservation. He speaks a little Sioux and believes in Sioux religion. When he heard there were Medicine People who could do a Yuwipi ceremony in New York, he asked for one. They were quite willing to do it for him. There was no money involved, as you cannot ask for money for that ceremony. His only obligation was to feed everybody. Every Indian in New York heard about it and came. They wanted to do a great Indian feast. Mary Crow Dog was supposed to cook, but suddenly she started menstruating. Which meant that she had to go to the menstruation hut, which was the farthest room away in our large apartment. This meant that Jean suddenly had to make an Indian meal. They had a runner going back and forth to the menstruation hut and back to the kitchen with instructions. [Laughter]

The only trouble we had was that the Yuwipi ceremony is also a dog feast. We had no dog for this purpose. Old Henry Lame Deer took me over to the window and said, "Look down there. Look at that man. He has a nice plump dog." I said, "No way, no way!" He said, "But go down and tell the man what an honor it is. Tell the dog what an honor it is." I said, "That's a New York dog. He has no sense of honor whatsoever." So he said, "Okay, get beef." So we had a beef soup instead. [Laughter]

I understand that you escaped from Germany during World War II. That certainly set the stage for some incredible experience. How did you manage to get out of there?

I belonged to a group of kids who came out of the German Youth Movement and who became more and more anti-fascist in the process. When the Nazis came to power I was at the Berlin Art Academy which, before the Nazis, was a very great institution. We published a little underground newspaper which I illustrated with very fat Goerings, and very un-germanic Hitlers and Goebbels.

I had a friend whose father had a little print shop. When his father closed up shop, he and I went in there and he printed my stuff. We were betrayed, and my friend was caught and hanged. The family had to pay for the hanging. It was not free, it was a few thousand bucks. Yes, the family had to pay for the hanging. There is now a street named for him. Whether this does him much good I don't know.

I managed to escape due to a very fat cop. All the others were arrested by the SS or the Gestapo or the Brownshirts. But they had run out of these types by the time it got to me. They sent an old, fat flatfoot to arrest me. He took me out into a central park at 5:00 in the morning, there was nobody there. He went into one of those evil smelling lavatories that they have in Europe. He said, "I'm going in to take a leak. You wait here." I said to myself that I knew what he wanted to do, he wants to shoot me in the back. "Shot while trying to escape," which happened frequently, daily, then. Then they saved themselves the trouble of the trial. So, I didn't run away, I stayed.

He came out and said, "You idiot! What are you doing here?" I said, "Well, if you want to shoot me in the back, it won't work. If you want to shoot me, you'll have to do it right now from the front."

Whereupon he burst into tears. He said, "Oh my God. You thought I was one of those swine. No, I have a kid like you at home. For heaven sake, run! Don't call your mama and papa. Go right to the railway station and go back to Vienna where you belong."

At that time Austria was still independent. He even gave me money for the train ticket. Otherwise I would be dead. Some of my friends spent all their young lives in concentration camps. One of them survived until they heard the firing of the American artillery, then he was killed at the last moment because the commandant didn't want any witnesses. But for this fat cop I wouldn't be here.

I read that at one point during your escape you actually ran into Hitler himself.

Yes. Two years after I escaped to Vienna, the Nazis came and took over Austria. I immediately went underground, because in the meantime I had added to my sins by working for the two anti-nazi newspapers in Vienna. I took refuge with my cousin, I was hiding in her attic. But I had to go out. I had to try to get an American visa, I had to make a living and sell paintings on the sly under another name, and so on.

In order to evade being caught... in the inner city of Vienna the houses are very baroque, the houses go back to the 16th and 17th centuries and they have these houses which have an entrance on two sides of a street, and in the middle is a big courtyard. Now, the thing you had to evade were the raids where, suddenly, on both ends of a street appeared two or three truck-loads of Gestapo or police who immediately form a line. Then the two lines move towards each other, everybody who is in between is stopped for papers and identification. If you have no papers they take you in and find out about you. If you have papers they check to see if you are on the wanted list.

To be wanted and to be on the street was not advisable because they did this all the time. They came upon you with the suddenness of a heart-attack. What I did was to go in one entrance of these houses, run through the house, come out on another street, run kitty-corner to another house, and so on. I knew the old city very well. In this way I was not on the street very much.

One time I came out of one these houses and there in front of me was a line of SS men standing at attention. On the other side of the line was Adolph Hitler. I had forgotten something. On that spot where I had come out one of the Nazi murderers of Chancellor Dalphous had, while fleeing the assassination, been shot down by the Austrian police. Hitler was there planting an oak tree in commemoration.

There were people behind me blocking my exit. I felt that if I became conspicuous they would see me and then beat me to death. So, I decided to stand there and watch. He tried to make a hole with a spade. He couldn't. He was the most unsporting character that you can imagine. He was tripping on his tiptoes, his mustache was going up and down, I started to laugh. But I couldn't laugh in his face, they would have killed me. He was hopping and carrying on, it was like a clown performance. If he hadn't been so horrible and killed so many millions he would have been very funny, a horrid, murderous Charlie Chaplin figure.

I didn't know what to do. If you feel laughter coming on, and know that you cannot laugh, it becomes irresistible. People had always said that he looked funny, but that he had these demonic eyes, that even the greatest statesmen fell under their spell. So I decided to concentrate on his eyes so as to not laugh. However, his eyes were expressionless, protruding, and without any magic in them. They reminded me of something, I didn't know what, but I had seen them before. I tried to concentrate on finding out whose eyes they were. Unfortunately, I found out.

They were the eyes of a calf named Bookshie, which in Hungarian means idiot. An aunt of mine had a farm where I had spent many summers. One of my chores there was to feed the calf Bookshie. The moment this realization came to me, I bent over with hysterical laughter. Then I knew that they would beat me to death and I would die laughing.

Then I heard Hitler say, "Yes, my boy. I am weeping too." They thought I was weeping! I set off a crying jag amongst those sadistic SS men who were standing at attention! They had tears streaming down. Hitler went into an ecstasy of joy because he thought I was weeping. I went along with it, "Ohhh, I'm overcome. I saw the Fuhrer. Ohhh." I backed into the house pretending to faint from emotion and got out of it. Voila!

Had it gone slightly differently, you might have missed out on a remarkable lifetime.

Yes, I would not have seen a Sun Dance or a Ghost Dance.

Ken Carey

Reflection of a Landscape

"The psychological process leading to awakening,
though it can be described in many ways, is fun-
damentally a process of identity shift from a linguis-
tically defined sense of self, rooted in your ego and an
exaggerated sense of your vulnerability, to a sense of
identity rooted in the unified field of consciousness
that lies behind and within all individuality. During
the process your sense of self blossoms into an ac-
curate awareness of who you are. This transformed
awareness includes your former sense of being one
among many, but it also includes an awareness of a
reality greater than the ever-changing worlds of form,
an awareness rooted in the singularity of Eternal
Being from which all individuality unfolds."

Ken Carey—Starseed: The Third Millennium

T he respect for Ken Carey's work with the written word of the heart runs deep. The accolades he has received are richly deserved. His poetic affinity with Spirit has moved many a reader to transcendent comprehension, along with an enhanced capacity and desire for illumination. Many a tear-stained copy of *The Starseed Transmissions* or *Return of the Bird Tribes* has been quietly closed in the warm afternoon sunlight, by the bank of a river or with back against a tree, experiencing a soft, tremulous shudder of recognition and reunion. His work has been a gift, a beacon, a tap straight from, and into, the heart.

An unassuming family man with seven children, Ken Carey never really intended to be anything other than a husband, father and carpenter. Now, the carpentry has fallen away and, literally as a result of public demand, he is a widely-acknowledged author. Despite this, his family still comes first.

Our first discourse took place in September of 1988. I had read his previous volumes and was quite struck by them. His then newest volume, *Return of The Bird Tribes*, had just been released and I was completely enthralled. As it turned out, Ken was just beginning a promotional tour for this volume, Seattle would be his first stop and, yes, he would have time for an interview. This was quickly arranged and I set about my perceived task of organizing a meaningful line of questioning.

At that time I was still fairly new to being a record-keeper. Fortunately, Ken Carey is an extremely affable person, a regular guy, and wonderfully conversational. Despite my mistakes it went very well and the finished product worked quite nicely. At that time I knew we would do it again. It was strikingly obvious, even to a greenhorn such as myself, that here was definitely a person with something most remarkable and meaningful to communicate.

Upon the publication of *Starseed: The Third Millennium*, the opportunity graciously presented itself. Fortunately for me, Ken wasn't planning any tours for that book. I felt that an interview conducted in his own element, in his everyday environment and his personal space, would afford the reader a better overview of the man and his work. Ken, in his typically amiable manner, courteously agreed to my request for an afternoon of his time and in the Spring of 1991, Aymie and I took a trip to Missouri.

Let's set the stage: Driving along the back-country roads of the Missouri Ozarks is a tranquil experience. The frequently sighted hawks and turkey-buzzards become a parable for the natural world as one goes up and down and around hill after hill through the oldest mountain range in the continental United States. They are no longer the highest mountains by any means. Millions of years have worn them down to foothills, ravines and valleys.

Gone also, but for different reasons, are the extensive soft-wood forests that once dominated this land. The pine has long since been felled for wood-products and the land cleared. The forest that does remain has gradually been overtaken by hardwoods. Oak trees, guided by inherent wisdom, sensed the changing conditions and now spread majestically over the landscape. Crossing the scenic Jacks Fork River one has to stop to admire the cool, clear Ozark water. A hawk glides effortlessly overhead; a crayfish glides effortlessly beneath the river's surface.

I mention all this because I appreciated it at the time, and it holds all-important consequence for Carey's evolutionary process. This was the area to which he and his family were led. This land would hold the sparks of potential that would culminate in some rather extraordinary co-creative, albeit symbiotic, developments.

We finally figured out which mailbox signified the all-important turn and a rutted and parched dirt road led us further back into the landscape. Another turn, perhaps the correct one, meanders up a small hill. On the other side there stands a gate with a small white sign. Ken has placed the sign there to remind a constant stream of casual visitors that he needs his space and his time.

A modest man not driven or swayed by ego-attachment or projection, Ken has led an interesting life. He and his wife Sherry, and the first few Carey children, migrated from California to this area in the 1960s to find a connection with the land. They gardened extensively and raised most of their own food. They worked long hours to insure their self-sufficiency. They founded the Greenwood School so their children and others in the area would have a space in their lives for that learning that the Carey's felt to be most important.

Ken apprenticed himself to a local Amish carpenter in order to learn a time-honored craft in a time-honored tradition and pursue a livelihood for his family. He rode a bicycle six miles each way, to work for $2 an hour, ten hours a day. In short, they risked. They had a dream and they took the often difficult and demanding steps to follow through with it.

In the winter of 1978, Spirit came to visit.

The result of that encounter was *The Starseed Transmissions*. The manuscript was destined to lie in his desk for four years. In the meantime, Ken and Sherry were busy with another project. The Spirit of Greenwood Forest required their cooperation and efforts to insure its continued vitality.

Public acclaim for xeroxed and randomly distributed copies of *The Starseed Transmissions* eventually led to a publisher and its subsequent publication. It was followed by *Terra Christa, Vision, Notes To My Children* and the classic *Return of the Bird Tribes*. Unfortunately, there were unforseen problems. Ken is a very trusting sort of fellow and when his publisher encountered a difficult economic period, followed ultimately by bankruptcy, the Careys never realized an appropriate or fair compensation.

The latest, and perhaps last, of the Starseed volumes, *Starseed: The Third Millennium*, is now in release. The evocative imagery and expression of the Starseed tradition pours forth in this work. In the hands of a new publisher it is now a more distinct possibility that Ken's writing will gain the attention and distribution that it merits. Also, as you will discover, he is beginning a new phase with his written efforts. The evolution continues in a pragmatic vein, with elevated awareness and consciousness attuned to everyday reality; a real down-home spiritual adventure guide. It sounds perfect, and well timed; we must be ready.

Clearly, to my mind, Ken Carey's work to date has been superlative. The degree to which his harmonic texts can touch the timeless, deeper recesses of our hearts and minds has simply amazed me time and time again. The transfer of that kind of communication requires a very clear conduit. Many have tried; very few, for whatever reasons, succeed. Ken's material works.

In the interview that follows we are afforded a glimpse of the man who has provided such a clear voice for that which, in many ways, is outside mere words.

"Trust in God is trusting in the God who lives within you, trusting your spirit's ability to respond to each situation beautifully, impeccably, individually, and creatively...

"Without the acquisition of another skill, without the acquisition of anything but complete and total trust in Creator and in yourself, you have everything you need to interact optimally, creatively, and productively with every situation you encounter. There are no exceptions."

Ken Carey—*Return of the Bird Tribes*

Clearly this land has a lot to do with your work. Just how integral has it been?

The type of work that I've been doing is definitely coming out of the landscape. Maybe I'm being too generous to myself, but I like to think that the highest definition of my role is that I represent aspects of the natural world that can't speak for themselves with human voice. I try to represent them in the human community so that they can get the level of respect both that they need for their own continuance and well-being, and that humans need for their wholeness and completion—a wholeness that doesn't really begin to occur until we welcome aspects of the natural world as parts of ourselves, and see ourselves reflected in the trees, the river, the flower, and the creatures of the forest.

Learning to live in that awareness is an ongoing process. In many ways it's an ongoing experiment, because there's a certain amount of trial and error involved with it.

Your work has always embodied the concept of seeing the Earth as a living organism.

I think that seeing the Earth as a single, living organism and having the intellectual realization that it is, and that we as human beings are a part of it, is the first step. It probably opens the doors and removes some of the mental blocks toward a fuller and deeper perception which actually becomes an experience, and there are no words for that. I've never been able to find words for that; my books are an attempt. For me, the real challenge as an individual is to experience the Earth as a single, integral organism and simultaneously experience myself as a part of that. It's hard to explain the distinction, but it's more than just an intellectual concept when there's the experience.

To try and sustain that awareness and go about your business as a human being is the second challenge. I find that in a culture of other human beings who don't recognize that reality, let alone that awareness, it's very difficult. Though I'm sure that certain groups of people specifically dedicated to that can achieve a certain success in sustaining that awareness, I find that it's enough of a challenge for me to sustain it in the course of working in the garden or relating to people in my own household. That's been interesting enough. [Laughter]

I don't have much success maintaining that awareness all the time. It comes and goes. There are times when it's there and I'm grateful for it. It's difficult to maintain that experience of being part of a single organism that includes yourself, the Earth and others in your human community.

You've been here in the Ozarks 20 years now. How did that come about? How is it that you've ended up here?

It's an interesting story. I think of it as a nice example of the left-brain and right-brain working in tandem. Sherry and I decided, when we met in the 1960s, that we wanted to buy some land and move to the country. We began researching different parts of the United States that, first of all, had land available in our price range and secondly, had adequate rainfall and a climate conducive to growing most of our own food. Other factors, like population density and the fact that, at that time, Missouri didn't have any nuclear power plants, played into it. We finally concluded from that left-brain research that the Ozarks was our first choice.

I was working at the post office and managed to save about half of my salary toward buying land. After about two years I had $5500 saved up. Then, one night I had a dream. I can go into the details if you want.

Definitely. Dreams can be great fun, and this one certainly sounds important.

Well, it doesn't make sense, rationally, but it made sense to me at the time. I was awakened in the middle of the night by a literal, audible voice. It was like I had a pair of stereo headphones on. This doesn't happen to me too much. Normally, when I bring through a book, I don't hear an audible voice, it's more of a telepathic thing. In this case, I heard a very loud voice right in my ears.

It said, "It's the second day of the second month." I sat up in bed with my heart racing, I'd been asleep, and I thought, "What the hell was that?" I looked over at the clock and it was two minutes after two. I thought, "This is really strange. Someone spoke these words to me, what does it mean?" I looked at the clock again. It turned out it was the second minute of the second hour of the second day of the second month of the second year of the

second decade of the second half of the 20th century. [Laughter]
I knew it had to mean something.

The long and short of it was I knew that I should immediately
go, without hesitating, and take what money we had saved,
immediately go to the Ozarks and buy some land. I literally
jumped in the truck and drove to the Ozarks. I didn't question it.
I just knew it was the right thing to do, even though that might
not make sense to a lot of people. It just felt like the right thing
to do.

I walked into the first real estate office that I had ever been
in. Among all the towns that we had circled for having cheap
land this one was centrally located. I told the realtor that I was
looking for an old farm, preferably about 80 acres with 1/3 of it
cleared. That it would be nice if it had a spring and an old house
on it, nothing in real good shape because we wanted to keep the
price down, but something we could live in while we built
something else. The other thing I asked for was that it be at the
end of a dirt road. Basically, I described this place. She drove me
out here. This was the first farm I looked at.

I stepped out of her jeep and as soon as my feet hit the ground
I felt this overwhelming rush of emotion. The tears came to my
eyes and it was like joy and sorrow all mixed together. The sense
I had was of a lot of experience here, for myself and my family
and maybe future generations. I just about started crying, but I
realized it might ruin my bargaining position. [Laughter] I knew
I would buy it and I did.

**That was 1972? The first book didn't come until 1979. I don't
think it was published until 1981?**

It wasn't published until 1982. In fact, another amazing
chain of events is that *The Starseed Transmissions* were written in
1978-79 but weren't published for four years. Almost immediately

after it was written this whole Greenwood Forest Project came up.

I've seen that on the backs of your books. Do you want to tell us about it?

In many ways I, personally, wasn't ready to have *The Starseed Transmissions* published. Those four years proved to be a real valuable teaching about how to relate to people. During the first seven years that we lived here we hardly saw anybody. I remember years when only two or three vehicles, besides our own, came down that road during the whole year.

A couple of weeks after I had received *The Starseed Transmissions* a neighbor came over one day and told me that all the forest between our farm and the Jacks Fork River was going to be sold to a logging firm, and clear-cut. We felt that we couldn't let that happen. We got together with others and came up with this idea to prevent the forest from being sold to a logging firm.

Within a matter of months we had NBC coming down here doing a televised report. We had reporters from all the major papers. *Mother Earth News* and *Organic Gardening* did stories. I suddenly found myself relating to a lot of people for a change. Other than my carpentry crew and the Amish family we use to do Bible study with, we didn't really have that many friends in those days. Then when the project started to happen, suddenly we had as many as 100 people a week coming through. That lasted almost three years.

By the time that was done—we had successfully sold about 1/3 of the endangered forest in order to buy the whole thing and brought the project to a completion—I had picked up skills relating to the media that I certainly didn't have before. It was after that experience that *Starseed* was published.

So the project was about saving the land and the trees?

Exactly. We didn't want to get into a protest, confrontational sort of thing with the loggers because we all use wood products, and that is one of the big industries here. However, we felt that particular land—where we considered many of the trees to be our friends, there are some very special trees out there—had a higher use, a better use than turning it all into charcoal and pallets, which is mostly what they do with the forests when they clear-cut them here.

Our scheme was basically to sell about 1/3 of the property in five and ten acre parcels to owner-members who then became owners of what we call the common land, which is the larger 2/3's of the property. It was the first development in the United States to require composting toilets. Usually you have trouble getting permits for composting toilets. It was fun to actually have them be mandatory.

Our initial plan was to offer the owner the smallest amount that we thought he might accept, we came up with the arbitrary figure of $5000, to hold the property for six months. If we could succeed in getting that much done, then we would take the next step.

A friend, an unsuccessful congressional candidate from the Ozarks, helped us draft the specifics of how the project could proceed. He found a woman who donated the $5000 which we went and offered the owner if he would stall off for six months. To our amazement he agreed. We told him we would pay him the balance in six months, which was almost a quarter of a million dollars. At that point we had no idea of how we would get it.

We were within two weeks of that deadline and had only sold one parcel. We needed to sell fifteen just to reach the minimum amount, which would enable us to borrow the rest from the bank and pull the whole thing off.

Then, this friend of mine from Toronto called late one night. He was real excited. I never heard him so excited. He says, "Ken, you won't believe this but for some reason I went to hear this psychic speak tonight. This woman went into a deep trance and suddenly started channeling what she called the Spirit of Greenwood Forest. She told me to tell you that everything is going to be okay and that the project is going to succeed." This is with like two weeks to go and we needed $250,000. [Laughter] But we believed it! I don't know why, we were just naive or innocent, but I do think we had a lot of faith. The whole thing was run on faith. Almost immediately people began showing up and buying parcels.

It ended up being successful. I can take you back there and show you where there are windmills, photo-voltaic cells, and passive-solar homes amongst the once-threatened trees. Ten years ago we turned the whole management over to the owners, so we've got nothing to do with it anymore. It was just one of those things we did for a few years. It was a tremendous experience. We learned so many things.

What do you consider to have been the most meaningful lesson?

What we noticed was that whenever our anxiety level was high and we got to worrying, people stopped coming to look at the land, people didn't buy parcels, things didn't happen, the project didn't work. When we were able to release attachment to results and say, "Look, we're going to do our best. The least that we're going to get out of this is a hell of an education. But we've got to let go of our fear of what might happen if we don't succeed. Let's look upon it all as an opportunity. Naturally, we'll hope for the best and work for the results we hope to achieve but, let go of that fear."

As soon as we would do that, people would start coming to see the land and buying parcels or a reporter would come down and another favorable article would come out. It was really graphic. It was about three years altogether, by the end of which I had almost completely forgotten about *The Starseed Transmissions*.

Your book, *Return of the Bird Tribes*, was a definite departure, a wonderfully synergistic departure, from your earlier works.

I would describe the difference by saying that *Return of the Bird Tribes* speaks a good deal about the past. Initially this really came as a surprise to me. In *The Starseed Transmissions* there was such an emphasis on the importance of being in the present moment, that when I began to see these pictures of past-oriented events, which in this case were significant moments of angelic/human exchange in pre-columbian times, it seemed quite incongruous to me. I didn't quite understand how it fit.

At that point I was under the impression that we pretty much needed to release and let go of the past. It was explained to me that to have some understanding of the purpose of history—which has been education—and the incredible momentum that lies behind these times in which we live, the long millennia of preparation that have led us to these present decades, really helps one appreciate the opportunities that we have. It makes me feel a much deeper awareness of the vast support that we have as we face our challenges and problems. That can be real helpful because sometimes, looking around the world, if not looking around our own household, our problems can seem rather overwhelming. It's nice to have a sense that we're not in this alone;

that there's a whole historical momentum behind the healing that we're experiencing in these times.

Would you tell us who the Bird Tribes are?

The Bird Tribes are those beings who, in the Judeo-Christian tradition, have been called Angels. They are the reality of our perfect human spirits, before and after our involvement with matter and, hopefully, to a large extent, they have a role to play in our lives in blending with our human egos and helping to guide our society in a creative and positive direction.

And your thought is that the Bird Tribes were in very close alignment with the Native American cultures?

Very much. Not only with the Native American cultures, but in just about every Earth tradition you find images of birds as dieties. There is a Native American term that comes from the Iroquois language, specifically the Seneca; the word is Hokseda [Hawk-saw-dah]. It refers to an individual member of the Bird Tribes. It is pretty much interchangeable with what people today are calling the Higher Self. The Hokseda is that eternal, spiritual entity who comes to Earth and through its vibrational presence draws the atomic substance of our bodies into their present forms and patterns. But in consciousness, we have not been historically aware of them. This is a time when they're making their presence known, and are involved in a process of incarnation wherever there are egos who will make them welcome.

Could you go on with that? How are they making their presence known and what are you seeing as happening?

Well, what I'm seeing is a reversal of the ancient historical pattern of the ego's rejection of Spirit. The human ego, as I use the term, is not a bad thing. It's not something that needs to be repressed, denied or somehow shoved to the side. The human ego is in fact an essential component of human identity. It's designed to help care for the physical body. However, in a healthy state the ego is a secondary component of identity.

In a healthy state it is Eternal Spirit which forms one's primary sense of Self. Many people have come to see that the old programming, the fear motivated ways of behavior, are just not proving effective. They are looking for new ways, new insight, some new thought. When an ego begins to experience this openness, then the Hokseda or Higher Self can begin to make it's presence known.

Many people will give a name to the Hokseda, and initially see it as something completely and entirely apart from themselves. This communication, which initially re-acquaints the ego with the Hokseda, needs to continue until it deepens into a communion, into a union, and ultimately into the incarnation of the Hokseda. That's the process I see taking place in many, many people, although they have different terms for describing it and different ways of talking about it.

I noticed that the year 2011 has come up in some of your work, as it has in other sources.

The Mayans did not see time in the linear manner that we do in the West, nor did they see it in the cyclical way that they do in the East. Their understanding of time was a sort of synthesis of the linear and cyclical. They saw time as moving in great spiralling tides, like DNA, or like the galaxies. According to the Maya, the last great tide of time went out at approximately 3114 B.C., and is due to return in again bringing with it, according to their tradition, a new age of the gods in the year 2011. I find it significant that on a calendar carved in stone in the Yucutan jungle, in 500 B.C., that the Mayans actually pinpointed the years between 1987 and 2011 as the time of the great transition, when human kind would leave the orientation of fear and move into a whole new state, which would bring renewed harmony with the Earth and her creatures and with the stars. I don't believe that because the Mayans said so; it's because it correlates with my own intuition and my own inner sensing.

Maybe we're at a point where I should ask about your process.

I feel that anyone who chooses to relax their individual sense of self, their ego, not attempt to repress it or push it out of the way, but just to take themselves lightly, and take all their self images lightly—their concepts, their ideas, their beliefs—has an opportunity to expand into a universal awareness of Self. When I do this, I usually close my eyes, because if my eyes are open I'm very aware of my physical body. That body-associated sense of self, which is another term for the ego, is harder to release. When I close my eyes and relax my self-images, I find myself expanding in awareness into a non-linear perception of time.

In that experience of time I feel all the love that has ever been in expression among the members of the human family. Wherever two people have loved, or wherever a human community has shared in the expression of love, it leaves traces in the ethers. It leaves emotional alterations in the very texture of the universe. They're still there because love is eternal.

When I allow my awareness to cover the whole span of a human presence on this Earth, I feel there has been a steady and consistent increase in both the quality and quantity of love in expression among incarnate human beings. When you go back tens of thousands of years, the increase in the quality and quantity of love in expression was very slight from century to century. But I feel there was a major increase in the love in expression approximately 2,000 years ago. I feel another amplification of the love energy beginning about 300 years ago.

My sense is that in this century the love energies are increasing at a phenomenal rate; they're actually increasing at an exponential rate. The point where that exponential curve really begins to take off, approximately coincides with the Mayan dates of 1987 to 2011. That also coincides with what other Native American traditions call "The Great Day of Purification," when many things that were forgotten will be remembered, where many things that have not been seen will be seen again. When we'll become more conscious of where we are coming from in our behavior, and make the decision to live as loving and compassionate beings rather than as fearful beings.

Your work on love has definitely been some of your best material.

The beings that brought me much of the information in *Return of the Bird Tribes* shared with me that throughout the stars, throughout the galaxies, it's common knowledge among all conscious beings that love motivation leads to the development of potential. Love motivation fosters creation, and fear motivation holds back that unfoldment. At one point the entity who was in communion with me as I wrote the book said "There are no star wars, or advanced and fearsome civilizations beyond your own. If civilizations are fearsome they don't advance beyond your own."

As I heard that I was simultaneously flooded with this being's understanding of the universe. I felt this system of interrelated frequencies... I felt this universal harmony... I realized then how presumptuous it is, how arrogant it is, how anthropomorphic in the extreme it is, to project our present state of disharmony and disease out there beyond the stars, where it doesn't exist and never will. Ultimately our role, as I see it, is not limited to this earth. But we've got to clean up our own backyard first.

In the afterword of *Bird Tribes,* you recall a remarkable pre-incarnational experience which involved the Circle of the Faithful.

Intuitively, I sense that the Circle of the Faithful of the Stars included most of the baby-boom generation. I don't see it as a small or elite group. I have the feeling that it included most of our particular generation, and certainly others of other generations as well. Most of our particular generation came here, voluntarily, for the specific purpose of helping to ease this great transition. And we knew that we might forget why we came. As we begin to wake up and remember, to whatever degree, we talk about it with one another. I find that that sharing helps us all to remember. Little by little we fill out all the pieces of the picture, get a better view of why we came to the Earth and what we are here to do.

You're now at a point where you've accomplished a very respectable body of work. How do you feel about that? What does it mean for you?

I feel that I've reached a point of completion with a certain type of writing. I hesitate to use the term channeled because it means so many different things to different people. What I do isn't quite what most people probably mean by channeled. I don't think I'm going to publish any more books that are like *Starseed, The Third Millennium* or *The Starseed Transmissions.* I think my emphasis in the future is on application, and how it relates on a day-to-day level. What does it mean in practice? That's what it's all about.

What type of format will that take?

My emphasis at the moment is basically a description of a few days in May, here in the woods. It goes into a lot of detail about the wildflowers, the plants and the birds. Then there's some sharing of my thoughts; what it has been like to live here, the challenges we faced when we moved here without electricity or plumbing, growing our own food, raising small children.

It's a mellow experiencing of the world around me from the consciousness that I write about in my books, and from that practical, everyday consciousness that you need to interact with the human community. I find there's a gradual integration between what some might call higher consciousness and the consciousness that you use when you go to the grocery store or the gas station. Somewhere between those two archetypes, is a new way of being which I think we are all learning about. How it interacts with the world is really a moment-to-moment, play-it-by-ear, ad-lib experience. Writing about that is more of what I'm interested in right now. You know, my whole writing career is like trying to find a way to say something that language doesn't really lend itself to that well.

You've certainly done an excellent job with it.

Well, maybe it's because I have an idea of what the job is. But I feel that everything I've done so far falls short. The nature of language is such that it is a symbolic form of expression. There's no way that it's ever going to wholly and completely convey a multi-dimensional universe, a multi-dimensional reality. But since people are so oriented to language—in fact since people's entire lives tend to revolve around language and around their conceptual understanding—I feel it is worthwhile to allow to be reflected in words some kind of sense of what is out there.

One of the things I feel that I still haven't conveyed adequately is just what it is like every day; what's it like to walk outside, what's it like to just walk through the woods and be conscious. I've conveyed a lot of the broader landscape of the overall general context in which each one of us lives an individual human life, but for each of us the bottom line is what we see when we open our eyes each morning. How an awareness of the richness and magnificence of God, Nature, and the larger reality that we live in alters your perception, each day, moment-to-moment. It's something that I hope I can begin to convey.

And yet you feel a completion with the process that led to the four books along the Starseed line.

I knew that even when I got the first Starseed Transmissions that the 1987 to 1989 cycle would be the last conceptual input from that source, for me. So, even going into *Starseed: The Third Millennium* I knew it would be my last book of that nature. Yet I think it's appropriate. There's an evolution that happens where you have to begin to internalize that awareness.

There will always be certain advantages to expressing information in the way that it's put in *The Starseed Transmissions*, because you can allow the Earth to speak with a voice. You can represent in that way the voice of the Creator or the larger Spirit that is the sum total of collective human consciousness. There is an advantage to hearing that represented as a single voice, which in a very real sense it is.

However, individually our challenge is to find that point of awakening where, like riding the edge of the wave, unity become multiplicity. Where we have that awareness of being part of the One, but we're also aware of being an individual human being in a world of others, some of which are human and some of which are not. And acting as an individual, not denying our individuality in any way—in fact, celebrating our individuality—but doing it in a way that honors the whole, and all the other individualized expressions of the whole. That's really the next and ultimate step; where you embody the consciousness and make it a part of your life. That's the frontier for me and, I'm sure, for many of us right now.

You've written quite a bit about children and communication. You and Sherry founded the Greenwood School. You've had seven kids. I have to ask you about children.

Children, naturally, have the experience of the Earth as a single organism and of themselves as a projection of that, a part of that, an aspect of it. I don't think that it's possible to raise kids today without them losing that awareness at some point. As adults what we can do is help prolong it, help them live in that consciousness longer when they're younger. And make it easier for them to get it back when they show an interest in getting it back, if they are still at home. Most often that doesn't seem to occur until they are young adults and on their own.

I think that it's inevitable that each individual takes a fall at some point in their individual incarnation. That's the way collective human consciousness is right now and we've got to be a part of it. There's no way to isolate ourselves from it entirely. We tried that when we first moved here. We were the only family back here in many square mile of forest, we were the only human beings. Yet, we saw undeniable evidence of the effects of collective consciousness on both Sherry and the kids, who weren't even having any interaction.

There were things that we noticed with the children. Things we purposively made a point not to expose them to, that they picked up. They literally got it from the surrounding field of collective consciousness. I think our healing, our awakening, our incarnation, whatever you want to call it, is through that field, not somehow trying to bypass it. So it really wouldn't be desirable to protect kids from that altogether.

What parents have to do is help their children learn that it's okay to interact creatively with their environment, and encourage them in their own natural tendencies to interact crea-

tively with their environment. Once a child learns to interact creatively with one environment, that's a skill they can transpose to any environment. All little kids have that confidence, that sense that they know what to do, that instinctual way of being that isn't so full of self-doubt and excessive self-reflection like adults have, that they pick up in school and from so-called authority figures as they move through life. Help them to retain their inherent self-confidence in themselves. Help them be creative people which is their natural tendency anyway.

Probably the most important thing for parents to realize is that there is no way they are going to score 100% on implementing and embodying all their ideals. They just have to do their best and let go, because it's real easy to get down on yourself and get overly critical. As long as you're doing your best, you can feel okay about the process. They're all going to have their ups and downs, their nosedives. There's no way to avoid that completely.

In the introduction to *Starseed: The Third Millennium,* you wrote about the differences between what you're doing and channeling. You termed your work as being metapersonal.

Meta simply means beyond. Meta-personal means beyond personal. It describes something that includes the personal. I think this a real important feature of it; it includes the personal but it is not limited exclusively to the personal.

One way that I like to think of it is that God, the Creator, the Great Spirit or Source, is like a big light, a great, great light. Each one of us is like a lens that focuses that light. Basically our bodies, our bio-circuitry, focuses that light into an ego, a sense of individualized self that is valid because it does have to do with that particular aspect of God. But we forget that the light is coming from the whole. The light is coming from a Source that is common to all beings, in fact all matter. So, it's like relaxing your definitions of self, relaxing your individualized focus and letting that light become diffused again, and feeling your awareness extend into realms that are not necessarily associated with your physical body.

I know for a fact that this is something that not only everybody can do, but that everybody has done as children, and often still do without recognizing or realizing it. One of the things you run into in that larger field of awareness is that there is thought and there's consciousness but it's not verbal, it's not centered around language. One of the things we've been conditioned to believe subconsciously, if not consciously, is that if thought cannot be put into words it's not real. We've been taught to not even recognize non-verbal thought. Non-verbal thought to most people, even though they may experience it, does not even register. It's there but it's not there, because they don't give it any credibility.

It has a lot to do with our value systems. We're taught to value what we can put into words, we're taught to value language. If things can't be put into words, we're taught as very young children to consider them irrelevant, meaningless or possibly even to be afraid of them, maybe even consider them evil. It's all part of the subconscious programming that kids go through.

For me, it is just relaxing my individualized focus and feeling myself as part of the larger field of awareness. It can go through different levels, like a series of step-down transformers. You can go through a sort of regional level. I experience—there's no words for it—something like a Landscape Angel right around this immediate part of the forest. I can commune with that, blend with it, experience it, perceive reality a bit like it experiences it. I can expand further and feel a Spirit of this local forest, or a larger sort of bioregional entity, which is like that aspect of God that draws out all the life in this particular part of the world. Or, go beyond that and experience the Earth. All these other things are all parts of that. Then you can go beyond that to solar, galactic and universal lenses.

I've seen some material that seemingly purports to define them as chains of command.

No! It's not chains of command! A lot of these spiritual groups perceive it as chains of command because they've grown up in these military cultures and they can't imagine a series of lights flowing through prisms without a spiritual hierarchy of some sort. It isn't that way at all. It's a little hard to find words for it without implying that, but I don't experience any hierarchy. To me, I know this probably offends a lot of people, but hierarchy is a real human projection. It comes from our feudal traditions and often militaristic past.

In the universe, as I experience it, all beings are equal. The tiniest little being associated with an insect is not inferior to beings that manifest as stars, and have things to communicate and teach them, and vice versa. In a spiritual sense, all beings are equal. There are just some that know it, and some that don't.

Dorothy Maclean was telling us about Earth Angels. She's been exploring Devas of countries. You've also touched on that with some of your work on national psychology.

Yeah! She knows that stuff! Dorothy Maclean and the whole Findhorn phenomena have really done some pioneering work with that. I might put this in different words, but my understanding parallels hers very well.

In the course of universal awareness, or these larger fields of thought and non-verbal consciousness, there is a level where people have been called group souls. I've heard that term used in a way that I don't always mean it, but that's a good term I guess. Nations, depending on how well they correlate with their geography and their indigenous people, are spiritual and psychological entities.

One of the biggest breakthroughs in recent years is the realization that a nation can have a pathological structure, a psychological distortion in the way that it thinks of itself and the way that its people and leadership thinks of itself. These things can lead to wars. If they are recognized, diagnosed and treated there are a lot of conflicts that can be avoided. It's always to the people's advantage to do that, which is the neat thing about it.

If there's understanding of how such a structure can reflect the people's spirit, the real essential spirits of the people, then they can do it better and the people will prosper under that type of government. To the degree that present day governments do that, whether consciously or not, there are varying degrees of prosperity amongst the people of different nations. On the other hand, people really suffer when the government is out of tune with the spirit of the people they represent, and the government has a hard time. There's a lot of work to be done in that whole realm.

How are you feeling about the state of the world these days with the Gulf War and all?

Right on course. I think we've seen unbelievably positive developments in the last few years. Right up until the Gulf War people were positively euphoric about Eastern Europe, the Berlin Wall coming down and apartheid at least being lightened up a little in South Africa. They've still got a ways to go but then everybody saw the Gulf War as being like a relapse.

Believe me, it touched me very deeply. Sherry and I did a lot of meditating on it, with it, with the Earth, with the larger field of human consciousness. Even from the beginning, even when things were at their darkest, I got a very strong sense that it was part of the healing, part of the cleansing, part of the purification.

It's hard to explain, but picture a globe in a dark room. There's a narrow-beam flashlight that moves around shining at different parts of it during different times for the healing and purification. The whole thing needs to be purified and uplifted. A holistic healer will normally begin not by addressing the disease, but by addressing everything that's already right, by strengthening everything that's already right and healthy in a person. Then, after the overall systemic health of the individual has been brought to its fullest level, then quickly go in and address the disease if it hasn't already healed itself by that point.

There are, and were, some changes in the Middle East that absolutely had to happen before humankind could move into the next dimension of awakening, or next level of incarnation. This whole conflict has been a part of that. It's been a positive thing. I really believe that, though I know it didn't always look that way on the news.

Your books have all suggested that we're entering a period where a lot of that work you have been talking about will be done. Where do you see it going in this country?

The most fundamental change that we're approaching and beginning to experience now, and will more so in the future, is to recognize what the United States has been doing right along. And to continue as we have been to create governmental and administrative structures to facilitate that rather than inhibit it. What that is, in a most fundamental sense, is that we are a nation of many tribes, a nation of real ethnic diversity. That's our strength, that's our richness, that's our power. Beyond our resources and everything else, America is the strength that it is because of that ethnic diversity. I think that is definitely more recognized today than it was 10 or 20 years ago.

Needless to say, the Native American dimension is certainly something we need more of in our national psyche and in our government specifically, and it is happening. I think that all of the other changes are going to follow from that. The environmental consciousness that's been spreading over the last couple of decades is tied in very closely to greater acceptance of Native American people and values. There is a correlation there.

The other thing we have to accept is that the other nations of the world look to us for an example, whether we like it or not. Who's to say whether or not we should be in that role, but we're in it. By taking it a little more seriously, and living up to that responsibility more honorably, we'll be a greater light in the world than we have been, and I do think we've been a light in the world. Despite all of our faults and foreign policy blunders, I know that we have been a very positive global influence. I see that continuing and we'll do an even better job of it in the future.

It seems to me that some people give up on their dreams. You've stuck with it because you obviously believe in what you're doing. What kind of advice do you have for people about that?

One way that I like to think of it is to imagine the headlights of a vehicle shining into the fog of a dark night. The headlights will light up a certain pathway through that fog. I think that each one of us has a purpose-beam. That purpose-beam is not a predestined script we have to follow. It's a range of behavior that is very directly related to the skills, talents, attributes and capacities that we've designed into our physical bodies and the passions that we feel in our soul and emotional realm.

If we stay within the range of that purpose-beam in pursuing our purpose—I won't say that we will never have challenges or problems—by and large, our material support is there for us. If we are fulfilling our purpose it's like the whole universe conspires to see that we keep doing it. The Earth longs for people that will pursue their purposes. That purpose is related to why we incarnated and why our spirits have chosen to dress in these material forms. There is a tremendous amount of energy there.

On the other hand, I've seen quite a number of people who go to the other extreme. They have some sudden realization that their purpose-beam is, for example, to be a writer and they refuse to do anything else. And they don't make it, they have problems and they want to know why. Part of it is a very practical willingness to—talking about struggle and challenge—care about your purpose-beam enough, to do whatever it takes to make it manifest in your life. Sometimes that might mean doing something else for a while so the overall picture works out. There have been a lot of times in my life where I've done things that maybe other people wouldn't have done and that's partly, I believe, why I've been given some of the gifts I've been given.

Sometimes we might project or concoct some resistance...

Sometimes your body might have a resistance to a certain path of action, but it might be really good for your soul and for your spirit. Sometimes it's hard for a person to distinguish in their own minds where the resistance is coming from, because most people don't have it sorted out; "Well, that's my body talking," or "that's my spirit talking" or "that's my past programming talking," or "that's my parent's voice talking." There are many aspects of self. To do your purpose-beam you've got to follow your heart, your soul and your spirit. Ultimately whatever those aspects of self are that might want to resist will enjoy it, and it will be good for them too.

How about an example from your personal experience?

For awhile we tried to do without a vehicle. We reached a point of trying to simplify, simplify, simplify. We were at our ultimate point of trying to simplify. We were already living without electricity, plumbing, television and we tried to do without a vehicle too.

I was working for an Amish carpenter back then. I had to meet him at his house every morning. He was four miles on the other side of town. I had a ten-speed bike. I'd have to leave at 5:30, before it was light, and walk the bike down the dirt road because I couldn't ride it on the gravel. Then ride it to town, through town, and four miles on the other side, get to his house, have a cup of coffee and jump into another guy's truck—because the Amish don't have trucks—and it would take us another half-hour to get to work. Then I would start getting paid $2 an

hour for eight hours of physical labor, and then ride the bike home after dark. I did that for about six months. It was interesting, the little spirit-ego dialogues. I ought to write about it sometime.

I'd be laying concrete blocks all day and then I'd pedal this bicycle home. [Laughter] It was cold and windy, and it was raining. [Laughter] My ego and my body have been pretty willing, for the most part, to go along with my Spirit's enthusiastic ideas. But I was coming down the river hill knowing that I'd have to pedal up the other side after a day of laying concrete blocks and it was dark, and my ego said, "Spirit, I've had enough of this!" [Laughter]

It was interesting. My Spirit actually learned something from my ego at that point. A lot of people who are into this whole ego-spirit symbiosis, dialogue and blending, tend to think it's mostly the ego that learns from the Spirit, but the Spirit learns from the ego sometimes too. Eternal Spirits, with their vast backgrounds in the fields of light, don't take fully into account all the realities of physical plane existence. And, basically, that's what egos are for.

But that was part of my purpose-beam. My body didn't really like it at first, but it really got to appreciate and even enjoy it. It was only toward the end when Fall came and it started to get cold that I decided that enough was enough. I had some incredible experiences... in the early morning, coasting down a hill, total silence, gliding past feeding deer... I think that's an example of the kind of willingness that is required to really manifest your life on your purpose-beam. For me, in those days, my purpose-beam really was carpentry work. I was really aware of that.

Sometimes we get bogged down in aspects of our greater pictures and never get beyond that.

Oh yeah, for sure. That's exactly right. William Irwin Thompson has an analogy that he uses. He says it's like a fly on the ceiling of the Sistine Chapel. All it sees is a bunch of little dots. [Laughter] Sometimes you've got to get back to see the larger picture. On the other hand, those little dots are pretty important too. In fact, the greater picture is made up of nothing but those little dots.

The ultimate challenge is to ride the wave at the edge where unity and the universal awareness spills over into individualized awareness. That way you can really celebrate the diversity, the individuality, the texture, of each totally unique moment and place. And you can also understand something of how it fits into the greater picture. That only contributes to its wonder. It makes it even more special and precious.

How are you feeling about the overall picture of your purpose-beam? Where's it going?

Well, it's always changing. I've never thought of myself as a writer even though I write. If I've got anything valuable to say it comes out of my experience. So, really, my purpose-beam is larger than being a writer. It's just that, now, it's a way that I can make this a better world. I've gotten enough feedback and enough indications from within, as well as without, that it's a talent that I came here on Earth to utilize and develop in this lifetime. But what I express and what I share is coming from a different sort of identity. It's not coming from anything you can label quite so easily. I'm definitely at a juncture right now. I know that what I do with the rest of this life is going to have to do with communication. I also know that communication takes many forms. I'm sure that my purpose-beam will continue to take written form, I really do enjoy it.

We communicate a lot more than we realize by just being; being in the garden, being with one another. I think that when someone picks up one of my books, that maybe the author should be the forest or some of these rocks we're sitting on. In my introductions I try to convey how much of that has come out of the Earth and the role that the Earth has played in allowing those thoughts to come. In part, the reason that I wrote *The Starseed Transmissions* was because that was the kind of stuff I always wondered about my whole life and nobody ever taught me. There's a void in understanding why we are here, why the Earth is here, what the larger picture is.

My initial writing had to do with filling the void I missed when I was a kid and making sure there is something there for others who might try to grow and blossom on these rocks. I realize that others are doing it too, I know that mine aren't the only ones. Everybody has their own unique way of expressing their experience of truth, the universe, life. Yet, it is all pretty much the frosting, there is a whole lot of cake underneath. [Laughter] In the future that's what I want to write more about; the day-to-day, more related to the application department.

Can we relate that application to trees for a moment. I know you feel a great harmony with them.

We have sat at the bases of trees and felt their peaceful energy, experienced an attunement with them, a blending with them, a comfort with them, for many years, even before we moved here. I've long felt a certain affinity for trees. My first experience of actually realizing that trees were smart, that they could talk and communicate in terms that were quite intelligent, was early on in the Greenwood Forest Project.

One night under a full moon, Sherry and I took a walk out there. We visualized the whole forest coming under the stewardship of people who would love it and care for it. That visualization, I'm sure, is a part of what helped make the project succeed. At the furthest point out, a point overlooking the Jacks Fork River, we sat under these old trees. I sat at the base of a pine and Sherry sat at the base of an oak. All of a sudden I heard a voice; it's very rare that it happens, that dream I told you about was one other time. It was like I had stereo headphones on. The voice said, "Hoya, Honansta Hoya!"

Fortunately, I had enough training with tuning into nature and spiritual things, this was after *The Starseed Transmissions*, that I knew enough not to react and jump out of my skin and say "What the hell was that?" [Laughter] I just sat there real still. I took a couple of deep breaths and let the reverberations of that voice ripple through me.

Then I understood. It was a term for a certain type of tree that the Native Americans would use for a certain type of blending. Certain types of trees could do this better than others, usually it was the older, more mature trees. When it happened, a person would sit at the base of a tree, like this one, and in a meditative state the branches, cones, and needles or leaves, would become an extension of the human being's nervous system. As I allowed that to happen, I could feel and perceive as the tree perceived.

It was interesting. Even though this was a highly individualized, older tree—only the older ones are individualized, by the way—the tree still knew it was a part of the surrounding hills. It didn't really think of itself as separate from the hills. It understood itself as a tree, yes, but not like humans think of themselves as individuals. I could feel, as the tree felt, the forest-covered hills around the river almost as if it were my own skin. I could feel the animals moving through the forest. It was a very beautiful thing. That was one of my first real conscious exchanges with a tree. After that I did it more on purpose.

Those particular trees—there's seven big oaks, probably 250-300 years old in a circle down there—they were our council of advisors. They gave us direction as to how to go about the forest project. They were never worried, they seemed to know that it would be okay. Since then, we've had a tremendous amount of appreciation from the trees around here.

Talk about support; support isn't just financial. I've had hard times, challenging, difficult, frustrating hard times and just walked in the woods and been almost massaged, vibrationally or psychically, by the trees. They really like me. That probably provides a lot more support than I realize. From time to time I take the time to notice it, but it's always there, underlying everything.

I want to ask you about the connection between what you term extra-terrestrial sources and being grounded with, and in, the Earth.

I don't think that it's as apparent as it needs to be. If you put a television antenna on your roof, what's the next thing that you do? You ground it. If you don't ground it, it doesn't work. I think that a lot of people assume that there are higher frequencies of thought that they can access without the grounding that really brings them in and makes it clear, intelligible, practical and meaningful. The grounding is an on-going process. It isn't something that you do once and then it's done for the rest of your life. I have to definitely make sure that I have time in the woods, with the trees, because if I don't, I begin to feel that sense of being disconnected.

Then, too, the Earth is starlight, stardust. It is literally a part of a star. It's just a little cooler. Because of the temperature range that the Earth is in, it's been able to go through a tremendously detailed differentiation process and experience of individualization and multiple life-forms. But it is still, essentially, not totally different from the Sun and other stars. It's all part of the same fabric. By grounding in the Earth there's something there that helps you understand the language of the stars, of the higher vibrational frequencies where information is communicated on lightwaves, rather than soundwaves or in atomic structure.

I recall that you once wrote, "The most destructive decision that an individual can make is to give away his or her decision-making authority."

I've thought of the whole process of awakening—or some call it enlightenment or incarnation—as a process of reclaiming, at least for us humans, that individual decision-making responsibility. What we've done historically is to give that away to the surrounding culture. Societies' filters, created through the languages and cultural biases, have left us little better than automatons. Historically, we haven't had much real individual decision-making responsibility. If you look at history, especially the last couple of centuries, you see it's a process whereby individuals are taking back their right to make their own decisions.

The beauty of this is that when people really make decisions from their gut, their heart, their soul and their spirit, they agree. They're not at odds with the decisions that others are making from their hearts, souls and spirit.

We are like cells in a single organism. If we're healthy cells, making our own choices, we're not going to run into the kind of conflicts that we've run into historically, where cultures and arbitrary structures of interpretation are imposed on people by some dominant belief system, feudal lord or hierarchical structure. Maybe if everyone towed the line within that structure they would have harmony, but look what happens when those structures bump into other structures that are trying to do the same to their people. You get the kind of chaos that we've had throughout the history of the world.

The only way that is going to end is by people awakening, and allowing their Spirits to come back into their lives. By allowing those Spirits to make their decisions. And, more importantly, then having the courage to live their lives based on those decisions. It's one thing to make the decision and then not do it. [Laughter] "Nice input, Spirit—maybe tomorrow." [Laughter]

Re-establishing belief systems, seeing through imposed illusion... is that getting easier these days?

I find that it isn't hard to let go of that programming. For me, it's not difficult to let go of that anymore. It's not that hard to do it in a situation like this.

What I find challenging, what I think is the real frontier of human experience in general right now, is to bring that awareness into the workplace, into the marketplace, into our government and financial institutions. Into the very structures that are dominating human energy and exchange, and guiding the whole, at least superficial, direction of the human aspect of the planet. That's where you really run into the old thoughts and the old programming.

There are a lot of people within those institutions that have clearly seen that they can't go on the way they have been, and are really open to change. There's a lot going on out there that is really encouraging.

Marcel Vogel

Touching the Spark

"A thought is an act of creation. It is what we are here for, to create, to bring into being ourself by means of thinking. The way a thought can be observed and measured by a simple life form, a plant, shows a wonderful relationship between man and plant. When we love, we release our thought energy and transpose it to the recipient of our love. Our primary responsibility is to love."

Marcel Vogel

D r. Marcel Vogel was a research scientist, author, philosopher and proponent of the Divine. Many will remember him for his years of research and development for IBM. There his work led to the magnetic coating used in computer hard disks, liquid crystals used in digital displays and the red hue on your TV. Many will remember him for his work with plants and his coverage in the book, *The Secret Life of Plants*, which dealt with just that subject. Many will remember him for his pioneering work with crystals and water. All of this is, and will be, worth remembering. To the above we may also commemorate his warm nature, moving smile, compassion and his cultivated and enlightened sense of self.

Dr. Vogel's interview was originally published in the July & August 1989 issues of *The Light*. In that introduction I wrote, "We have in Dr. Vogel a singularly sensitive and developed individual. A man whose work will, in all probability, not be generally appreciated for years to come." In retrospect I will add that when his work is fully realized we will be a changed people. Given both the speed and tediousness of change that we are undergoing these days it still remains to be seen whether or not we will witness it personally. However, I do find that his work has all the potential to radically, though with intense sensitivity, alter many of our common beliefs.

Fittingly enough, it was a challenge of imagination that led Dr. Vogel to his legacy. He had been asked to facilitate a course in creativity for IBM engineers. At one point a student referred him to the work of Cleve Backster regarding the possibility of plants possessing emotion. Logical scientist that he was, the good Doctor promptly dismissed the notion. Later, however, his curiosity was piqued and the decision was made to do some experimentation. The class was divided into three groups and rallied to attempt a duplication of Backster's results. None of the three teams made any headway. However, Dr. Vogel working on his own, did.

All of this soon led to a number of, metaphorically speaking, doors. I imagine that if he had turned away from these doorways our story would stop here, or would never have been written. However, being the curious, motivated and sensitive researcher that he was, these gateways were indeed spread wide, their hallways thoroughly inspected and the vestibules graciously observed. These doors would remain open for the remainder of his life.

These doors led Dr. Vogel to the Psycho-Galvanic Response of plants, psychic energy, information bands, pre-forms, life force and the power of love. Though he was busy with plant life and later, water and crystals, it was apparent to him that what he was really functioning with was the power of the mind. His belief was that the mind working in conjunction with the other life-forms would produce the synergy he sought. This was a radical notion in the 1970s, less so now and perhaps, as Vogel believed, common knowledge a generation from now.

His endeavors were thoroughly rooted in a new awareness of consciousness. He was most careful to avoid the more blatant, and inaccurate, labeling of his undertakings by not stressing the aspects of phenomena in the adventure. You will notice that he speaks to this in the interview. For Dr. Vogel the message of the work, as it related to a higher view of all life, was far deeper than the momentary outward surprise of misunderstood recognition. It was not parlor games that he was after, he was not content with mere sleight of hand. The substance of his discoveries was magic enough.

The interview begins in an altogether different manner than all the others. Our scheduled time together had been arranged by another who had not passed on to Dr. Vogel any of the materials I had sent to help familiarize him with our publication. We had never met and he had never seen a copy of *The Light,* which at that time was still looking for its identity.

After introductions and some small talk it seemed appropriate to begin our discourse. At this point the good doctor remembered that he was not familiar with our work and asked to see a copy. This was quickly presented and he spent some time with it. Then he indicated he was ready and started to speak. I felt at the time, and still do, that his opening remarks were a completely intuitive digestion and interaction with what I was looking for. With his candor and sensitivity we instantly cut out a great deal of meaningless posturing and got right down to the heart of things. When he began to speak I was initially surprised but still quite prepared to go with the flow. I had no idea where he was going to go with these opening remarks. However it was quickly apparent that they were the perfect salvo to open a number of lines of inquiry. The learning was in the listening and he presented a magnificent earful of that. It was a tremendous lesson, one that would be repeated later in a few subsequent interviews with other individuals, equally as brilliant.

I had misgivings about some of the questions that I anticipated asking him. I was concerned that they might be awkward or even inappropriate to the occasion. Despite this I, of course, went ahead. Fortunately, he was not put off and even provided a framework for their inclusion himself. I was quite relieved. When he spoke of his childhood experiences I knew that all would be well. He had witnessed the Light at the end of the tunnel at very young age. It would shape his being for the rest of his life. He would remain eternally grateful for the experience. He travelled to the tunnel again in 1991. This time he stayed. I imagine that he danced all the way.

"You have heard it said so often that we are made to the image and likeness of God. It's true. There is that divine spark that we each have. There's a tremendous joy in living to activate that and get that going. That to me is the joy of living."

Marcel Vogel

Marcel Vogel: Tomorrow is the Feast of the Holy Trinity. The expression by God of His love for mankind. The third person in the Blessed Trinity is love. Once we can open ourselves to be loving, we then take on the divine aspects. Too few people ever really know how to love... to see the good in another person, and not to be discriminating—not to put it into a box and categorize it.

Basically we are trained almost from infancy to use our rational mind, that which comes to us through our senses. But where is the training given to us for our intuition, that wonderful inner aspect that guides us, which transcends the senses? When we can let that operate, and not be fearful of it, we bring that into balance. When we bring these two together, the intuition operating with the physical senses, that becomes love. But one or the other, just by themselves, is not a complete aspect.

I've had my sensitive faculties going all of my life, since earliest childhood. As far back as I can remember I've always had a deep love for my guardian angel. I would go out in the back yard and sit down and talk to my guardian angel, bring them a little gift. I never saw them, it wasn't necessary. I could feel the vibration. There is a teaching in the Roman Catholic church: to every soul is given a spiritual companion, a guide. I fully understood and accepted this and I've used it throughout my life. It has been a wonderful asset.

I've expanded that into using the guardian angel as a messenger to help me when I get into very difficult problems of technical natures. Now there's another adjunct in the overall hegemony of doing things, and it works, it's wonderful. And... channeling is a perfectly natural thing, if it's done properly. But if it's done blindly it becomes stupid.

What's the qualifier?

The qualifier is the integrity and intensity of the reason for the channeling. Integrity is number one. Then, the type of question you ask. If you sit down and let a person blindly channel for you, you get blind information. Channeling is only as good as the depth of your thinking and the questions that you ask. Otherwise you don't get anything. If you don't put out a good carrier wave you are not going to get a good signal. If you just sit back and say, "Now give me a reading," you may get a bit, but the real information comes when you move to a higher state of consciousness, then the two of you dialogue together.

I've done that most of my life. It's nothing magical or mysterious. I'll exhaust my senses, I'll use every ounce of strength and knowledge that I have, then I'll go to the next level. Exhaust that, then go to the next level. At times I've pushed myself till I've moved up to a very, very high level. And there's a great difficulty in that. A very great difficulty... you don't want to come back. It's a very wonderful, peaceful feeling and it's a great temptation to stay there.

What were you experiencing?

A tremendous sense of peace. Being at home. Joy. Joy like you don't find in any other expression here on this Earth plane. And you don't need any drug, you just do it with the breath. You see, I've done my best to develop all of the faculties, not limiting them only to the technical and scientific. Yes, I've developed my scientific interests, but also the spiritual. The key is to bring them together in harmony, not competing one against the other. There is no competition.

What strikes you, and honestly and truly it hits you like a brick wall, is the tremendous limitation that each of our senses have. I've put a lifetime of work in research and I've gotten just a minute smidgeon of information, real information, and I've worked hard. If you're really honest with yourself it hits you like a ton of bricks, about how little you really know on any subject you've done intensive study and research on.

Right now I'm studying water. I've now done over five years of study on the structuring of water, the nature of the water molecule itself. It's the most demanding structure that we have to study. There is no solid theory on how water exists in the fluidic state. What I'm doing is putting love into water. The way I do that is to put the thought of love and well-being into a crystal, then I spin the water around it, around a stainless steel coil. When that water spins around that crystal it takes on that charge from the crystal and is changed. Then I spin it again, and again. Each time it changes further, and I suddenly have a completely different state of water. It has a vital energy to it. The water gets smoother, softer and when you drink it you feel as if you're

floating. It takes you right out of your body. I'm working on this to make water healthy again.

With this we can feed it to plants so that we can have healthy, strong vegetables again, or give it to animals so we can have healthy animals. We don't have healthy water. I'm also working to purify the water to remove unwanted pollutants and I'm able to do that. It's fun. Now, you have some questions for me.

Well, I'd like to go on with this and ask you about your impressions about the state of the planet.

There's a great deal of sadness. When I grew up as a child we had this tremendous desire to achieve—the Horatio Alger syndrome—where a person could by guts, determination and work, achieve and move ahead in life. I've applied that to my own life and have done that. But, you take the youth nowadays and they don't seem to have that type of drive in them. We suffer from a pollution in the press, a pollution with television, an obsession with sex and lower activities. It becomes almost sad. The young people when they watch it, that is their guideline for the life they are to lead. We're not doing much reading. Nowadays with the younger people, you don't find this type of developing mind. It saddens me.

We must build again people with a real sense of spirituality; that they do have a soul, that they do have a higher sense within them. That they're not only a body and a mind, but that there is a Spirit. That they are a reflection of a Divine Mind. If people learn to talk to that—to friends they have in space—they can be guided and they can be directed. They're not out wandering alone.

How do you recommend people do that?

To learn how to pray. To learn to go within. Take a moment of silence. Not meditation, there's been too much focus on meditation this, meditation that. But, dialogue with yourself, "Why am I here? What am I to do with my life? What is my purpose now in living? How can I find my objective reason for living?" When you focus on that it comes through. That's what I call meditation. Asking questions, real questions, and then hanging in there.

For example, I was dying of pneumonia at the age of six and was given the Last Sacraments of the Roman Catholic Church. I was totally prepared for transition. First, Holy Communion and the Last Rites, the doctor was there, the priest was there, my father and mother. I went out of body and went into that tunnel you read about. I was in that tunnel. I looked at my body and it became smaller and smaller. I saw that beautiful light at the end of the tunnel. I loved it. I wanted to keep going. But, whoosh, back into my body. The next day I was well. Suddenly, I was well.

So I asked my parents, "Why am I alive? Why didn't I die?" Of course, they couldn't answer. So I went, every morning, to 5:30 mass. It was in San Francisco. I walked a mile and a half, attended mass, and set down and asked, "Dear Jesus, I want to know, why am I still here on this earth? There must be a reason. There must be a purpose. Give me an answer." Four years, I had to do that every day. Four years, no word. Nothing. I wouldn't quit. I hung in. Suddenly, at ten years of age, I'll never forget this, 'a voice spoke within me. Loud and clear. It said, "You will be a phosphor chemist. You will write a book on luminescence. You will then build your own corporation and do fundamental research on rare earth phosphors." Everyone of those I accomplished.

Could you have understood that direction at the age of six?

No. That's why I had to wait for four years. I then went right into chemistry. By the time I was eleven I had a full-blown chemistry laboratory in my backyard. I didn't waste any time. And, I ask questions.

I think you are persistent too.

Once I go after something I never quit. I just hang in and hang in. That's where you gain knowledge.

Are you still relying on that voice?

All the time. What is it but your soul, your Higher Self speaking? That's a God within you, within me, each one of us. Once you activate that, it speaks—when it's right and proper for you to hear. That is the God within each one of us.

You hear it said so often that we are made to the image and likeness of God. It's true. There is that Divine Spark that we each have. There's a tremendous joy in living to activate that and get that going. That to me is the joy of living.

Once you can begin to love yourself, then you start healing. Most people are ill because they don't forgive themselves. They maintain a rejection of themselves. They literally beat their body for things that have happened. The body finally crumbles and breaks down. We've got to learn forgiveness and, above all, acceptance of things as they are, and then move on.

What have you moved on into lately?

I was able, this last year, to create something absolutely new. It's about as near unusual as anything you'll find. I've developed a technology for finishing wine. I can bring wine to a state of completion by one pass around a crystal, and it comes out as a completely finished wine, in a manner of seconds. I've done that at the Sycamore Creek Winery with ten different lots of wine. The wine develops a whole new absorption band in the ultraviolet, it changes in the infrared spectrum... it immediately ages without having to be cask aged or put into a bottle and stored for awhile. It's all done with love. I've done it.

What are the mechanics of that? How does it work?

I put a program into a crystal that I've specially cut. Then I spin the wine I want to test around the crystal a certain number of times. Then we test these wines, we taste them. Then I test them with the instrumentation and we determine which pass gives us the best wine. In the fourth pass we get the wine at its maximum taste and evaluation. We take that vibration, which we have the equipment to measure, and put that vibration right into the industrial crystal we have. Then we put that into the apparatus and spin the wine once around it and it reproduces it. And the wine comes out that way. It's that simple. It works. I've filed patents on this now. In July, we'll be presenting this at the U.S. Psychotronic Association. It's like magic but it works. It's just the beginning. I'm just beginning to let go now that I've retired.

How frustrating is it for you and your work to be so far ahead of your time?

Without prayer, without my spiritual base, I couldn't, wouldn't, be alive. Yes, it's terribly frustrating. Because you see, when you move ahead this way... I know what things are going to be. And, I've seen it again and again and I just proceed to go ahead and build it. But people are fearful. Many times it's five or ten years ahead of its time. That's about what it takes, a decade of time. You have to be so darn persistent. In 1960 I saw liquid crystals as a viable means for display, on watches and flat panel television screens. I went back to the laboratory, bought a microscope and started to make these compounds for that purpose. 1960 mind you, long before anybody got into it. It was difficult, because IBM didn't know how to cope with it. To deal with a creative person, you're not talking about a normal time-frame, mode of experience or language. The average businessman doesn't think more than one to three years ahead. The average truly creative person thinks about five years ahead. If they're lucky they can bring it down to three, but the norm is five.

The average businessman might not necessarily think about crystals and love either.

Right. The key vibration I put into it is love, not power.

How did you learn that?

Practice. Persistence. Trial and error, and having the equipment in the laboratory to measure it. Without that I wouldn't be able to talk to you the way I'm now doing, or be able to communicate. It would just be arbitrary feelings. Because all you can feel when you charge a crystal is a vibration, a tingling sensation, that's as far as you can go. But with the equipment I can quantify that into a numerical value. I can transfer that vibration into water now and measure it with spectrophotometry. I can get the force that is being created... it's impact on matter, so I can put it into translatable energetic units. That's what I've worked to do; to build it into a science. It's really the first time that it has been done.

What I'm getting here is that you've measured, albeit quantified in some fashion, love.

Yes, the power of love. Love is a force, a force that coheres matter, it brings matter into order and balance. Okay, two key words: order and balance. When you can bring order and balance into matter it then manifests itself; it comes to self-recognition. Same thing for you and I. When I love you, I give you a sense of self-awareness; I recognize you. Not necessarily for any particular attribute but for the intrinsic totalness of what I experience looking at you and being one with you.

I'd like to ask you, as you see it now or maybe ten years down the road, about the inroads that you've made on traditional medicine.

It's a tough job. Medicine is ruled by the A.M.A. It's ruled by fear. I mean traditional medicine. I tried for four years lecturing to a group of MD's and did my best to pass on what I knew to them. What the real answer is on this I do not know. I tried my best, first to go to the medical profession, because I felt a responsibility to try to pass it on to them. I've gone now to the lay practitioners and to the lay public in making this knowledge available to them. So they can learn to relieve the stresses and the tensions from their bodies and to then do the self-healing that they are capable of doing.

We have been too deeply absorbed in trying to counteract most illness with drugs, chemical agents and surgery. The average person, given half an opportunity, can heal themselves. Of anything. Too often we give up and do not take responsibility for our bodies and then whole acts of healing are inhibited and we struggle.

The other thing that should be looked at... the laying on of hands is quite real. People praying together for the good of a person I think is very important and very meaningful. If they pray with any degree of sincerity it has a tremendous benefit.

The first part of next year I'll be coming out with my book. It will be Marcel Vogel on crystals. It will be a textbook. It will give about 120 case histories of treatments that have been given, the follow-ups, and a systematic methodology on how to use crystals to do this type of therapy. It's all done now, it's been written and put into the hands of the publishers. Now I'll be moving into chemistry and physics and applying the crystals for technical application... the structuring of fluids, the purification of water, and the preparation of fuels.

Fuels?

Oh yeah. Energy sources. That is in the beginning stages, so I can't say too much on that. There's no limit. Because you deal with your mind and you can create with that thought and your crystal and operate with it. It's a computer, a micro-computer. You've seen them haven't you? They are highly tuned and finished instruments.

We're seeing a great deal of bridging between science and metaphysics these days. Your work is certainly there. Where is it going?

Yes, this is a bridging of science and metaphysics. I'm giving a logic, a reasoning, a language, to metaphysics. Once the language can be gotten and the mathematics that go with it, then science can step in, accept it and put it to work.

Now, the language is the following: In the consideration of the energy bands that surround a substance, I believe we have another band, which I call the information band. A band of information in which the substance, whatever it may be, stores information of itself. When you learn how to contact that information band you can interact with that object, modify it, alter it if you want, without the use of energy as we normally think of it, either heat, light, or other types of electromagnetic energy. Because the information will act directly from one information band to another and the transformation takes place immediately. That's what I've discovered. It's a major discovery.

consciousness that you're talking about?

right. I know how to communicate directly, consciously, with one object to another.

Should we consider this to be some manner of telepathic maneuver in the etheric sense?

Right. I know how to talk to water, to wine, a crystal, and create a change. I'm doing it. For over five years now.

So... how? People would probably want to know, "Well, how is Marcel doing that? How's he talking to that wine, or water?"

Alright. I take a sip of the wine, a young wine, and wonder what needs to be done to it. I let the wine tell me what I feel needs to be done, the changes that should be made. I mentally think that out. I have the crystal in my hand, and project that thought into the crystal. Then I put it into the holder and spin the wine around it, and test it again. And it changes. There's no energy, no light, no electricity, no heat... purely thought.

You see, consciousness precedes matter. It sets the stage. It develops a pre-form on which matter then grows and builds. Before matter comes into being, it suddenly manifests itself. In the growth of a crystal I have seen it as a flash of light.

When you take an object like a liquid crystal and heat it, it goes into a molten state. It's now randomly dancing about, all these molecules of a compound. You slowly cool it, under a microscope and you watch it. Suddenly you will see, boom, a flash of light, a blue flash. Immediately after that there is a liquid crystal state, it takes on a structure. The preceding of the formation into an organized state is preceded by a flash of light. That is the information band that I'm talking about. It's real. I've seen it. And that persists then around that object. Once you know how to contact that you know how to move that around, at will. Do you realize the impact... what the meaning of that is?

Sure. You've just transformed society.

That's right. It can.

How long will it take?

Probably another generation.

Do we have that much time?

Just about. We're coming to a critical phase right now. I'm talking about our youth, and the way we are acting. We're polluting at a tremendously accelerated rate. We have to stop polluting. You see, we think of physical pollutants, but we've totally neglected mental pollution, emotional pollution, those are equally as bad. Have you ever gone into a room where two people have had a fight? You can feel that energy. It persists. Those forces are not in the electromagnetic spectrum, they are not limited by time or space. They can persist for thousands of years. You catch what I'm saying?

So, how do you clear it? Two simple ways. One of the key ways to clear is incense. It is not an accidental thing that the Roman Catholic church incense the altar before and during the ceremony of High Mass. Incensing purifies and clears the atmosphere of negative patterns. It is not accidental that Christ was given, as a babe by the three wise men or astrologers, gold, frankincense and myrrh. The symbolism of those is that they are instruments of purification. Other cultures use them too. They precipitate out thoughtforms.

I'm reminded of something that Ken Carey said, that wherever two people have loved that it leaves etheric imprints forever.

For all times. Yeah. Absolutely. What I'm doing right now is I have these samples of rocks from Ireland. From all the various sacred spots in Ireland. I have this wonderful woman, Mary Lampson, we've sat for hours now taking each rock and we tune into it and she speaks out the information contained in the rock. We've gotten a remarkable bibliography of information. One of these days it will be put into a book. But the information is still all locked into the rocks.

That's a nice lead in to the crystal skulls.

Yeah. They're information transfer devices. I've worked with four or five skulls already. I've worked with the Mitchell-Hedges skull. What I saw was that the skull was very effective in taking information that is contained in the brain of one person, store it in the skull, then transfer it to young children. I found exactly the same thing with the other skulls. The others didn't have the articulated jaw that the Hedges did. You don't need a skull. You can do the same thing with a terminated crystal. Just as you're holding information now with your tape recorder, you can hold information at a higher subliminal level with those crystals.

When I worked with the Hedges skull, I charged it and it lit up and became luminous. Easily seen in the dark. I went back and saw them cutting the skull and carving it. They were made in South America, not in space, ground and cut by sanding. They are rare achievements. That one had remarkable lenses cut in, so that the light would come from below, go through the eye sockets giving you points of light beaming out. It would scare the pants off of you. They could turn on the hidden light source and the eyes would suddenly light up and frighten the people. They really don't interest me. Next question.

What is your legacy? How do you want people to follow up on your work and research?

What I would like to see is them repeating the work I'm doing with water and do careful scientific measurements, infrared, ultraviolet spectrophotometry, surface tension measurements, and use water as an index of measurement of the information transfer that takes place in either humans or in various bodies. Because water, I believe, is a vehicle for the transfer of information, in the body and in other vehicles we have. I think we should get a consortium of people together and do a very careful, serious study on this.

We have done too much study of phenomena, and you get no place fast. When you look at something like the bending of a metal or a spoon, it's nice, it's interesting, but you don't gain insight into what the fundamental teaching is. I'm after coming to grips with what are these forces within us that give us these types of capacity to act and to do.

I'm particularly interested in having a deeper understanding of how we can know ourselves in a more meaningful way, and develop the ability to communicate more deeply with our higher self. I'd also like to see channeling being given its proper respect and position, and not treated as, say, psychic phenomena. I'd like to see those who are skilled in this being given a position of respect and consulted. I've used sensitives throughout the latter ten years and I deeply respect them. One woman that I work with, Kay VanDamm, I deeply owe a vote of respect and gratitude towards. She helped me immensely in working through very difficult technical problems.

In developing the technology and science I had no textbook, nobody to turn to. I was standing alone. Basically I was the first person to cut crystals, tune them and make them into these forms. I stood against everyone else in the field. Everyone preached that crystals were to be left alone and used naturally. I said no.

The discovery I made was that when I cut a crystal and tuned it properly I then found we had a crystal that was attuned to water. It had the same vibrational characteristics as water itself. When I measured it with the radionic type instruments, I got the number 454 for both water and the crystal. Whatever information I could put into the crystal, I could immediately transfer it to the water. I tried it with the natural crystals and it wouldn't work. It only worked when I cut them to the proper form. So, I could create information with my mind, put it into a crystal, and then transfer it into water. Just as now you're hearing my voice, and we're transferring it through the electronics into the tape via the magnetic pulses that are being created on to the ferromagnetic material on the tape. Now, just visualize, instead of all that... I could take a thoughtform, all of the information that I said to you and in one breath put it into a crystal and then act. That's a big jump. Now, how long science will take to absorb this and begin to appreciate it, I don't know. I retired from IBM, supported myself through the lectures, beholden to no one, let my mind go, and brought this technology into being. I was determined to create, and I did. That's a good place to end.

How about some parting words while I take some pictures?
You're endless aren't you? Okay. We must all begin to take a bit of time to work and serve our fellow man, because we are part of a total society. Being part of a society means that we each have a responsibility to help each other. We work together, not separately and... it's not easy.

Fred Alan Wolf

The Shaman of Physics

"For me, reality consists of a gigantic superspace—the mathematical space of all possibilities. We might think of this as the 'mind of God.' Each dimension in the space is like a dimension in our ordinary three-dimensional space. Each dimension of the space also points or indicates a 'direction.' This direction is a possibility. In this space something called mind floats and freely associates. It puts together—for a fleeting moment, which could be an eternity, depending on the time scale one is looking at—any two or more dimensions, and it asks what about this combination?

"Our minds are thus tuned or are tunable to multiple dimensions, multiple realities. The freely associating mind is able to pass across time barriers, sensing the future and reappraising the past. Our minds are time machines, able to sense the flow of possibility waves from both the past and the future. In my view there cannot be anything like existence without this higher form of quantum reality."

Fred Alan Wolf—*Parallel Universes*

A
h, yes... science and spirit, the interesting debate. For the better part of 2,000 years some of our concepts of science have been at odds with some of our concepts of the Higher Realms. Of course the concepts of science have been argued, discussed and disputed many times over. The same is true of the concepts of spirit. As a species we have long wondered, theorized and even warred over our concepts. And where does it inevitably—by education, time, death and a host of other reasons—and invariably lead? To new concepts. Concepts that, at times, can literally shake the foundations of culture and mankind. Perhaps we have entered into just such a period.

Perhaps no group of theoretical scientists is making more forays into the nature of consciousness and the energetic life processes than physicists. It's an interesting situation and a cause for wonder. Is it because these folks are so non-linear in their process? Are their strange and often bizarre musings actually facilitated by their ability to break through, and thus beyond, convention? To pursue the abstract while being completely supported by extraordinarily complex, weirdly mystical and socially approved mathematical models might indeed yield the truth in wholly new ways.

Dr. Wolf would have you know that just as God and man are not separate so neither are God and science. It is through the mathematical models of the new physics that our good doctor provides challenging theoretical insight into the workings of time, reality and the human consciousness. It is through the heart-based intentions of his own perceptions that he pursues these avenues of focus. The combination of science and man as presented by the man himself has coalesced into a wellspring of insight, intuition and imagination.

Fred Alan Wolf is the author of six popular and informative books, *Parallel Universes, The Body Quantum, Star Wave, Taking the Quantum Leap, Space, Time, & Beyond* (with Bob Toben) and

The Eagle's Quest. His remarkable efforts with *Taking The Quantum Leap* were rewarded with the American Book Award in 1982. Dr. Wolf holds his doctorate in theoretical physics from UCLA, was a Research Fellow at the University of London, and has illumined, lectured and taught literally all over the planet.

Sitting on the rocks by the sea, recording two-dimensional imagery (the taking of the photographs) of a notably multidimensional personality, I was half-expecting a quark of illumination to pierce my stuff at any moment. It had certainly felt as though the timing for this interview was singularly apropos. What I didn't know yet was just where it would go. It was a quantum leap alright. But while I had thought we might bareback some theoretical neutrinos somewheres, Dr. Fred was intent on surfing the quantum wave in the jungles of Peru!

I can only say that initially I was surprised, if not shocked. I had no idea that the interview would go this way. However, after a few moments, it was all working quite nicely and I felt that this was indeed a bigger gift than I had ever expected from this encounter... and I had expected a lot. To hear of Dr. Wolf's adventures with the shamans of the Peruvian jungle added an entirely new vista to my appreciation of this "new physicist." My mind took great delight in visualizing the scene. It was entirely conceivable to imagine this wise man sitting in the dirt with indigenous wise men discussing the plant people. It sounded like great fun to me but what took me to the next level was the intuitive understanding that the good Doctor had not only the inner capacity to learn from the shamans but also the desire, and the recognition that their wisdom and knowledge may well be, in many ways, superior and certainly more balanced than our own.

There's one further story involved here. The interview with Dr. Wolf was a coincidental gift of such magnitude that, at the time, I could hardly believe it was happening. Aside from holding the distinction of being the first interview in *The Light* in its inaugural magazine format, his was also one of the most seren-dipitous. Here's an overview of the situation at the time.

We were a mere four weeks from going to print with the debut issue. Of course I was nervous and somewhat apprehensive at that point. Ordinarily (but not always!) I would have an interview ready to go at that late date. However, the one I was anticipating was put off at the last moment! Panic struck! What was I going to do in that short a notice? Sleepless nights coincided with my anxious days when, out of nowhere, there came a phone call. Dr. Wolf was within 150 miles, would I be interested in an interview? Whoa! I would have been interested had it been 250 miles and I had three pieces all ready to go, let alone nothing for the first issue. It was incredible and it provided me a glimpse of what might be accomplished with some good intentions, patience and, of course, benevolent intervention.

What followed was a thoughtful view of his then current book project, and some surprising insight. Dr. Wolf once wrote about a topic he calls visionary physics. He considers it to be an art form based upon scientific fact and, through extrapolation, conscious-ness. He suggests that if visionary physics are to have any value or practical application they must provide a doorway to insight. His works to date deliver a universe of magic, mysticism and mystery.

"*Just as I feel my foot as my foot and see the star in the star's position in the sky, I am able to project my inner world onto the outer world. This experience of projection provides the double-edged blade of separateness from the world and perception of the world as it occurs in space and time. This is the life we all 'sense.' It is important to recognize, early in the game, our mental roles in the universe. This leads to an intuitive-inductive sense that while somehow I am not separate from that physical world, yet I feel so alone and apart from it. This double sense of aloneness/apartness and togetherness/perception is the identification 'process' itself. It is also the realization of certain qualities or perceptions about the world.*

"*At some level of this projection the very existence of the physical world is 'created.'*"

Fred Alan Wolf—Star Wave

What can you tell us about your book, *The Eagle's Quest?*

It's probably the most unusual of all my books and a new standard in my writing. One that I'm hoping will give me the opportunity to explore areas that are more on the outside of physics but still within the framework of my own interests, my own development and my own insights to nature. This book is called, *The Eagle's Quest, A Physicists' Journey into the Heart of the Shamanic World*.

"Into the Heart of the Shamanic World?" Whoa... that's a pretty deep space.

That's what I discovered. I didn't know that until it all integrated together. I originally wrote a 160,000 word manuscript that was a chronological journey, from early childhood to the present, of all the magical and shamanic experiences I've ever had, with a number of dialogs with Shamans I have met. It will make better reading when I restructure the book and separate out the various categories of shamanic activity, shape shifting, time travel, healing, animism, lucid dreaming—a number of different sections which all the Shamans spoke about.

By grouping it under these different sub-categories I hope to give the reader an insight into the commonality of all the shamans around the world. A kind of, if you will, 'shaman physics' or 'shamanic technology' which is totally foreign to our western thinking. It's a way of seeing that we are rapidly losing, aside from such obvious influences as Buddhist teachings and the current interest in shamanism. Mainstream America has no idea what this way of seeing is. Carlos Castaneda wrote about it and Mircea Eliade has written about it, and others. But all the writings up to now have been, except Castaneda's, intellectual studies. Castaneda's were first hand experiential reports.

What I want to do is be a first hand experiencer of that world. I also want to bring to it my knowledge as a Western physicist and see how those two overlap, with some possibility of under-standing or explanation.

In your other books you have often shared some of your experiences. Would you feel comfortable doing that now?

Once one gets involved with the shamanic worldview, once one sees it, it acts as a rekindling. It awakens you to memories of experiences or things in your life that you may have had as a child. It rekindles your enchantment with the world. It rekindles the magical child within. It gives you a feeling of greater trust. A feeling that no matter what happens to you or how bad, horrible or wonderful things are, that things are going to change. It gives you that reawakening, that quickening.

The experiences that you have are often very brief and fleeting. They're not long drawn out experiences. They're brief glimpses, but they're so profound that you can't really nail them down. The lucid dream that I recounted in *Star Wave*, [a trip to an astral plane and a subsequent meeting with some interesting souls], that's a very incredible experience. It's a bilateral, biworld, parallel world vision. Not many people have had an opportunity to do that. I was having those experiences well before I knew about anything shamanic. But when I integrate them with my shamanic experience it all fits together.

I had an experience in the early 70's in which I found myself flying over England. I could smell the air. I could see myself coming into the coastal area of Wales. When I got back there I felt a deep sense of connection, of being. I could see myself flying into the castles on the coast of Wales. I remembered the vision so strikingly that when I went to Wales I searched for those castles, and I found them. I was having a vision that was of some direct experience.

The most recent experiences I had were in Peru. I think the Peruvian journey was probably the most deeply disturbing yet moving and heart-opening. I had experiences with consciousness that I imagine would be difficult to understand if you're in a normal waking state of consciousness.

One of my experiences was that my mind split into three different minds. Each one spoke with a different voice. One of them was like an old father who was very wise and had all the wisdom in the world, all the answers, and knew from deep experiential knowledge. Another was like a child who was very eager to find out what this was all about; why was he suffering, why was he going through this? The third was like somebody who just sat back, watched, witnessed and never said a word, but his presence was clearly felt. I was, simultaneously, all three people.

Talk about parallel selves—they were all there. I could feel every one of them. It gave me an insight that if one was able to understand consciousness totally—as one understands matter through the quantum model for example—one should be able to see that ordinary waking consciousness is a composite of perhaps an infinite number of different voices that all speak as one through the egoic state. When the ego state is removed those voices will splinter apart. As, for example, a child who is locked in a closet at a young age and becomes a multiple personality. Or possibly in the case of a schizophrenic who suffers some trauma or chemical imbalance in the brain which causes the ego to shatter, and as a result these different voices can be heard. I went through a shattering of my egoic state.

What brought all this on?

What brings it on is not too hard to understand. I will tell you about it. I had an experience in which I was able to see the Spirits of the Ayahuasca plant. They looked at me, they beckoned me to join them. They were very unusual looking, they don't look human. I could see them. They showed themselves to me.

The voices lasted a good five or ten minutes. I was having a conversation, this active conversation in which I wanted to know what was going on. The third witness person would say to me, "Fred, clean up your act." What I took that to mean was that in everything that I do, from now on, be honest, tell the truth. Whatever you say, tell the truth. Tell it from your own experience. Don't lie about it, don't exaggerate it, try to stay within the framework of the truth. I decided from that point on I would have to lead my life that way. I can't go back to the person that I was. You know what I mean?

Oh yeah. It's easy for us to forget about the responsibility of it. We tend to ooh and ah about spiritual stories but we sometimes forget that the trust works both ways... and all the time.

Yeah, it applies to everyday life. I mean, if you're uncomfortable about something which you know is not pleasant you still must tell the truth about your discomfort. You don't injure other people with it, but you must tell the truth. You can't lie, you just can't. So I watch myself: "Are you telling the truth, Fred?" And if I'm not I'll get a feeling or a sense that I'm not and I'll try to listen again to see why I'm having difficulty, what is blocking me, what am I hiding?

Marcel Vogel once told me that we each have basic responsibilities and that they weren't easy. Since then I've found that he was very, very right.

From the point of view of allowing the truth to come out in this society, which is just totally fraught with basic dishonesty, at the very core... I mean, do you know what would happen if we could just tell the truth to each other, how simple the world would be? How wonderful it would be?

So, the message from the jungle was very, very clear. It came so loud that it literally knocked me over, "Tell the truth. Clean up your act Fred."

So, how did these Peruvian adventures begin?

When I first began the shamanic book, which was about a year and a half ago, I saw that I would be going to Peru. I saw that I would be with the shamans in the jungle. It frightened the living daylights out of me. It was about the last thing in the world I wanted to do. I knew that anytime you go into shamanic activity you must make a sacrifice. I wasn't prepared to make that sacrifice.

I didn't know what it might be. I didn't want to make it but I saw it.

I had met a shaman in Santa Fe. He also happened to be a professor of education at the University of San Martin, in Peru. I interviewed him, and asked him a lot of questions. My main questions were like, "How do you heal somebody? What do you do? What do you sense about somebody when they are ill?"

He would say, "I sense their vibration." I said, "Oh." You hear people talking about good vibes and vibration all the time. What is that supposed to mean? I said "What do you mean?" He took hold of my arm and held my wrist. I thought he meant the pulse but he meant something more than that. I kept asking him but he had a difficult time explaining because it wasn't something that he could tangibly point to. I kept asking him questions. Finally, he said that he was doing a ceremony that evening, would I like to stay? Well, ceremony meant the imbibing of Ayahuasca.

Imbibing? I think I'm getting the drift here.

So we did this ceremony, it was an evening ceremony, it began at 7:00 p.m. It begins with each person coming up to the Shaman, who sits crosslegged in front of a little shrine in which you place items that you wish to have blessed. I placed before him two of my books, Taking The Quantum Leap and Parallel Universes, which I offered as a gift to him to use as he wished. When it came my turn to take the Ayahuasca it was given to me in a small ·cup.

I feel that you're going someplace interesting with this. Could you tell me a bit more about this plant before you do?

Ayahuasca is a vine that grows in the Peruvian jungle. It grows in the Upper Amazon and Amazon Basin regions. It doesn't grow anyplace else. It's very common there. They put it into a pot of water with other essential ingredients that each shaman uses, but don't reveal what they use. The brewing of Ayahuasca itself is a whole science, a whole pharmacology. There's somewhere between 100-300 different species of medicinal plants that are used in these types of ceremonies with Ayahuasca being the major substance.

So this is some manner of psychotropic vehicle?

Hallucinogenic, intoxicant, psychotropic, whatever you want to use. No word is quite fair. No word quite describes what these substances do. However, they generally fit under that type of pharmacology. They brew this up for 24 to 48 hours. What comes out is this thick, viscous, brown liquid that is bittersweet tasting. It's a purgative and can definitely clean out your intestinal tract.

I've definitely got the drift now.

There were about 20 people in the room. There's a ceremony to the drinking. My shaman would blow tobacco smoke into the mixture. So, you imbibe this, you sit down and then you start to hear sounds. At first I thought they were coming from outside, the sounds of the movement of birds and bird sounds. Then the shaman would start his chant. The chanting, called an *Icaro*, is an important part of the ceremony.

Then you're transported. You leave where you are and you find yourself feeling like you are someplace in the jungle. Then the shaman moved around to each of the people. He spent an inordinate amount of time with me. The room is dark, so you really can't see very well. Because of the effect of the plant you're beginning to feel dizzy, slightly nauseous and you're beginning to have visions.

Part of the visionary experience is the vision of the shaman himself. He changes—he doesn't have the same appearance all the time. I saw an old Indian with long white hair wearing a white robe, which is not how he looks at all. He's a young man with black, curly hair. He looked very different. He came up to me speaking in Spanish—which I have some knowledge of but nowhere near fluency—and I was able to understand him.

He came to me and he took something from his heart which looked like a glowing ball. He took the glowing ball and he passed it to me. My natural instinct was to reach up and take it with my hands and put it into my heart. Then he held his hands out and I took from my heart all my pain and sorrow and I gave it to him, and he took it into his heart. Then he acknowledged what I had done in total, clear communication, as if we were speaking to each other fluently. I found it amazing.

Then I began to have visions. I had a number of major experiences. The "clean up your act" voice came in. I saw myself as an eagle flying over a field. I had omnivision of the whole field below me and of the air and the clouds. It was like I could see 360 degrees. I could see the movement of everything below. Then I saw how the eagle saw. I saw that when the eagle goes for its prey it looks for something out of balance, something which is moving out of harmony. A mouse moves in fear, out of harmony, and suddenly the eagle's vision goes from omnisphere into tunnel vision. He dives with total clarity for the prey he is going for. It's an amazing thing that eagles can do this. I never knew how an eagle hunted before. Did you?

Only that they are far more attuned to the natural world than I am and have an impeccable eyesight.

But that's not good enough is it, because what do you see? Then I had a vision of being on a mountain place where there was a ceremonial temple. I was part of a sacrificial act in which I could either be the one who was sacrificed or the one who would do the sacrifice. I chose to be sacrificed, which meant my heart was going to be cut out from my body and taken away. The vision was very clear.

Then, of course, I was getting very sick and nauseous. This is kind of funny. There were throw-up bowls all around us. I was so sick that the voice inside of me was saying, "Fred, you're such an ass. Look what you're doing to yourself. What are you doing? Are you crazy?" This voice would constantly complain and complain. Finally I heard myself say, "I know that this is horrible for you but it doesn't do any good to complain. It makes it worse." [Laughter]

There were all kinds of experiences like this. They'll be in my next book. There were so many, but they were all of this kind, clarifying, getting in tune with my animal spirits.

Sounds like an elemental connection with the Planet.

Definitely. When I finally went to Peru, my shamanic experiences took place in the jungle. You can't imagine... the jungle life is so verdant, so alive. I felt totally clear about the Mother Earth element, the Mother element of it. As if I was in the womb of the Great Mother and that all life proliferated here. All the processes of life were going on there in the jungle. The sounds are incredible. As a result it has changed me. It has definitely changed me.

The new book, and the new Fred, seem as though they might be quite a departure from what you've been doing.

The book is a real jumping-off point from what I've written before. Rather than explication I'm getting into narrative and story-telling which is something I like to do.

Your intention is to blend the physics and the theory into it?

Yes, definitely. A number of insights to consciousness and how the mind works arose.

Well that's about where I thought this would start. [Laughter] But first I have to ask about your experiences with the Spirits of the Ayahuasca.

They were little people, about five feet tall, very thin, very brown skinned. Completely naked and hairless with two exceptions. They wore about their waists a white skirt-like towel, like the Egyptians wore. They were totally hairless except for hair which grew like a mohawk from the forehead all the way back to the nape of the neck. The hair was like a porcupines', sticking up, almost 12 inches high. They were very unusual looking.

When I told the shaman about what I had seen, he said, "Oh yeah, we know those guys." I said, "Well, who are they?"

"You were very fortunate that they showed themselves to you," he said. "They are the Spirits of the Ayahuasca. The Spirits of the vine itself. You were being invited." I thought that was kind of nice.

You were conscious of them, they were conscious of you, what did you garner about the nature of consciousness?

That what is being revealed to you is your own consciousness. Of course, with the Ayahuasca your consciousness is being mixed with the plant consciousness, so you're beginning to see beyond your own. However, it is still within your own integration of experience that you see these things.

During the latter part of my visit I had a chance to spend time with a neurosurgeon. He is also one of the primary researchers into these substances in Peru. He had a wealth of insights and stories to tell. He is a former student of Wilder Penfield in Canada, so he knew a lot about consciousness and he was certainly well aware of these substances. He related to me a model of it that I think applies.

He said that you have to think of your consciousness as a kind of searchlight in your brain which is very focused, like a beam. When you normally use your consciousness, when you are normally attempting to find information in your memory storage, that searchlight will scan and move back and forth looking for the information. When it shines on a file of some sort it will get the information, but sometimes some files get hidden behind the file cabinet and you don't see them. Under Ayahuasca the whole file cabinet gets ignited at once, they're all giving back information and you don't need the searchlight anymore.

Now, without the searchlight there is no willful activity as to what to look for. You just have it all, and all happening at once. So the whole unconscious mind becomes alit. For most people this experience would be akin to going crazy. I mean, how do you orientate yourself when your normal mode of orientation is to direct the searchlight? When the search-light is out and everything is lit, being seen and witnessed at once, how do you manage? Well, the shamans have had years to figure that out, because that's the state of consciousness that they're in. They know how to move about in that world. Whereas the techniques and training that we've had to move in that world just don't work. I thought it an interesting model.

It is interesting and it sounds practical. What did you get from it that has bearing on processing information in an everyday state?

A lot of our information is stimulus-response; you step on a stone, you feel it. In order for that feeling to take place, information has to travel up your foot to your brain and then back down again. That takes time. Yet, we know almost instantly when that happens, but the brain—the part of the cortex which fires in association with that stimulus—won't fire for about a half second after that stimulus. It won't show that the message has even been cognated upon, yet we know instantly.

I wrote a paper about a model I had in which consciousness does not work in time as we normally think of time. Our consciousness actually moves both forward and backward in time. It moves into previous experience and into future experience. The future experience is probably much more important than we've ever realized. A lot of what we anticipate, our ability to form words, to change in accordance with new information that's coming in, has to do with what we think is happening next.

Baseball players hit home runs when, if you calculate how long it takes to send a neural impulse to the wrists to move the bat, to swing it, and the time it takes for the ball to get over the plate... you're at the level where there's no way you can swing the bat unless you anticipate where the ball is going to be before it's thrown, or maybe at the time it's leaving the pitcher's hand. The neurophysiology of the brain, the brain-arm-hand reaction, would not allow that to take place unless there was some ability to go beyond the normal mechanisms.

So I made this model of how information can travel backwards in time, from the brain into the stimulus site, so you have a probability field at the site where you are receiving the stimulus. You would move according to the most probable way you think things are going to happen. That information has come from your brain in the future. It's not happening now, it's happening a half-second later.

Your hands are there, you send a stimulus to the brain. The whole brain receives the message, but the most likely pathways are going to be associated with the cortical region that connect to your hands. The message that will most likely come back to your hands is most likely from that particular region of the brain. However, all the parts of your brain are responding too, but receiving their message is less probable. If you were to dope the brain in some way or block out the normal pathway, then these other pathways would be experienced as being real. So, alternate reality experiences might take place, so-called crossover phenomenon where you might hear a color or smell a sound, but the normal cortical pathways would most probably be associated with the usual stimulus-response.

In your book, *Star Wave*, you brought up a number of questions relating to how the nature of the future might be influencing the present.

The title of that book refers to how quantum physicists calculate the probabilities for events. Probabilities are numerical measures of likelihoods of things to take place. What quantum physics allows you to do—this is a rather paradoxical statement to make—is to calculate with certainty the probability of any event, but it does not allow you to calculate with certainty an event itself. All it gives you is a probability field, a map in space of where and when something is likely to occur but not when and where it will occur.

To calculate this probability you have to multiply two basic entities, two basic fields, together. One is called the quantum wave function and one is called the complex conjugate quantum wave function. The quantum wave function itself can be seen to be a wave-form which begins, like any waveform, from an initial stimulus or input and the wave moves forward in time. Quantum waves also have a rather peculiar property in that they travel in speeds in excess of light-speed.

They are not material, they are simply probability fields. The fact that they are probability fields and the fact that I believe that they are real means they have a quality of mind already present. Probability is a mind thing. It's not a physical thing. Physical things are either there or they ain't there. Probability fields are a lot of maybe's.

The star wave, the complex conjugate wave, can be seen to be a wave that starts from a future event travelling backwards in time to the present event. Between any present and any future event there is this double movement; a flow forward, and a flow backward. The two modulate each other, actually producing the field of probability at the initial event. You then have a measure of what's likely to occur based upon what future events are likely to be connected with that present event. The more in resonance the two events are with each other, the more likely those two events are going to have a meaningful connection.

What do you mean by a meaningful connection?

In a certain sense I'm giving a definition for something that has never been defined before, which is a definition of meaning.

There cannot be any meaning to a single event—single events are meaningless. There is only meaning when there are two events in comparison with each other. What is meaningful simply means what is probably the connection between the two events. So, the more meaningful an event is, the more likely the connection is between the two events.

I have an event A, an event B, C, D. Say B, C, and D are in the future and A is in the present. B may be the most likely event connecting with A, C less likely, and D even less likely. Nevertheless there is a meaningful association with those events. This simple model would explain a number of different phenomena.

It would explain the nature of human development. Why are humans so different? What makes one person better at something than another person? It's simply a question of human being #1 having B-A developed, while human being #2 has C-A developed, and human being #3 has D-A developed, or something of that sort. In other words, it's a matter of what is considered to be meaningful to that human being.

And the transformation of what is meaningful... some of it is somewhat hard-wired but some of it isn't. I mean, it's certainly meaningful that we walk. The connections that will produce willful activity into the movement of feet and finally the growth and rapid development of the child into adult through the ability to walk and move hands and feet and so forth, is probably reasonably hard-wired. It's part of the mechanisms that are developed. However, if a person loses a limb or one of their senses then the other, rarer, future senses have to become more important. So, a person who loses his eyes hears a lot differently than a person who has his eyes.

This would explain why that happens. If you block out the major pathways, the minor pathways become more important. They then become the major pathway.

If you look through the principles of physics you find that there are a number of interesting little things that happen, just in the mathematics of it or, if you will, just the way things arrange themselves. There is a principle that we call the Principle of Least Action. This says that between any two events there is a least action pathway.

If you look at all the pathways between two events you will find that some of them are wild and weird and some of them are very clear and linear. Nature will favor the least action pathways. If you go to all the pathways that exist between two events and look at the ones in the neighborhood of reasonable, logical, linear, least-time pathways you find that the movement or change as you go from one to the other is very slight. However, if you go to the hinterlands of other pathways, the other ways of going from A to B, you find that as you move from one pathway to another pathway the action changes radically.

What nature seems to do is to find, always, the least action pathways to get from A to B. If you block off a particular least action pathway then other areas become least action pathways. Nature is always adaptable, infinitely merciful, in the sense of being able to provide alternatives when certain avenues are blocked or broken.

How does consciousness fit in with the pathways?

All pathways are between present, past and future. In fact, the pathway is the construction of time itself. Time is the construction of pathways. The natural development of nature, probably through the expansion of the universe and the big bang model, is a tendency to follow the least action pathways for development and consciousness seems to play a big role in it.

The role of consciousness is the ability to choose pathways that aren't necessarily the least action pathways, and by doing so creating new least action pathways. How consciousness does that is not always a clear process. It certainly has something to do with these probability fields, but not always.

If intent can work in a certain way, it's possible that intent can begin to construct that least probable way as something which will be more likely to occur the next time. Which means it's altering the probability game in some way. It's weighting the swing and hedging the bets in some particular way. That would explain why unusual development can sometimes take place, why there's genius that occurs every once in a while.

Everybody has moments of genius, but what do we do with them? If we suppress them, become fearful of them, we go back to mundaneness, the everyday world life, the life as we're used to

living it and doing the same thing over and over again. Nature will always throw you a curve because it's a probability game. When that happens how does your consciousness deal with it? Do you suppress it or do you enhance it by bringing it out, and by doing so make it more likely to occur again the next time?

My feeling is that consciousness allows one to choose reality. It's not that you have to make a real choice. You simply have to be aware of what is happening to you when it happens. Most of the time you will be aware of the ordinary body/mind states of consciousness, but there is no clear barrier to anything. Quantum physics allows you to leak through these barriers.

So, I think that responsibility is nothing more than the ability to respond to novel situations. Bring them into the light of awareness, not dismiss them as fantasy but bring them into the manifestation of possibility by continuing to have the intent that it happen that way rather than follow the old pathway.

What about probability theory and God?

That's a good question. How does God play the game? Does God play the game? I think that God and consciousness are one. The only way that the material world can even exist is through the presence of consciousness in the material world. That meant that things can never be certain. Once things become certain there would be no purpose or meaning to life, no myth to life. It would just be a mechanical world, no point to it all.

What is important is novelty, change, transformation. Those can only happen if nature allows them to happen. It isn't that you have to force them to happen. You just go along doing the everyday thing until you see the light. When it happens make sure you have the intent to see it. Nature kind of invites you in every once in a while to the deeper secrets of what your life can be. But if you don't wish to see those secrets, you won't.

Because of our various addictions of consciousness, belief systems, patterns, and so on?

Right. Once you become addicted to certain substances, whether they be money, sex, a way of seeing or whatever, then that pathway becomes a least action pathway. The one that you are going to repeat. All habits are addictions. All habits arise out of a desire to repeat but nature itself, the quantum world itself, never allows you to repeat exactly what has happened. There's always novelty. Our minds tend to tune out the novelty.

It seems to me that there is a rare opportunity here in the world, if we become more quantum conscious, that we can begin to see the nature of consciousness and its effects.

Like the dynamics of one expression or another? The physics of love, the physics of fear?

Love is an interesting topic. Is there love in the material world? Yes, but it doesn't act through the matter itself. Love is actually contained in light. Light itself has the properties allowing the love properties to occur. It's a rather beautiful metaphor. I thinks it's real but some people might say I'm being anthropomorphic to speak about light being love in this sense.

Wait a minute. We've been talking about little plant spirits with porcupine mohawks. Do you really think anyone who's reading this will be concerned that you're being anthropomorphic about light and love? [Laughter] Don't worry, we wouldn't.

All right. In 1945 a concept was developed which enabled the first laser to be built. Laser means light amplification by stimulated emission of radiation. It refers to something that light has as a property which matter itself... electrons for example... you breathe in oxygen and you think its oxygen that you need to survive. Oxygen is not what you need. What you need is a molecule capable of allowing electrons to land on them so they can give up their energy. That's why we take oxygen in. It's an electron transport phenomenon rather than our needing the material oxygen. We need something to take in those electron energies and fall into the oxygen molecule and give up energy in doing so.

When they give up their energy what is that energy? The energy is light energy. It's light energy that really fuels everything that's going on in our bodies. So we are really bodies of light. But we don't identify with the body of light, we identify with the body of matter.

The human spirit is capable of undergoing a transformation of identity. One direction is to identify with the material body. That leads to the problems that we're having in the Western world. The other aspects of spirit are to identify with the body of light, to become light-body. The material body is not ignored in this case, not by any means. In fact it is listened to more carefully. But the light body is where the person sees themselves residing. That's the choice of consciousness. It's simply a matter of your intent. What do I intend to be? What am I?

Where do you think people should start with that manner of soul-searching process?

I would say you begin with what you know. What every human being knows is suffering and compassion. If you can understand and identify with suffering then you can see it as not being the suffering but being apart from the suffering. The suffering can be there but you're not it, you're just seeing it. So you have an understanding of it.

Compassion is the ability to move outside of your suffering into someone else's suffering. When you begin to see and resonate with that, you're beginning to move into your light body. Because the only body that's going to see suffering and compassion is the light body. That's the only thing that resonates, that's the only thing that goes beyond space and time. It's the only thing that's the laser of action in which my photons and your photons are no longer able to see themselves as separate. They begin to sense that they are part of a group state. Therein I think lies the great hope, the great dream, of the human condition.

So, Dr. Fred would like to see all of us cleaning up our acts.

When you get into heart communication or truth-telling you're really getting into a more spiritual light-beingness. That's why spiritual development in the Western world is so difficult. We've created situations in which the material body is almost necessary for survival. In the shamanic world material identification with the material body is not the important thing.

When I went around the world I realized there were other ways of seeing and being that I was not seeing and being. When I got back I was very confused. I thought physics would answer everything. Now I would say that physics is just a part of the total answer, a very profound part, but there's another thing going on. I see that great things can come from the light body; great peace, understanding of differences.

Light is love. The models of physics suggest light is love. If you can identify with your light you become love itself. You don't have to love or be loved, you are love. You are that essence. I can't see any reason why that's not possible.

If it's all probability fields and intent is what forms which of those fields are to develop as they occur... then what's to prevent us from doing that?

Tara Singh

"We do not miss holy relationship because we have never known it. We have never known what it means to lead an impersonal life. A life untouched by desire or fear must have its own resources, its own integrity. We thought that maybe mankind would be moving in that direction. But it is the other way around. It gives the appearance that we are progressing but in actuality, we have lost touch with something essential."

Tara Singh—Awakening The Child From Within

For Tara Singh the Course In Miracles is the direct Thoughts of God. Perhaps we should think on that for a moment, or for a lifetime. It is not an idle comment. It is presented to us in all sincerity by a man who knows it takes commitment, conviction and determination to step beyond thought.

Tara Singh is best known for his efforts and lifework of teaching, instructing and sharing with students the principles of the inspirational text, *A Course In Miracles*. Volumes of material have been written concerning the Course and its lessons. It is a singularly unique and important volume. Quite possibly it is the finest work on self-transformation to have ever graced our planet. And, quite possibly, it is even more.

For many the Course is a modern day scripture. Indeed, it is difficult to read this work and not be struck by its content. Its words certainly do resonate with what might be considered the core of human response to the holy. For those who endeavor to live, share and teach the Course there clearly is a deep heartfelt response to its message.

Much of the Course In Miracles is aimed at undoing our limited belief systems. This in turn allows us to examine the self and socially imposed illusions through which we allow ourselves to believe, feel and think we are separated from Spirit. Sound familiar? It seems as though we all go through it. Perhaps that's the point of it, to go through it and find the sacred space at the other side. But, the Course points out that there is no other side, that the other is just our illusions and that the Daughters and Sons of God are just a perception away from the Holy Instant.

Born in Punjab, India, and having lived in Central America, Europe and the Himalayas, Tara Singh first came to America in 1947. He has had close relationships with Mahatma Gandhi, Krishnamurti, the teacher of the Dalai Lama, Eleanor Roosevelt and many other world leaders and thinkers.

After working closely with Dr. Helen Schucman, who brought the Course into physical manifestation, and Dr. William Thetford, the scribe of the Course, and after a period of 100 days of intensive study, reflection and "special aloneness" Mr. Singh devoted himself towards bringing the Course into application. He found that it was indeed possible to do this. Countless numbers of students and readers have since benefitted from this discovery.

From Easter 1983 to Easter 1984 Tara Singh facilitated a one year, non-commercialized study of the Course for a group of serious students. Approximately 50 dedicated and sincere pupils from across the United States were sufficiently moved to join him in Los Angeles. This must have been an interesting group of people. Their commitment surely was as honest as the mind is deep. Obviously their goal was not in any way related to some manner of material, career or financial gain. They made these journeys solely to find within themselves a truth. And what does it say of the teacher that provided them with that sort of ambition, commitment and trust?

Not surprisingly, out of this intensive study and from this core group of seekers there evolved the Foundation for Life Action. It conducts itself as a non-profit, educational foundation dedicated to the Course In Miracles, its teachings and the application of these teachings. The author of some 10 books on the Course, Mr. Singh's work is also available in video and cassette formats and continues to become more and more widely visible.

There is another aspect to the work of Tara Singh and the Foundation that should be considered. It is a principle which seemingly involves many spiritual movements. According to Tara Singh and, of course, many others the Thoughts of God cannot be commercialized. That is a simple statement and it certainly seems basic enough. Upon reflection, few would disagree. Yet, we have all seen the disregard with which various "truths" have been applied in the marketplace. Further, we have all seen the seeming folly, energy and economic support that they have attracted to themselves. And, for what? Frequently, it would seem, all it fosters is a continued sense of isolation, separation and fear. But, I digress. What we are concerned with here is the cure. And what I have found in the work of Tara Singh is an honest, clear and straightforward approach to our self and socially imposed puzzlements of reality and illusion. He would not tell you that it's easy or wouldn't require effort. However, he would encourage you to find the light of truth that does, inevitably, reside within us all.

Of singular importance to the Foundation's work is the bringing of the Course to application. This is accomplished through the sharing of the text and by service. For Tara Singh, the concept of service and thus the giving of one's self, of one's own, is of vital importance. It provides one with what Mr. Singh would call clear direction. "When you have clear direction, you look at things in a different way. Clear direction ends our wandering through experience without purpose." The purpose is then presented as taken from *A Course In Miracles:* "I am here only to be truly helpful." It is easy to appreciate, recognize and understand the changes in our lives, our insights and our perceptions such clear directives might bring.

The timing for this particular interview proved to be most fortunate. A few months later Tara Singh entered into a one year period of silence. This was not the first time he had entered into such a dedicated and meaningful state. Previously, for periods of two and three years, he had done the same. When I first heard of this I was amazed. It struck me as such a beautiful thing; to consciously entertain the silence in such a fashion. I imagined it on the order of an extended vision quest and decided that such a person must be truly remarkable. I was not wrong.

Tara Singh and the Foundation conduct various workshops around the country and for this particular weekend he was to be in Portland, Oregon. With directions and scheduling assistance from the Foundation people in Los Angeles and after a quick three hour trip, I was there. Although I generally feel somewhat nervous about meeting the people I interview, in this case I believed that I was actually prepared. This conviction lasted about five minutes into our session. As soon as he said, "It was at a place where choices don't matter anymore," all of my pretense was melted.

Clearly here was a man who had discovered a high state within himself. And I, who have remarkably tenacious struggles with all the confusion of my choices, knew that I was definitely in the presence of a true teacher. Such meetings are a gift, and I got lucky.

Following the interview and over the course of time I have had the opportunity to speak with several of Tara Singh's students and fellow travelers. It is quite clear that they love him deeply and have done so for quite some time. Perhaps no higher praise is possible.

In the time that I spent with him and the time I have spent with his words I have concluded that there is a sincere integrity behind his actions, there is a love in his heart. His words are simple, profound, and always eloquently directed towards "something essential."

"To extend the Will of God is our true function. But right now we are extending fear and the illusion of thought. And the world is in chaos. We are part of that chaos because we are part of the illusion of thought that made it. Ultimately we have to conquer fear, for fear is the biggest illusion. To overcome fear we will need conviction."

Tara Singh—*Nothing Real Can Be Threatened*

I'd like to ask you about the events that led up to your association with *A Course In Miracles*.

I think that some things are very profound because you didn't do anything, but you discovered that life prepared you for something. When the encounter takes place you say, "Good God!"

In the case of *A Course In Miracles*, I think I had a good deal of background in religious life. I spent about four years on the Himalayas meditating... lots of gurus. Finally I spent time with Mr. Krishnamurti, a very life-transforming experience.

Then I had some great yearning within to spend some time in silence. It wasn't a wish and a want. It was just something you can't help. You don't know where it came from, you don't know how long it's going to last, but it's that way. Like when you are hungry or have to urinate, there's nothing you can do.

That took place when I was in India. My feeling was that I was too well known in India, people won't leave me alone. I will go to Switzerland or Italy and maybe settle down. I didn't know how long it was going to take, but there was an urgency about it.

It was like, let the dead bury the dead and get on with it. I mean, you can't delay anything that has that kind of urgency, power, with no haste and no pressure. It's just factual. So, I made arrangements to get settled in Switzerland. Something tells me, no, I have to go to America.

It was at a place where choices don't matter anymore. Once you're free from your choices, you're free from your advantages, you're a newborn person. No choices, no opinions, they have no meaning anymore. So, "You have to go to America." Very well, I came. I spent three years in silence in Carmel, California. It took me two years to just normalize myself.

At the same time *A Course In Miracles* is evolving on the other coast, in New York City. So how can one say where the action begins? Then I came across the Course In Miracles and it says something. Right away, somewhere—not mentally, not intellectually—I knew there was a connection with this. It was like the function of my life.

You actually met and worked with Dr. Helen Schucman. So little is known about her, I'd like to ask you about that experience.

I met with Bill Thetford, the one who took the dictation, and with Dr. Helen Schucman later on. She was a delight. Her intensity, her purity is unbelievable. For such a being to be in that presence, and yet so totally obnoxious, so totally contrary. It would turn you right off. If you haven't mastered reactions and were going to judge, you would never get near her. And the whole Course is based on non-judgment and forgiveness. She didn't want anybody who was going to judge, you know, who was all wrapped up in their knowing.

She puts me through the whole thing, but I can't react. I've seen something else as to who she is. It's like if you see who Jesus is, if behind the temple he's turning the tables and the money-lenders off and so forth, you have no doubt in yourself because you relate it to something. The world of appearance doesn't control you anymore. When you meet at that level it's not subject to ideas, it's direct contact. Then I knew right away, it's this.

I would say I learned from her directly what The Course is, what it means. It's become part of my function in life. I feel very honored and blessed. I was then told to teach The Course. I said, "But I don't know the truth. I love The Course. It makes a lot of sense to me, it's a great wisdom, but I don't know the truth. And I don't want to teach something that I don't know the reality of. I have all these obstacles. If Heaven would help get me over these obstacles then this is the thing I would like to do."

They said the obstacles were necessary, because if I didn't have them I would be very arrogant. And the second thing is, when I start removing other people's obstacles then mine would get removed. I saw the truth of that. I started to love my obstacles. That's how I got started sharing the Course.

These two, Dr. Helen Schucman and Dr. Thetford were psychiatrists. They were at the top of their field. They had a tremendous work. It was work to them, they really put their hearts into it. In the middle of that work the Course started to come. And, it's not channeled, she rose to that state and met it. She could do it anytime. She did it all the time with me when I called her. Then, when I didn't have a question, when I was going this way and that way, she was more ordinary than me. Whenever I had a question there was just the Light, just the clarity. That is my direct experience. It was the same thing with Krishnamurti too.

So, here are these two people and she started with the Course. None of us discovered that they had jobs, that their lives were full and content. They had to give up all the outlets in order to make space for the new. It's not easy. The Course says wherever you are, whatever you're doing, that's where you should be. That's a fact. You start doing it and as you awaken the outer circumstances will change also. This is fantastic. All the time you were indoctrinated; you have to join an order, you have to go to the Himalayas, you have to sit in a monastery. This says no, you belong where you are. And once you have outgrown certain things, you've mastered it and you'll be somewhere else. But it's no longer your concern. It says do whatever you would do that would be the greatest delight to you... so you're not denying anything.

One of the failings of religion is that it makes you deny all kinds of things and suppress yourself. That is bad, it's awful. It takes the passion away, the fire away. Then you can't see anything beautiful because your mind is wondering. There's great beauty in the sky, in the face of a child, or the face of a man and a woman, and you're going to hide yourself away? It's a temptation? No, it's not a temptation. It's a temptation if you have unfulfillments. If you have something to give, it may not be.

I was so startled. Then the next thing that it does, it says start doing the daily lesson, don't try to understand it, don't expect anything. If you don't like it, you do it. If you like it, you do it. If you understand it, you do it. If you don't understand, you do it. Just do what the lesson says. I thought, "My word, this is unbelievable!" That you would see just by doing whatever, to bring to remembrance, that it awakens you. It doesn't care what you're mentally like or what you know. No, that doesn't mean anything.

Then the Course says, "Nothing real can be threatened, nothing unreal exists." So we are still caught in the unreality of

"I like it this way." There is no other scripture in the world that tells you how to get out of it. Here it says don't bother with it, just start awakening yourself. It doesn't even use that word, it doesn't promise anything. It says you do this and you'll see the result. Then it's your discovery, not what I'm saying. And everything with such compassion, every line you read. It's a blessing of life to be part of it.

It's for anyone who has it. It doesn't want to start a cult or organization. It has no aim of rescuing the world. You want to be rescued, you find it. That's all. It's so simple, and so profound.

How did your actual teaching of the Course, and the Foundation, start?

It's very simple. I took about 100 days off to see if it could be brought to application. See how simple it is? It's like the child coming into your life; what you do with it is who you are. You discover, not what you want to do but what you are doing. I spent 100 days alone, by myself, did the lessons exactly as it says, and I saw that it could be brought to application. When I learned that, I could no longer commercialize that which is true knowledge. No saint or prophet of God ever commercialized true knowledge. They don't even own anything. Jesus never owned a home. I come from the Sikh, the Guru Nannek, he never owned anything. We don't own property. We don't accept donations or ask for charity... so something new takes place.

So, I said I would share the Course for a year, noncommercially, nobody has to pay tuition. About fifty-odd people came. We thought it would be somewhere out in the country, a serene place. We spent a lot of money trying to find a place. We actually spent $26,000 trying to find a place. But, we just couldn't. See, you can get a place for a weekend, or two weeks. But when you want to do something extraordinarily different, it doesn't work.

We tried everything, but we couldn't get a place for a year. Finally, we can't manage and some people have given notice at their jobs, and they're coming and we can't find a place. They arrived in Los Angeles. What happened? Can you imagine that within six days, 50 some people had found places? They got together, 5-6 people, and rented houses. Now we didn't have to sign the lease. Can you imagine? Then one began to see the wisdom of not going to the country... because then you confirm the idea that you can only know God out where the greenery is and away from society. So you let life teach you.

It's amazing to me that you do your work and have the Foundation in Los Angeles. You also do longer retreats, don't you?

When you do a weekend workshop it's not enough. It's barely enough to introduce it. You have to spend time together. This might sound very pretentious but, Jesus spent three years—this Prince of Peace, one of the greatest beings that walked the earth—three years, and they still didn't have it when he left. They went back to the old fishing again. He told them, "I'll send the comforter," because he didn't want to make them dependent on himself. He said, "You can do what I have done, and more."

It's discovery, it's not something you seek. It either is or it isn't. When it isn't, that's when you start preaching. That's a danger. This preaching thing, I'm scared of it. Once you have it you don't preach. Then whoever you are related with, there's some kind of sharing. You're not building an ashram and you're not dependent, but there is a relationship. In relationship there is no exploitation. We are related because we're part of Sonship, Sonship of God. One life. If that's not enough, nothing is going to be enough.

I wanted to ask you about your book, *How To Raise A Child of God*. How did that project get started?

These things are not premeditated. All action begins that way. Otherwise we project it, then pursue it. We never do anything that just happens because we respond to it. That's a very difficult thing in this society today, to have that spontaneity, and the space for it.

It began because of this little girl, Crystal. She was about three. The father used to be with us in Los Angeles, at the Foundation. He brought the little child over. The parents are divorced, the wife lives with the child in San Jose. The child is very beautiful, very sensitive, and usually sick. Quite bright, very sensitive.

I'm drawn to children, they're drawn to me. There was a wonderful relationship. One time I had picked her up and some-one else was there. My attention went to the other person, and she got down. Then she just wouldn't come near me. I wondered why. I saw that if I'm carrying her and thinking of someone or something else, my attention is off, then this child is so sensitive as to end this. I was very upset inside. I said, "I'm very grateful for the lesson. I will be present with whatever I am doing, with whoever I am doing it with, wherever I am. That's how I want to live." This child has introduced me to that.

I didn't know how to make friends with her again, because she just wouldn't. I'm wondering what to do. Ask the father, give her more ice-cream... what do we do? Then she comes running up the stairs, "Taraji! Taraji!" She's totally forgotten. I thought, "How blessed are the children! That they can totally come to a new day on another day!"

When she was five, we said to the father, "She's such a sensitive child. How come you're divorced?" He said he didn't like his wife and he's with another girlfriend. I said, "You should have some other thoughts than just yourself. You can't tell me you love the child. You call that love? It might just be attachment."

This child is so intelligent. I got a card from her. On the card she writes, "Taraji, I want to thank you for teaching me not to be controlled by my wantings." I think, "Good God, she's going to teach us all something." I mean is there anyone not controlled by wanting? The whole television system would fall apart. Can you imagine what it would do to the present society?

I wrote a letter to her mother. I said, "I'm not seeing you, but I have seen Crystal. I met your daughter. You must be very exceptional to give birth to such a child. I wish that you would come and visit with us." So the mother comes. The father and his sweetheart are also at the Foundation. So I said to John, "Listen, maybe you'll give it another try, you know, for the sake of the child. The wife is coming, let's see if something can work through. Just be open. I'm not going to force you but let's see. There's a responsibility there, the child. The child is very gifted and probably we should examine the situation. Let's explore into it." So he's somewhat receptive.

The mother comes and the sweetheart, Sandy, she's falling apart. We asked the mother if she'd like to move to Los Angeles. We said we would work at it and, "if you put away your resentments and reactions of John, probably he would too and we'll give it some space. Maybe things would work."

Now to Sandy, I said, "Sandy, you're going to do the noblest thing of your life. You're going to make this child's life whole. You will be blessed for that. I'll fill your gap. We will be friends. We won't leave you abandoned. You will be surrounded by love." She thought that wasn't a bad idea.

Out of this incident came the book, *How To Raise A Child Of God*. Crystal is extraordinary. She's ten now. When she was seven years old she was just leaning on her mother. I said, "Crystal, why are you always holding on to your mother's apron and leaning on her?" She said, "When I'm 10, I'll depend on no one!" She has a voice that is so vertical. We never heard that kind of voice. I said, "I thought you were going to take care of me when I get old?" She started thinking. I said, "Which is it?" She said, "Well, I'll take care of you." And she started to learn cooking.

When she was ten, so she would have the right relationship, I said, "Crystal, would you like to make your own bed? Do you think you're old enough to do it? Would you like to try it?" She said, "I'll try it." It went this way and that way and I said, "Don't ever do it if you don't feel like doing it. Never be false to yourself." Wonderful things started to take place with her.

She took her mother for granted, and her dad somewhat like that. I asked her, "Who do you love?" "I love my mommy." "How about your dad?" "Mm, he's okay." This child would never lie. I said, "Crystal, can you promise me something? Will you have respect for your parents? I don't want to hear the word okay. They're doing something for you. We're all going to grow together. Will you have reverence for them? Will you love them?" She said, "Yes, I will."

Now she's learning ballet. She's read all the stories about Helen Keller, Mother Theresa, all the noble people and their lives. She's very interested in classical music. Feels very close to Jesus, and everybody else; it could be Buddha. I suggest a state of being that person represents, and another enlightened being represents the same state.

As she got older a new book came into being, *The Awakening Of The Child From Within*. It expands on a lot more than Crystal. It goes into how does the adult awaken.

Well, that should lead us into our next question. How does the adult awaken?

I think they have to have love for honesty. Without that nothing works. It is not a learning. I think that man has gotten caught in learning, and learning has become an indulgence. It doesn't introduce one to anything that's real. It introduces one to every-thing about reality, but not reality. What it does is really make us more harmful to nature, to man, to our own self. I don't think society is going to change but the individual can, you and I, and it must start there.

So, you ask the question—how does one awaken? To see the false as the false. Have a sense of discrimination. Then stick to it. Whether it's difficult or easy is not the issue anymore, you have conviction. When you change then you've made a contribution. Whatever you would do, it will have your goodness in it.

I think that the illusions of "ism's" is over. Democracy is no better than communism. They both started with wonderful ideals. But it's concentration of power into the hands of a few so the military-industrial complex can control society here, there, everywhere. It's so difficult now for the "new" person to rise. The media totally has got you and you're isolated. Every country has some small segment of society that's objective, that's sane. They have different values but they're not very fashionable and not in the forefront.

In India, there were the wise men in the villages. In my time there were 550,000 villages in India, and not one single policeman. When there were disagreements they would go to the wise person and he would say, "You've definitely come here to quarrel over something. You must rise above it. Come to nobleness." He helped them to rise above it. Now you have lawyers. Where there is one lawyer, he hardly makes a living. Where there is two, they both flourish. It's a very wasteful society and terribly artificial. But the human being is always there, that one person, solely human beings. Not Americans and not democrats, communists and socialists; all that is just dogmas.

The tragedy is that all our institutions of education divide man from man. Politics divide man from man. Religions divide man from man. There is no wholeness anywhere. That's for you and I to find. It's as simple as that. When that is what we see, then you are in command of your own potentials. We all have the potential to do it. Simple, but difficult.

Where does the difficulty lie?

I think the difficulty is to give up our attachments, our laziness, our projections, and how we are conditioned. It's not difficult, letting go of false values is difficult.

Where is the correlation between inner peace and national peace? What about disillusionment?

National peace is never going to be there. Not on that scale. Let us say, that where there is half-truth there is no peace. It doesn't make any difference whether you are Iraqi or you are American. Both live by half-truth and partial attention. But the other is possible. Neither your organized religion, nor your universities, nor your politics, nor your economy is going to lead you to that. You have to see the false as the false first. One must come to disillusionment first and not be bitter.

Before coming to disillusionment I want to make a call as to how bad society is. So, I want to have another society of my own. I say that's reaction. That's worse than half-truth. When you see that as a fact, then you're disillusioned but you're not judgmental of anything. You've outgrown the duality in you. Then what you would do would not be projected, not premeditated.

It can start with a child, it can be anything, then someone gets inspired. The letters I write to Crystal, that she writes to me... anyhow, they are happily married now. They have a nice home and good family. Sandy began to see that she did something noble for the child, for the man she was supposedly in love with and so on. The man, John, and his wife have a little tension. I say, "Now don't be petty about that. You're doing a noble thing by coming from San Jose. He's a good man, making it work." So, they are, all three, happy.

Since you're talking about personal sacrifice, I'm wondering if some people might have problems with what you're saying.

Yes, I think so. But if they have friendship and support they won't. I mean, if I give advice and don't have to give my life... You see, we often give advice but we don't follow through. So, we did.

You can't advise if you're not going to put your life into it. Simple advice, "do the right thing," and then I'm not going to see you again. It's like planting something and never watering it. The wise never get involved with whatever he commits himself to, you stick to it. Then what you say is what you mean. Otherwise it's empty words.

We hear so much about self-reliance, and yet very few seem to accomplish it. I understand it to be a basic principle at the Foundation.

You know how difficult that is? It's difficult, but it's good. It's not for the weak person. You have to be competent, you have to be factual. You have to have order in life—especially when you're not going to build a community, you're not even going to own any property—so no one can exploit you. Whoever is there can come and they can go. You want to come to self-reliance, you have to work twelve hours. If you don't like it, then get yourself a job. We are neither for or against anything.

The foundation started with us having to be self-reliant. No charity, you have to work and therefore awaken yourself, do you see? If you can do it with that love in you, more attention. We are trying to outgrow partial attention. Then once you get there then maybe you will find out what your intrinsic calling is. Self-reliance is intrinsic work that you love what you are doing. It energizes you, you don't need outlets. But if there's a good play, a good ballet, a good movie... don't cut yourself short because those are the fruits of the city, be sensitive. But don't let your boredom and loneliness rule you. So, you become productive.

We started that way. We stuck to it. We still don't have much money but we've never missed a meal, we paid all the bills. As a matter of fact, every couple of years we raise the rent without the landlord ever asking us. That's part of rightness. If we can't live with rightness let's close the place. If the landlord has to ask us for a raise, then we are oblivious of rightness and we're only thinking of ourselves.

Everything that we're going to do... the first thing: is it right? Is it noble to do so. Don't do it to please and flatter because then you're going to miss out on some meals. You become responsible for what you say, and responsible for what you do. Dr. Schucman said that the Course is to be lived and not to be learned. We have made very good progress in the external about self-reliance. We have made very little improvement in inner changes. The internal change is the bigger challenge.

Then we said, "Look we're self-reliant, we're doing fairly well." We made some money, we paid everybody's debts. After that I said, "We've been together too long, we should disband. Six years we've been together. The ending has wisdom in it." I asked how they felt. They all wrote long, nice letters and not one of them was attached to staying or to leaving. Not one of them. They said that they wouldn't teach the Course. Why? "We don't know it. It would be deceptive." I said, "Wherever you are, if you won't teach the Course, you'll be an example of it. That's teaching the Course, not pretending you know it."

I was somewhere in Connecticut reading all the letters. It was so unbelievable; that they are willing to leave and they are willing to stay. They are not afraid. I got very inspired and said I would do a retreat, and I would give them all the proceeds from the retreat so they can have some money to do what they need to do. I did the retreat and we made about $15,000. I said it was for them, I didn't want them to go back into the world empty-handed.

Never in the seven years has there ever been a quarrel among them. Not once has anyone come to me to complain about another. I gave them the money. They never took a penny. They said, "You've given us life. You gave us six years of your life and never charged us a penny. We're different beings. We have self-confidence. We can't pay you. We won't accept this money." That was very inspiring.

I said to them, "What would you really like? Since we're not caught in choices and preferences, what would you really like?" With one voice they said they would like to stay and make this thing really work and grow. They really became self-reliant. It was quite an interesting experiment. That it worked is amazing.

Do people send you money?

People send us money. Some people said they wanted to give us a big property. We said, "No, if you have goodness in your heart you need the property to do the good work. Give expression to your goodness in your own way. We don't want to get involved." One person sent a $25,000 check. I said, "You're interfering in our self-reliance. Have mercy on us. What are we going to do with this? Please take it back."

There was one woman, an elderly actress in New York. She just forced us... "The Lord told me." Once they say the Lord I get scared. That's just a projected thing. I'd rather depend on somebody's common sense than the lord of their imagination, then I'm asking for trouble! She kept sending money and she won't listen. Charles is our accountant. I say, "Charles, she is very...

keep the money. She's going to need it. Just open another account somewhere. We know it's her money." After a few years she did need it and the money was returned to her.

We don't go by any projected thing. When the situation occurs we learn what to do from it. To accept is beautiful, to not accept is beautiful. You have to see which it is. Each thing, at that given moment, the clarity of that moment is valid. Not what I assessed yesterday or 10 years ago. No, we must look at the situation the way it is. Somewhere that sense of insecurity is fading away from the group. If there is nothing in the world we will serve man.

So, we have moved from jobs to work, from work to intrinsic work. Now we are taking the next step, to serve. While the buying power is still there we will sell books and tapes to support ourselves. When that is not there... if there is an earthquake in Los Angeles we have nowhere to go but where people are in need, to help.

That's our next step. Wherever the human being is in need we are going to help them. And it's becoming natural because it's a growth. We had never planned it that way, we never knew it was going to be this. We sit down and decide together. Each person comes out with something very unique. So, it's not one guru, I make mistakes. They can't put me on a pedestal. It's a good friendship and relationship.

I'd like to ask you more about service.
Service is supreme. You know, I met Helen Keller, a wonderful lady. There's this Carnegie Endowment for International Peace, a large foundation. They have a building that they built, close to the United Nations. All the offices were occupied by foreign countries. They were selling their craft, and trying to bring the

world together. For the opening ceremony they invited the President and all the big people. I happened to be there. People made these tremendous speeches. Helen Keller was there. She said, "Work is worship. Service is supreme." She silenced all the intellectuality with those few words.

There's nothing like service. Then motivations go away because you care for another. It's a different way of loving one another. Then your caring is not a cliche, it's in application.

As we begin to see that this thing is not going to work for so long, the way it is, we must learn to serve. One day, some years ago, I said that our work is going to become very similar to Mother Theresa, that we have some similarity. But one thing is clear, the Foundation is a school. It's not social work, we're never going to confuse the issues. This is a school to bring the Course to application, to come to self-reliance and not working for another and so on.

Hers [Mother Theresa's] is very different, yet an extension of the same kind of spirit. So I said to them, "Why don't you find out about it and what they are doing. Why don't you go." We have a girl with us, she's the only one who's vegetarian, Connie. Very strong person. Very dependable and reliable. Connie called and some of the people from the Foundation went. They came back so inspired. They said, "The Sisters never get involved. If you have questions, they answer. They have no conversation, they're not curious, they are blissful, they emanate a love for Christ. They are there when you need them, and then they disappear. If you have any questions you ask them. But if you want to find out things, they are not into it. They are alive, full of laughter." It's unbelievable.

Then some others went. We became familiar with them, and them with us. Their Mother Superior, Sister Angelina said, "The

day your group came we had prayed for help. And you all came."
There is some rapport there.

They said that they made these lunches together. They give
the food away, peanut butter, rice, and so on. They said they did
so many of these bags, but then when the people come it's just
not enough. So I said, "Look, we will give them $50 a week. We
could give them the money or buy the food, because we know
where to get it wholesale." We would like to start with $50 a week
because we will always be consistent. We could get enthusiastic
and say we'll do $100, and then our enthusiasm will have a flat
tire. We're going to do something with no flat tire, so there will

be consistency in what we do. Maybe other people can see that's the way to do things, not impulsively do it and then forget it. They were moved, but they said, "We don't like consistency. We like uncertainty." [Laughter] So, it's the same language, both speaking in a different way. Something very beautiful is developing.

Having something to give is the joy of life. No one has it to give until they have developed their own potentials. "If you give the money you have, you shouldn't have had it in the first place," says Gandhi. Thoreau said, "If I had it first to give then I'm a thief. I shouldn't of had it saved for myself." Having something to give of one's own: own energy, own wisdom, own goodwill, own space, that's a great gift.

You are about to enter into a year of silence.

Yes. It's very necessary, you see. It rejuvenates. In the Course, in the *Manual For Teachers*, they say a teacher goes and then they are given a long span—an extended period of silence—where different things take place. It's not just my wish and want, it's something evolving. This action is coming to its fullness. Then something else will blossom, I have no idea what.

In fact, I spend most of my time alone now. We have undertaken to do a few things, one is the book, *Awakening The Child From Within*. Aliana Scurlock is working with me on that. She's the one who worked on the book, *How To Raise A Child Of God*. We want to write about people free of pretense, and what self-reliance really is.

After that we want to do a book on how affluence without wisdom is self-destructive. I think we need to communicate that to people that are dependent on some "ism," or this and that. Just warn them that, "you have to awaken yourself." That's where safety is, that's where wisdom is, not on relying on someone else.

In American society... it's insane to grow food 3,000 miles away and then ship it. Why can't Utah or Carolina have their own self-reliance? The way we work things... all the profiteering minds doing this and that, it's not humanitarian. There's no humanism in it. We are not helpless, but if you are dependent on another you are. But we don't have to, and whatever we are dependent on is falling apart. There might be some virtue in that; so we can wake up.

Let's talk about the Joseph's plan. what does it mean and how does it work?

There are certain things that take place that are not premeditated. You see, I had brought loose ends to a head. It had taken me some years to bring them to a head, so I would know what to do. If you have a child you know what to do, if you have a wife you know what to do, if you have a job you know what to do, if you want fulfillment you know what to do. You bring loose ends to a head, where you can say, "Yes, I'm my own person now." Then something new takes place. You gain a lot of wisdom in the undoing of the dependencies, attachments, wishing, wanting, and you emerge into something else. So, I had brought loose ends to an end.

I was in London and it was given to me, the Joseph's Plan, and now everything from the past has ended. You see, Joseph was thrown into the ditch and all of that, but in his heart was goodwill. So, I have goodwill for even my enemy, it doesn't matter anymore. It's just misperception. If you have corrected it in yourself than you are the one who is blessed. Maybe the other one needs correction. If they will listen you can do so, but not that you are going to be a teacher, but just out of goodness and friendship.

Then the Joseph's plan started. I just loved that idea. We started the 40 day retreat in New Mexico. All the income from the tuitions would go into the Joseph fund, every penny. We bought Treasury Bills. We made so much money you won't believe it. Then the Foundation people said, "What about us?" I said, "The Foundation has nothing to do with this." So the Foundation sold $40,000 worth of books and tapes, the Lord gives to them too. They hadn't sold that much all year, so they had their own account taken care of! Isn't that something?

We have some very wise people, outside the Foundation even, who are on the board to decide what to do with it. This is my joy of what I'm doing now. Whatever you do, if it's intrinsic, it's blessed. After all these things are done, I think the Joseph's Plan will have a good deal of seed money. I have some kind of premonition that the Joseph's Plan would be unlimited, its resources would be unlimited. How or what, I don't know, but it won't lack. It's good that we have quite a number of people trained at the Foundation. I hope to convince people that it's easier to give and it's miserable to want and be a prisoner.

Earlier you said, "As we see this thing is not going to work for so long as it is." What are you seeing for the world?

I see the world goes on. I see America declining rapidly, making so many mistakes. I see more problems. When you are prosperous, problems go unresolved. When you are weak, they surface. The Black people will want their own Alabama, and there is nothing that you can do. There are a lot of unresolved issues. We've not been very kind to the Native Americans. Humanism has never touched America on that scale. You cannot assimilate the new, there is not that space. And now, the outlets have destroyed man, he cannot call upon the highest in him. We're drugged, chained.

The way we are spending money... here's a country in deficit, nearly bankrupt and you're fighting wars. You say Iraq attacked Kuwait and it's terrible, but you do this all the time. You attack Panama, you go to Libya and bomb. What example did you set as a world leader? What reason could you give for going to Korea? Six million people and you're still preaching they are doing it.

It was said that Iraq has 100,000 soldiers and that Kuwait only had 20,000, so Iraq went and took it. No. How many are you sending now compared to Iraq? It's all the time, "moving from strength." Well, moving from strength is what got us bankrupt. So this industrial-military complex, the concentration of power in the hands of a few, is going to play havoc. The corporations have the money, the government is broke, you can see what's ahead.

Each person has to come to something noble. Can we do things that are meaningful? That enriches your life and would help someone else. We have to be trustworthy as human beings. We have to come back to who we are, not what the institutions are.

I'd like to ask you about your thoughts on AIDS and how that fits in with your world-view.

It's quite obvious that man is suffering. We have to respond. And response is always adequate. If you can't respond adequately, then it's just a gesture.

I don't think that we can do certain things about AIDS. If a person has AIDS, that's a fact. Now, what we are going to do about it is who I am. I might have a totally different kind of AIDS, called miserliness or lovelessness. How does a non-AIDS person approach this thing. I think, again, from what goodness is there.

Out of crisis there are people who come to blossom with originality, and that originality is giving. It's Mother Theresa picking up a child, dehydrated, going to die, and picking him up because she sees the Light of Christ in him. That child dies knowing that there's love in the world. Then look at how it multiplies. It multiplies like fishes.

We can take care of AIDS when there is that love in our heart. Just doing duties—no. Shaw said, "When you ask a stupid man why is he doing a stupid thing, he always tells you he is doing his duty."

The AIDS is spreading. Do you know how much we waste, sir? Do you know how much we waste on dogs... when people are starving for food. Millions of dollars of butter got rancid and it couldn't be sent to Africa where there is starvation. We burn wheat and throw potatoes in the ocean rather than give it to a hungry world.

So, these problems are surrounding us more and more, aren't they? And our means of solving them are becoming more and more meager. But we always have money. It costs $50 million, daily, to have the army in Saudi Arabia and it's going up. So, we have lots of money. But for AIDS... it's a gesture. If the rich part of Santa Barbara, California catches fire, immediately the President sends money. Have they ever sent money to Harlem? The slums? The fate of AIDS is the fate of Harlem... gestures.

When you want to do something, you can invent Star Wars—profiteering. In order to kill humanity we have all the genius of science, universities, and everything behind it, to put a man on the moon with a flag. So if prestige and abstract things become important, what about the human being? What do we account for, this American civilization, at the end? What contribution have we made as a human race?

Every country, they don't have toilet paper, but they have tanks. We've intensified frictions everywhere. So, one sees the future. Man is not any closer to loving one another or to their own honesty, or to caring. More and more the population increases, and the more it increases the poverty increases. Then they have the job and all that energy builds a battleship.

This is the country that started the four-point program; "The only war we seek is the war on poverty, illiteracy and disease." How far we have degenerated in that. There's no justice anymore. All laws of justice have become subject to the laws of injustice. There's not much one can do, whether it's AIDS or aggression somewhere, it's the same thing.

But I think we can say that if you and I are going to make the change within ourselves, just criticizing the system is not good enough. The hippies did it. They were good people. It's sad that the country, the system, couldn't incorporate them. Isn't that something? It will never incorporate. That's the American way. It doesn't incorporate, but we think it does.

I've seen Tibetan children come, a small minority in New Jersey, and they go to school. They're teased because they're different and the children bleach their hair, they want to be like the others. If you go to some other country every person is dressed differently, they speak differently, and there is tolerance. Someone worships their God this way, another that way.

Here it demands conformity. Communism demands conformity, affluence demands conformity. Somewhere we have to see all of that in order to outgrow it, not to react to it. The only purpose of seeing it is that you outgrow it. If you try to make a cause... I say no, you're still dependent on people. One starts with one's self. And then it grows.

Afterword

Even though this appears to be the end of this book, it is quite possibly not the end of the process. As was suggested in the Introduction, you most probably did glimpse some aspects of yourself somewhere within the preceding pages. At some point something evoked a response. Once such things are noticed I've found that it can take a tremendous amount of energy to discount, ignore or invalidate such a response. The provisions might be better spent in a continuance of the recognized self-momentum. There's no telling about what rainbows could be waiting. One might start with some of the many noteworthy books our collective guests have themselves penned. It is conceivable that their volumes will lead some towards their own personal quests. While, most assuredly, the going will not always be easy, the path occasionally hard to find, and the torrents of doubt difficult to ford, the experience of it all will always be there.

Perhaps our experiences, or what we make of them, are all that we ultimately accomplish. Perhaps, in the beginning, if the experiences of the good souls in this book are any guide, that is all that we ever really wanted.